THREE STEPS, ONE BOW

Bhikshu Heng Ju, Bhikshu Heng Yo

Three Steps, One Bow

American Buddhist Monks' 1100-mile Journey for World Peace

BUDDHIST TEXT TRANSLATION SOCIETY

Three Steps, One Bow
American Buddhist Monks' 1100-Mile Journey for World Peace

© 2019 Buddhist Text Translation Society
　　　Dharma Realm Buddhist University
　　　Dharma Realm Buddhist Association®
　　　4951 Bodhi Way, Ukiah, CA 95482

All rights reserved. No part of this book may be reproduced in any form or by any electronic or mechanical means including information storage and retrieval systems without permission in writing from the publisher, except by a reviewer, who may quote brief passages in a review. For more extensive quotations, request the publisher's permission at the following address:

Buddhist Text Translation Society
Attn: Permissions Coordinator
4951 Bodhi Way, Ukiah, CA 95482
www.buddhisttexts.org　　info@buddhisttexts.org

First edition 1977, Second edition 2019

ISBN 978-1-60103-074-0 (second edition paperback)
ISBN 978-1-60103-073-3 (second edition ebook)

Printed in Malaysia on acid-free paper

Library of Congress Cataloging-in-Publication Data

Names: Heng Ju, Bhikshu, author. | Heng Yo, Bhikshu, author.
Title: Three steps, one bow : American Buddhist monks' 1,100-mile journey for world peace / Bhikshu Heng Ju, Bhikshu Heng Yo.
Description: Burlingame, California : Buddhist Text Translation Society, 2019. | Includes bibliographical references.
Identifiers: LCCN 2018046685 (print) | LCCN 2018047834 (ebook) | ISBN 9781601030733 (ebook) | ISBN 9781601030740 (pbk. : alk. paper)
Subjects: LCSH: Buddhist pilgrims and pilgrimages--United States. | Heng Ju, Bhikshu. | Heng Yo, Bhikshu. | Buddhist priests--United States--Biography.
Classification: LCC BQ6450.U6 (ebook) | LCC BQ6450.U6 H86 2019 (print) | DDC 294.3/4351092 [B] --dc23
LC record available at https://lccn.loc.gov/2018046685

Table of Contents

ix	Foreword
xii	Editor's Preface
xiv	Introduction by Jeanette Testu
xvi	Introduction by Heng Ju
xxiv	Introduction by Heng Yo
1	I. San Francisco to Garberville
71	II. Garberville to Coos Bay
130	III. Coos Bay to Marblemount
196	Notes
198	Glossary
200	Introduction to the Dharma Realm Buddhist Association
210	A Brief Account of the Life of the Venerable Master Hsuan Hua
216	DRBA Branches

> "To do what no one else can do, to be patient when no one can be patient; this is what it's all about!"
>
> —— *Venerable Master Hsuan Hua*

The Venerable Master Hsuan Hua with Heng Ju and Heng Yo

Foreword

In Memory of Tim Testu, the Monk Heng Ju

I met the future monk Heng Ju about a year before we became students of Buddhism and disciples of the Venerable Master Hua. He had recently retired from the Navy, primarily working on submarines touring the world's great oceans. His father was an executive in a large truck manufacturing company and I always thought Heng Ju's basic nature was not unlike a Semi-Truck: big, powerful, and made for the long haul. He also had an affinity with the ocean; his passion, drive, and motivation were vast and deep.

In 1970 I was living at the Buddhist Lecture Hall in San Francisco studying Buddhism with Master Hua. One day, Tim asked me what I was doing with my life. I answered that I was learning to benefit living beings, subdue my inner dragons, and end birth and death. This resonated with him and within days he arrived to live at the temple with the Master.

Because of his personal drive, he quickly aspired to practice the principles handed down through 2,500 years of Buddhist teachings. A little over a year after taking refuge in the Three Jewels, he shaved his head and was among the first Americans to become a novice monk. He felt it was both a path to understanding his own nature and a responsibility to living beings, to inspire them to understand their own deep wisdom and fundamental nature. It was an opportunity to go beyond theory and to practice a timeless way of compassion and wisdom, to plant the seeds of Buddhism on Western soil, and to become a future Buddha.

Less than a year later, Heng Ju found inspiration in the Buddhist practice of Three-Steps-One-Bow. Whatever he pursued, it was with a unique passion, and this idea of a pilgrimage became all-consuming. It was clear to him that the first step begins in one's own heart. In beginning this expedition, he found a way to honor his parents while seeking peace in this world. In preparation for the journey, I helped him design and build a cart for the two monks to carry their minimal provisions on the road to Seattle.

In sincerely exploring and cultivating the five main schools of Buddhist practice, one hopes to gain insight into the enduring questions of existence and find answers beyond one's intellectual mind. Sometimes Heng Ju would try to describe some of the states he experienced. At times he could see what we think of as mythical, or symbolic beings. It is said that dragons live in wild places and are commonly at home in the ocean and have a great deal to do with the weather on this planet. Perhaps this had something to do with his affinity and comfort living under the sea on submarines. Heng Ju seemed to have an affinity with dragons. Once he tried to show and describe to me the dragon that lived on the mountain overlooking the City of Ten Thousand Buddhas, but I was unable to see it. Another time, after he and Heng Yo had completed their bowing pilgrimage from San Francisco to Marble Mountain north of Seattle, they both saw a majestic dragon frolicking in the clouds. Another monk witnessed this as well, and when word of it got to the Master, he predicted that in the future, a Buddhist Monastery would be built there called Dragon Cloud Monastery and many people would live there and practice the Way.

Toward the end of the pilgrimage, nearer Seattle, the two monks noticed that the rain would stop when they were bowing and resume when they stopped. The Master would comment on this whenever he lectured before an audience. When the monks approached Seattle, the Master announced we would hold a Gathering for World Peace there. At that time there weren't any computers, we couldn't just check the weather in Seattle or see what the traffic was on the highway. We did find out that it had been raining in Seattle and it was a big storm. Seattle gets a lot of rain during the year and it was supposed to be raining for the next few weeks, just solid rain. Somebody mentioned this to the Master, and he said, "Oh, don't worry about that, I'll take care of it." Most people drove up to Seattle, but I flew with the Master on the plane, and when we got near the Seattle airport I was looking out the window. For a ten-mile radius, there was a perfect circle over Seattle where there were no clouds. It was just like somebody had taken a compass and drew a ten-mile circle and there were no rain or clouds within it.

When we drove into Seattle it was not raining. It was sunny, skies were clear and the grass on which we were holding the ceremonies was all dry. I don't know what the newspapers said about this, but we had our ceremonies and our world peace gathering. After that gathering, many people decided to take refuge or to leave the home life. Back on the plane returning home after the gathering we could see the circle disappearing as we left. I don't think anybody else got to see this and if I hadn't been on the airplane with Master Hua, I wouldn't have been able to see it either. To those on the ground, it just seemed like the clouds parted and it was nice that it wasn't raining, but from the sky you could see this very definite circle. It was all very uncommon.

It is said if you go too fast, then obstructions appear, and it is common to stumble. After the completion of his Pilgrimage for World Peace, Bhikshu Heng Ju had a trying time settling back into the day-to-day lifestyle of the Buddhist community. Whereas the pilgrimage had been a momentous effort and finite mission, when he returned to the peaceful practice of the everyday rituals of the community, his mind began to wander from his original resolve.

Although he had a deep respect for his teacher and the teachings of the Buddha, several years later he left the monastery. It was an extremely difficult time for him after he left the peace and quiet of the Buddhist community. Eventually, he did settle down after this and found a special person to share his life with. Together they had a daughter who has furthered the wonderful aspirations of her father and recently published a compelling autobiography that he left for posterity.

Tim always maintained his closeness to the Venerable Master, a special relationship that went far beyond his life as a monastic. After he returned to lay-life he spent a lot of time visiting the various temples that Master Hua had established, and offered his skills and time, doing whatever he could to benefit the Three Jewels.

Alan Nicholson   July 28, 2018

Editor's Preface

In 1883 at the age of 43, after having been a Buddhist monk for over 20 years, the Great Master Xu Yun (虛雲 Empty Cloud), set out on a pilgrimage to repay the kindness of his father and mother. His mother had died when she had given birth to the Master. During this pilgrimage, the Master did a full prostration every time he took three steps. While doing this "three steps, one bow" pilgrimage, the Master constantly recited the name of the Bodhisattva of Great Wisdom, Manjushri Bodhisattva. This incredible spiritual quest started at Pu Tuo Mountain in Zhe Jiang Province, which is the sacred mountain dedicated to the Bodhisattva of Great Compassion, Avalokiteshvara (Chinese: Guan Shi Yin) Bodhisattva. It ended three years later in 1886 at the famous Wu Tai Mountain in Shan Xi Province, which is dedicated to Manjushri Bodhisattva.

Venerable Tripitaka Master Hsuan Hua (Xuan Hua) said the following in his book "A Pictorial Biography of the Venerable Master Hsu Yun":

After having paid his respects on each peak of Wu Tai Mountain, the Master's vows were now complete. Joy filled his heart. On his way down the mountain he again bowed in gratitude to Manjushri Bodhisattva. Manjushri Bodhisattva emitted rays of light that reflected, shimmering, off ten milleniums of snow piled on those cold, craggy peaks. How splendid!

Eighty-seven years after the Great Master Xu Yun completed this 3000-mile spiritual journey, in 1973 Bhikshu Heng Ju was inspired to make a similar "three steps, one bow" pilgrimage here in modern America, from San Francisco to Seattle. His close friend on the spiritual path, Bhikshu Heng Yo, vowed to be his protector throughout this 1000-mile journey. During this arduous 10-month pilgrimage, the two monks bowed throughout the day and did their daily rituals and other spiritual practices in the early morning and late into the night. They did all of this without any shelter other than the tent that they carried along with them throughout their pilgrimage. Now the Great Master Xu Yun encountered life-threatening obstacles during his journey and was saved each time by a person who he later found out was a "transformation body" of Manjushri Bodhisattva. In reading this journal by Heng Ju and Heng Yo on their unique journey, there are many lessons to learn and also some rather amazing experiences. And at the culmination of this "three steps, one bow" pilgrimage, Heng Ju received a life-altering teaching and experience with a very wise and rather unusual person. This was an incredible and well-deserved reward for the completion of ten months of rigorous spiritual cultivation by the two monks.

It is my great pleasure to write this preface to a new printing of the journal of Heng Ju and Heng Yo on their remarkable "three steps, one bow" pilgrimage from San Francisco to Seattle in 1973-1974. Although the events described in this journal are nearly 45 years old, it is said the teachings of the "Dharma" are timeless. The truths of the Buddha's teachings are applicable to people regardless of the time or place. Just as "joy filled the heart" of the Great Master Xu Yun when he completed his pilgrimage, may you the reader also experience the joy of the Dharma as you read this wonderful book.

Bhikshu Heng Shün

Introduction

As a child, I didn't realize what a big, wonderful deal this bowing pilgrimage was. I thought everyone's parents went on great adventures in the 60's and 70's. I had no idea that there were dozens of newspaper articles written about my dad and his comrade, Heng Yo. I had no idea that it was the first pilgrimage of such a length in America. He said, "I wish to transfer any merit acquired to all living beings." I know he meant this statement because never once did I hear him brag about this trip or complain about the physical hardship. I was, however, warned about the dangers of poison oak, "leaves of three — let it be!"

Dad continued to fervently cultivate the Dharma after he returned to lay life. Some of my earliest memories are of us meditating together. We enjoyed vegetarian meals, swimming in Hood Canal, hiking, working on the property, and visiting Snow Mountain and Gold Summit Monasteries. It was a special treat to drive down highway 101 to The City of Ten Thousand Buddhas. If Shr Fu (Tripitaka Master Hsuan Hua) was visiting Gold Summit, we always spent an extra long time at the monastery. After what seemed like hours of sitting, reciting *sutras* and walking in circles, finally we would get to eat! The children were allowed to go sit at Shr Fu's feet while he gave the evening lecture. I was too young to remember what the talks were about but I have a clear memory of what it felt like to be in the lecture hall when Shr Fu was talking. It felt like being inside a big hollowed out candle-lit pumpkin. It felt light and warm and safe. It felt like the world outside the monastery walls ceased to exist.

When Dad was getting cancer treatment at Fred Hutchinson Cancer Research Center in Seattle, he would sometimes drop me off for babysitting with the *bhikshunis* (nuns). We didn't speak a common language, but we had lots of fun doing *taiji* with the pigeons and writing English words and Chinese characters on the blackboard. At The City of Ten Thousand Buddhas, I got to see the rigorous daily schedule of the monks, nuns, students and families. I saw all who live there joyfully working for the good of the community and human-kind.

My dad died when I was 18. I wish that we had more time together. Dad worked very hard every day from sun-up to sundown but he was always available to go on a walk and talk with me or help with a problem. Having a record of this journey is a way to hear his voice again and to honor his memory.

Jeanette Testu   August, 2014
On the 40th anniversary of the completion of the pilgrimage

Introduction by Heng Ju

In late 1973, a series of circumstances led me to decide to make a religious pilgrimage. Previously, I had heard the story of an elder Chinese Buddhist Meditation Master, the Venerable Hsu Yun (Xu Yun, or Empty Cloud), who at the turn of the century made a walking pilgrimage across China. As he walked, he bowed his head to the ground after every third step. In six years, he bowed a total of three thousand miles or what amounts to the entire breadth of China. During his trip, he encountered incredible hardships, suffering from hunger, thirst, and the cold, but he never gave up. Eventually, he was able to attain a state of mind which can only be described as "single-mindedness." That is, he was able to halt all of his thinking processes, and he experienced a radiant clarity of mind which he had never been able to attain before. His pilgrimage also had a very profound effect on the people he encountered.

Master Yun's trip had given me an idea which began to grow and develop. I had always thrived on adventure, and after so many years as a layman and then a monk inside a Buddhist monastery,

I was ready for a little change. I began to entertain the thought of making a bowing pilgrimage in America.

In the history of the world there have been many religious pilgrimages. Most of these came about as a response to the fighting and moral decadence of the times. People always need ways to express themselves: ways to display their religious feelings. As people gradually attain peace and understanding, they need ways to share them with humanity. Consequently, there have been countless pilgrimages; pilgrimages on horseback, on foot, in buses, pilgrimages all over the world, by large groups, by individuals. I felt that the conditions had become ripe for me to contribute this way to a great cause: the cause of world peace.

This would also be an excellent opportunity to improve my own cultivation of the Dharma. While I bowed along the road praying for world peace with the actions of my body, I would also be praying in my mind and simultaneously striving to master the six perfections of an enlightened being (a Bodhisattva): giving, morality, patience, vigor, concentration, and wisdom. The more that I thought about it, the more I became resolved on doing it.

I didn't tell anyone about my decision to bow. I figured since it didn't involve anyone else, why talk about it? I didn't even inform the Abbot. One night in early October, after everyone was asleep, I packed up a bag with some books, food, and clothing, and went bowing out the door onto the sidewalk of Fifteenth Street. I would take three long strides, and then stretch down on hands and knees, bringing my forehead down to within an inch of the pavement. The cement was very cold. The streets were empty; it was dark and I felt quite strange. The bag, which weighed about thirty pounds, was a problem. On the third step, I would toss it ahead, and then bow up to it. But this act of bowing was extremely invigorating; it was tremendous exercise! I bowed steadily in order to get in as much mileage and experience as possible before daybreak.

As I bowed along, I had the physical work pretty much under control, but my mind was full of conflicting emotions. "My God!" I kept thinking to myself, "I have done a lot of hard-to-explain things in my life, but this is going to take the cake." I kept bowing:

turned right on Dolores Street, across Market Street, through the big Safeway supermarket lot, and headed in the general direction of the Golden Gate Bridge. At daybreak, I was in the heart of the Tenderloin district ghetto, and I could feel the city coming to life. I could also feel the presence of the San Francisco police, who had been shadowing me for several blocks. I could imagine what they would be thinking.

By noon, I had reached the top of Russian Hill. A lot of people had seen me by now, but none had talked to me. They mostly just stared with their mouths open. One lady drove by in a big white Chrysler, and right in the middle of an intersection she slammed on the brakes and exclaimed in horror, "Oh my God!" I tried to keep my mind as centered as best I could, and ignoring the occasional pangs of embarrassment, I kept pounding the pavement. Somewhere down inside of me, beneath all the mixed feelings and scattered thoughts, there was a faint flicker of laughter.

After a miserable lunch of cold rice and some sidewalk weeds, I bowed down Russian Hill, and by late afternoon I made it to a little park just before the entrance to Golden Gate Bridge. I had bowed five miles!

I was quite exhausted, so I found a tree to lean against, and immediately fell asleep. Several hours later I awoke, but I didn't feel at all like the same person I had been earlier in the day. My body was wasted, completely drained of energy. I was filled with a silent terror. I had felt this terror before, but never quite so intense. I couldn't go on like this. I looked up at the little lake in front of me with the geese and all the beautiful shrubbery, and the happy couples strolling hand in hand along the shore. Wow! Thirty years old and this is how far I'd strayed from reality! How did I get so estranged from ordinary life? And bowing for world peace! How was a lost soul like me going to help world peace?

As I sat there in my despair, dressed in Tang dynasty robes with a freshly shaven head, I contemplated my life. As a child in the Pacific Northwest, I was always the wildest kid in the neighborhood—though I'd been born into a good family. And if I wasn't out raising the devil, then you could find me in dreamland. There, in my flights of imagination, I would perform every heroic act then known to man. Yes, I had won major sports car races throughout the world. Innumerable times, I had whipped the high school ruffian and rescued his girlfriend the cheerleader. And yet, though my mind was in dreamland, I passed successfully through school with only a token effort.

After high school, I plunged into six years of submarine service in the Pacific with the U.S. Navy. My ship, the U.S.S. Rock, visited exotic ports throughout the Pacific, and I was able to actualize many of my wildest schemes. I labored in the very cramped and hot engine rooms, trying to keep thirty tons worth of GMC Diesels and two ancient Badger distillers running properly. On occasion I acted as the ship's diver and performed some very exciting recovery and repair jobs down underneath that two-thousand-ton steel shark. I really enjoyed life in the sub, but those long weekends ashore were my downfall. The Executive Officers' report said it all: "Tim Testu is a genuine asset to the ship. His excellent service aboard is only offset by his horrifying conduct ashore."

There was the time when Frank Messerli and I, after a long night of whiskey and bennies, stole the Admirals' launch from the Royal Philippines Navy. We were well on our way out of the harbor before we noticed that there were two torpedo boats after us. Fortunately, we outmaneuvered them by heading for shallow water. When we brought the little boat in to the pier, we saw about fifty men and several outraged officers there waiting for us. I don't know how we did it, but we came in to that pier at full speed, and then at the very last second, shifted into all back emergency. The little boat shuddered and moaned, emitting a big puff of black smoke and churning up the crystal blue water. It came to a perfect stop, just inches from the pier, and the men on the dock erupted in wild cheering. But the officers weren't at all happy, and before the day was over, we were sentenced to two months of confinement. It was a typical escapade, but even so, I emerged from the service with a good record and an honorable discharge.

Afterward back in the States, I blended with the clamor and chaos of the late sixties. I did a little college, and then later worked as a carpenter, railroad mechanic, harbor diver, and even a fry cook in a topless restaurant (I couldn't see anything from the kitchen). I did well enough, but inside of me there was an overwhelming sense of loneliness and frustration. Eventually, I fell into drugs, unemployment, and bad company, but fortunately escaped unscathed and found my way to an anarchistic commune near the foot of Mount Rainier, Washington. For six months, I didn't have a care in the world, until the whole place burned down.

By my twenty-fifth year, my dilemma was at its peak, but then by a stroke of luck, I ran across a little temple in San Francisco where the teachings of the Buddha were being transmitted to America. It was like walking into a cave of precious treasures. The cave was my own mind, and the treasure was the multi-faceted Dharma. Most important, I found a teacher with real ability. He was an elder Chinese Buddhist *bhikshu* (monk) in the patriarchal succession of Chan Masters, and he had brought to America the whole range of Great Vehicle Buddhism: the Teachings, the Secret Doctrines, the Pure Land School, the Moral Precepts, and Chan. I saw in the Master a living example of the much-sought-after qualities of not only Buddhism but of Daoism and Confucianism as well.

During my first exposure to the Master, I was continually flooded with emotions of all kinds. In his teaching, he instructed us not to be moved or turned around by any kind of situation, but the direct, penetrating manner in which he dealt with my thoughts caused me to respond like an emotional faucet that's running first hot and then cold water. I was overwhelmed with love and respect for the Master. His wisdom, compassion, humor, tact, timing, and understanding of human nature, combined with his penetrating vision and other inconceivable spiritual powers put him far beyond the scope of any teacher in America. There was no question about it.

Every evening, in a most orthodox and traditional setting, he gave instruction in the Dharma, and what we heard was unspeakably wonderful. There, in that little incense-filled room with thirty or so other people, I experienced states of joy and dharma bliss that brought me to tears many times. For the first time I had met a person who totally understood me and who really cared about my spiritual welfare and was able to do something about it to the ultimate degree.

It soon became obvious that the Master somehow had access to all of our petty little thoughts: past, present, and future. He rarely left his little room in the back of the temple, yet he always knew what was going on, and it all came out in the lectures. His manner of speaking was very penetrating, cutting through the crap, and getting down to the problems that we constantly seemed to create for ourselves. Sometimes there would be scoldings. "I'm not scolding you, I'm scolding your ghosts," he once said. But most of the time was spent carefully explaining the ailments of the grasping, calculating mind, and showing us how to cure ourselves.

During my first year of studying Buddhism, I worked part-time as an orderly at the Jewish Home for the Aged in San Francisco. Seeing all the suffering, sickness and death there gave me a strong impression of the vanity of self-centered existence. I saw very clearly that, although we people of the West have a great flair for life, we have no idea how to prepare for a dignified exit from this world. We have a thousand false values ingrained in us which we cling to desperately right up to the last minute. Buddhism, I found, could help prepare us for this important transition. After a year as a Buddhist layperson, I shaved my head and became a novice monk. A year later, in 1972, I became a fully ordained bhikshu, a Buddhist monk.

Living in the monastery, I went through a lot of changes. I began sleeping sitting up and eating only once a day. I was surprised to find that these "ascetic" practices were not as difficult as they seemed, and as time progressed they became more natural. I think that is why in the Chan School there is a saying: "Bitter practice, sweet mind." There were others in the monastery who cultivated much harder than I, some eating only raw vegetables, some not touching money, some following other difficult practices; but we all studied the sutras—the sayings of the Buddha—and there was plenty of time devoted to meditation and the work of daily life. In late 1970, we moved to an old brick mattress factory in the Mission district which we converted into what is now Gold Mountain Monastery.[1] And now, after three years at the monastery—having already left my family, my jobs, and my old future—I'd left the monastery and my teacher as well to take some strange bowing pilgrimage in quest of some impossible goal. Sitting there in a state of quiet terror in the little park by the Golden Gate Bridge, I couldn't imagine why I had even started out in the first place. I picked up my bag and dragged my weary bones back to the monastery.

I slipped right back into my regular routine. No one had even noticed that I'd been gone. I tried to work up an interest in the activities at the temple, but my heart just wasn't in it. I kept thinking about that one day of bowing. Despite all my false thinking and doubts, I had still gone a very real five miles! And there was something about that experience that was impossible to describe, but which felt like it was reaching to the core. It didn't take long before I decided to take another crack at it.

This time, however, I decided to be a little wiser and a little less mysterious. I revealed my intentions to the Master, and requested his opinion and help. The Master was at first interested, and then delighted with the idea. He gave me encouragement, and I could feel myself beginning to overflow with what in Christianity is called the "Holy Spirit." The Master said that the best way to understand the Dharma is to undertake difficult practices: "To do what no one else can do, to be patient when no one can be patient; this is what it's all about!" He recommended that I wait two weeks and start on October 16. Then one evening at the Dharma lecture, he announced my intentions, and an awesome hush fell over the place. When he said, "Heng Ju is going to bow a thousand miles for the cause of peace," I really felt wonderful. He said it with such authority that it seemed like he was guaranteeing it to be a success. From that point onward, I entered into a very fine state of mind, and everyone else seemed to be delighted with the idea, too. I received all kinds of encouragement, offers of food, clothing, camping equipment, etc. Bhikshu Heng Yo, alias David Bernstein of Providence, Rhode Island, offered to come along to carry the supplies.

This journal is a record of our daily thoughts and actions while involved in bowing for world peace. It has been polished up and re-written from the original log that Heng Yo so meticulously kept during the entire trip. All of the events were real, and none of the names have been changed. Only the perspective has changed as we look back on the trip from the point of completion.

Speaking for both myself and Heng Yo, we would like to transfer any merit we may have acquired from this journey to living beings throughout the universe, hoping that they may quickly obtain the absolute, perfect enlightenment.

Introduction by Heng Yo

I was raised along with my two brothers in good surroundings which my parents worked hard to provide. As a child, I was moody, active, rebellious, and, in general, typical of the times. My life was tempered by a few occasions on which I got into minor trouble. I remember one incident when I spelled the junior high principal's name backward at an assembly. He just happened to be walking by as I laughed at the ridiculous-sounding name, but it wasn't so funny anymore as I sat in the jail of his office.

There were good times too. In the winter, the family would ski in New Hampshire, and we children would spend summers in that wonderful corner of the world called Maine. I indifferently passed through eighteen changes of the New England seasons before I left home to attend a small experimental college in rural Michigan. I was lulled by the illusory freedom which I enjoyed there. I could sleep as late as I wanted; I could eat whatever and whenever I wanted and nobody told me what to do. But when the first year came to a close, my rapture came to an abrupt halt; not surprisingly to anyone but myself, I had flunked out.

Entrenched in a deep depression, I went off to Cape Cod, trying to answer the riddle of my existence, trying to answer a question I could not even ask. I found that I could not run away from myself, for no matter how far from consciousness I fled, I inevitably came back to the same place. After a few months of living alone as a bum, I concluded that my life had nothing more than a veneer of worth. I had never really questioned what I was supposed to be doing with my life besides eating and sleeping and wearing clothes. I had been alienated and insulated from reality, living in a world which was terribly devoid of meaning. It was, as Bob Dylan said, a state which "your gravity fails, and negativity don't pull you through." I strove to find a way out of the vacuum.

Someone gave me a book on Daoism, and upon reading it, I wanted to slam my fist on the table and shout "Yes! THIS is what I mean." I stayed up all night reading. That book made more sense than my whole life had. I was caught up in a tide that sent me back to college. I found myself studying Chinese and Asian philosophy. I gradually became interested in Buddhism. I began to meditate with a friend. And yet, there was a slight but persistent gnawing deep inside me. What was it?

One night I was sitting alone in meditation in my room. Outside two feet of freshly fallen snow covered everything and every sound. The whole school was on Thanksgiving vacation, and it was intensely still. Suddenly I had a very strange experience: inside of my body and outside had merged into a single oneness. There was no separation, no integration, no defined space which was "me" or which "I" was in. Bright light was everywhere.

The state faded rapidly as all sorts of thoughts bubbled up to the surface of my consciousness. I didn't know how long it had lasted, but I was left with a crystal-clear knowledge that I had to find a teacher who could explain such experiences and guide me along the path. I noticed that the gnawing feeling inside of me was gone. I redoubled my efforts in school.

I heard that there was an enlightened Chan Master in San Francisco, and during the summer break of 1968 I went to see for myself if it was true. After passing through the tangle of mysterious and unfamiliar sensory contacts of Chinatown, San Francisco, I slowly climbed the four flights of stairs to the old Buddhist Lecture Hall, predecessor of Gold Mountain Monastery. The tiny room, a former Daoist temple, was crammed with people absorbed in reading Chinese, meditating and working. It was the first one-room schoolhouse I'd ever seen in operation. When I saw how the people there ate but one meal a day, and slept sitting up on the roof in meditation posture, I felt rather uncomfortable. The slight gnawing had returned, but I would not admit it to myself. I returned to the Midwest a little bewildered, writing off the whole experience as unimportant.

But two years later, at the end of 1970, after whizzing through school, that same uncomfortable feeling brought me back to San Francisco. Before long, I was helping with the construction of Gold Mountain Monastery, the new headquarters of the Sino-American Buddhist Association. The force and the magnitude of that gnawing feeling are hard to convey. Fundamentally, it can be described as the ripening fruit of karmic seeds planted in the past. We tend to forget things we have done because of our limited unenlightened state. Sometimes an encounter with an object or a word can trigger a flash memory of something that had been covered over, and we may be motivated to act.

I became a disciple of the Venerable Chan Master Hsuan Hua, Abbot of Gold Mountain, and later the same year became a novice monk. In 1972, along with Heng Ju, I was fully ordained as a bhikshu, and was given the name Heng Yo.

A year later, I heard that Heng Ju was about to embark on a thousand-mile pilgrimage. He planned to walk from San Francisco to Seattle, bowing every third step for the sake of world peace. I was overwhelmed. That same gnawing feeling I had had in my room at school and again in 1970 returned, but this time it was amplified tenfold. I walked around in a mild daze, trying to forget about the imminent pilgrimage, but there was no way I could get it out of my consciousness. Finally after three days of agonizing preoccupation with the idea, I spoke to Heng Ju, and volunteered to go along and contribute whatever aid I could along the way. It was at this time that I decided to keep a record of our experiences.

Even before we left San Francisco to begin the pilgrimage, people were doubtful about how and where we would obtain the basic requirements for survival—food, clothing and shelter. But the Master had said that if a person is completely sincere and genuine in what he does, then survival will never be a problem. The Master had completely proved this in his own life, and after a while on our trip, we too found that to be true without fail. We discovered very quickly, however, that what is tacitly assumed by this principle is equally true: if your heart is not sincere, then survival will be a problem!

This book is an account of our ten-month pilgrimage: some of the events that took place, and our feelings and observations along the way. It is impossible to mention all of the kind people who helped us in one way or another. This book, then, is an expression of gratitude to those people; to the Buddhas of the ten directions of the past, present and future; to our teacher, the Venerable Master Hua; and to our parents and fellow cultivators. My hope is that the book will evoke in the reader a response similar to what I felt when I first visited the old Buddhist Lecture Hall and remembered with a start that the path of cultivation is open to all who choose to follow it.

The Venerable Master Hsuan Hua, Abbot of Gold Mountain Monastery, with Heng Yo, foreground, and Heng Ju

I. San Francisco to Garberville

16 October 1973. The Very Beginning. Heng Ju writes:

This morning all the folks at Gold Mountain Monastery drove us down to this little park by Golden Gate Bridge, where I had previously given up. We didn't waste any time; I started bowing northward, and Heng Yo followed behind with a backpack full of supplies. The monks, nuns, and laypeople recited the 415-syllable Great Compassion Mantra while circling around us. There were about twenty people altogether. After bowing two blocks, I was preparing to cross the big highway in front of the Marina, when a bunch of fire trucks arrived and stopped right in front of us. There was general confusion for a while: we didn't know what they were doing and they wondered what we were doing. The street was too busy to cross in the bowing fashion, so I just stood there and bowed in place for a while. It must have been quite a spectacle. Finally, I decided to simply walk across, and I resumed bowing once I reached the other side. As we approached the long entrance-ramp to the bridge, the group departed, and Heng Yo and I were on our own.

Yo would go up ahead a few hundred feet with the equipment, and then bow in place until I passed him by; then he would pick up the gear and go bow up ahead some more.

At the Golden Gate Bridge, we met our first obstacle. A bridge official came running out and said if we were going to do "that" across his bridge, he was going to bust us. He said that we could "either walk across like normal human beings or not go at all." Then he said: "What is it? What are you going to do?" We could see that he was looking for trouble. I said, "We're going to think about for a while," which flustered him, but there was nothing he could say about that. We bowed in place for a while, and then decided that there was no choice but to walk across like "normal human beings." On the other side, in Marin County, we continued bowing and I suddenly remembered the Master's departing words: "Tomorrow Heng Ju and Heng Yo will cross the Golden Gate Bridge in a single thought."

From here, we plan to head on through Stinson Beach and all the way up Highway 1 to its end in Leggett, California. From there, we will take Highway 101 all the way up to the middle of Washington State, and then we'll head inland to Seattle. According to our map, we should encounter almost no freeways.

Right now we are camped under a little clump of trees just past the Golden Gate Bridge near the Sausalito exit.

17 October 1973. Heng Ju writes:

We turned off Highway 101 and headed down into Sausalito this sunny morning. Hordes of Porches and Volkswagens buzzed by us on their way to work in the big city. As we entered this peaceful little bay town, many folks along the sidewalks stopped to stare at us, but only one old woman stopped to talk, saying that the Buddha was dead. At noon, Kuo Rung Epstein and family and their friend Tom Yager appeared with a hot Chinese lunch. Dr. Epstein,[2] who is a philosophy instructor at San Francisco State University, expressed quite an interest in our practice. When lunch was over, we continued bowing, and a mangy-looking mutt started following us.

He whimpered and cried as he made circles around me, as if deeply ashamed of all the dog-like things he had done to warrant a dog's body, and then left.

In general, people stayed away from us. Perhaps they think it's a publicity stunt or something. I wonder how many realize what great possibilities there are in bowing. In the East, especially in India, China, and other Buddhist countries, bowing is a way of showing respect, salutation and obeisance. In old China, bowing was almost the same as shaking hands is in America. Workers bowed to the lords, lords bowed to the kings, kings bowed to the emperor, and on some occasions, the emperor would bow to enlightened Masters and ask them to help guide the country.

For us, though, bowing is a vehicle for meditation. It is most conducive to concentration, since it doesn't involve thinking or talking. The slow and graceful repetition of the motions is an exercise in awareness. The whole idea is to bring to a halt the wild ramblings of conscious thought, and thus reveal the underlying self-nature which is beyond all dualities and conceptualization. This self-nature is all-pervasive, like empty space; it is not born, nor does it die. The goal of Buddhist practice is to attain union with this nature. Bowing meditation is one of many methods of approach.

We bowed five miles today, and made it all the way through downtown Sausalito. Right now we are camped in the bushes next to Tamalpais junction. Tomorrow we head up over a big hill on a windy little road that leads to the coast.

18 October 1973. Heng Yo writes:

The road is narrow and full of curves bordered by a thin gravel shoulder. Heng Ju quickly learned how sharp the gravel was against his hands and knees. We tore up a shirt to wrap around his knees for protection.

I neglected to bring along an extra pair of pants, and the pair I was wearing has seen better days; the material had worn thin in several places. This morning, as I bowed in place waiting for Ju to bow by, the seat of my pants split apart. Fortunately, though, my robe covered the rip. I planned to sew the damage later in the day, but as I continued to bow, more rips began to open up. This would never do.

In the last couple of days, people have been shocked enough to see two monks bowing out here in public, but to see a monk bowing without a decent pair of trousers would be truly outrageous! I'd surely be arrested for indecent exposure. The cool Pacific breeze filtered through the holes and chilled me to the bone. When Heng Ju came bowing by, I mentioned that I was in dire need of a pair of pants, but there was nothing we could do. We didn't have any extra pants or any money to buy a replacement pair. People that passed by were giving me the strangest looks.

I picked up the pack and began walking ahead. Right around the first corner is a pile of brown cloth lying right in my path. Excitedly, I ran to it and picked it up. It was a pair of men's slacks, size 34 waist. Just my size! Not too small, not too big, but just right! I could hardly believe it. I jumped into the bushes and put them on; they were perfect. I don't know if it was a Bodhisattva or what that left these in my path, but I certainly am grateful!

Police have been driving by often without giving a second or prolonged look. Proceeding with minor incidents, we bowed through Tamalpais junction today and made six miles before making camp here on a hill in a cedar grove. We have no tent, but we are somewhat protected from the miserable rain by a sheet of plastic.

19 October 1973. Heng Yo writes:

We got an early start after some wild raspberry tea. Heng Ju bowed ahead while I packed up camp in the early morning. We are going slowly due to uphill and gravel roads.

Being outside for the first three days of our trip, I am confronted by millions of forms of life: plants, insects, and animals. Despite their countless numbers and varieties, though, everything with life must sooner or later die. The pattern for all life is birth, dwelling, decay, and emptiness. Birth is when certain elements come together and coalesce, forming into a body. Dwelling is the period of time that these elements remain in stable relationship. Decay is when the elements disperse and redistribute themselves. Emptiness is when the relationship is completely over, and the entity ceases to exist.

Out here in the open, my thoughts have no walls to bounce off. My mind radiates into the heavens and mingles with the stars. Unencumbered, I fathom the ageless questions of humanity: Who am I? Where am I going? The Sages tell me that the answers lie within. This journey, then, will be an inward one. When I crack through the shell of illusory selfness, all distinctions between inside and outside will vanish. I will see this world as being my very own body. That is why the Buddha taught compassion; when you know that you are really everything, you want to be nice to it all.

Kuo Jung came to offer lunch. About five miles to Stinson Beach to go, we made camp after gathering acorns and huckleberries. Despite light rain, we made fire anyway.

20 October 1973. Heng Yo writes:

Penetrating rain. We slowly made our way down the hill onto Highway One, and then north through Stinson Beach, where a drunk yelled out at Heng Ju (from a safe distance): "Hey clown, get lost!" After a really tiring day, we set up camp on a hilly cow-pasture overlooking the ocean. Now as I write the log, I gaze into the small fire that we managed to kindle. Will someone see the smoke from the wet wood and turn us in for trespassing? No, the strong ocean breeze carries it away into oblivion. We rig a makeshift tent with some plastic and settle down for a long cold night. Five miles is a long way to bow! Heng Ju says that he has always liked to travel, but I think that this trip is much more worthwhile than aimless wandering. We have a purpose and a goal. It feels right to be out here. When I think of all the time in my life that I squandered, all the energy that I've wasted, I resolve to become more vigorous each day.

21 October 1973. Heng Yo writes:

We awakened to the wind howling through the trees. It was pitch black when we broke camp and felt our way back to the road. Heng Ju wrenched his back while jumping the fence, but nevertheless he got out on the cold, wet, uninviting blacktop and started bowing.

When the Venerable Master Xu Yun started on his long pilgrimage, there were several monks who accompanied him, but they soon got tired, and turned back. We have been on the road for only five day now, but it is becoming very clear to me that bowing 1,000 miles is going to be a lot more difficult than I thought. I'm sure that if it weren't for the fact that Heng Ju is so determined to do this thing right, and to bring benefit to the world, that the whole thing would have folded already.

The severe wind has cluttered the road with large branches, and the culverts and rain ditches roar with the sound of rainwater. Kuo Tun came with hot water and lunch. A county sheriff checked us this afternoon to see if we were escaped criminals or madmen. He left with a disappointed look on his face when he found nothing he could book us for. We have set up out meager camp near the Bolinas turnoff.

22 October 1973. Heng Yo writes:

It's a cold and wet autumn here on the coast, but like the cows and the horses, we are adjusting to life in the elements. Passing through Five Rivers, a girl brought us hot tea.

I've been thinking more about the "inward journey." What does it really mean? We must look not at our projections, but at the very thought processes themselves. Our minds should become like mirrors, not like cameras, which can only take pictures of other things. It involves reversing the flow of attention. The mind should be developed in such a way that it does not move when confronted with sensory impressions. Buddhists have observed that although the functioning of the mind is extremely complex; its movements can be divided into two categories.

The first is grasping: the mind gravitates toward pleasurable states (hot tea!) and tries to make them last. The second tendency is rejection: the mind tends to withdraw from situations that it deems unpleasant (cold wet weather!). This movement of the mind oscillating between these two opposites is the reason we have lost touch with our inherent wisdom, which is basically still and undefiled.

The whole idea of cultivation, then, is to direct our attention "inward," and to learn to observe these movements and their causes. Next is to develop concentration so that no matter what happens, pleasant or unpleasant, the mind does not move. Eventually wisdom will grow. Now that we are out here on this highway, I can see that there are going to be plenty of opportunities to put these principles to the test.

23 October 1973. Heng Ju writes:

We bowed through Olema today, a small village just inland of Point Reyes National Seashore. It was very peaceful. In our past entries, I forgot to mention that several of the families from the monastery have been coming out to bring us hot vegetarian lunches. So far, Gwo Dun Schweig, Gwo Rung Epstein, Gwo Yo Linebarger, and their families have come out, and in each case, it has been a welcome surprise.

This afternoon, as we worked our way along these desolate flatlands, a lone wanderer with a small puppy joined our strange caravan. Now we are all three camped under an oak tee about a quarter mile from the highway on somebody's land. It isn't easy to find campsites around here, but Heng Yo has been finding them. Every evening, just about a half hour before I'm ready to quit for the day, he walks ahead to pick a spot. Almost every inch of land around here is private property, so the decisions are tough to make. At first, he wouldn't make the decisions, but would wait for me to catch up and decide. Now after seven days on the road, he has changed completely. By the time I get up to him, he generally has the whole camp dug in, the tent set up, and sometimes, if conditions permit, he even has a campfire going. This is a real reward after a long day of bowing.

Making decisions is an important aspect of spiritual growth. I remember an incident at Gold Mountain when I was trying to make a decision, but couldn't quite get it together. At the time I had just become a novice monk, I still had seventy dollars left over from when I was working on the outside. The money was burning a hole in my pocket, and I wanted to get rid of it. When the incident occurred, I was standing on the third floor landing at Gold Mountain, about one hundred feet down the hall from the Master's room. My hand was in my pocket fingering the cash. I was trying to figure out what to do with it. My original intention was to give it all to the monastery, but then some greedy thoughts began to arise. "Maybe I should keep a little for myself. Mmmm, how much should I keep?" I thought to myself. Pretty soon, a whole chain of ideas and arguments concerning the money arose. I stood there, unable to move or decide; my hand, which was holding the money, was sweating profusely. I felt like the neurotic donkey who was caught midway between two equally succulent bales of hay, and who went insane trying to figure out which one to eat.

As I stood there watching my brains battle it out, I heard the Master's door open somewhere in the distance. It was very much as if a door in my own mind had opened. I knew that he was "tuned in" on me. The Master has said, "When you obtain spiritual penetrations such as the heavenly eye, the heavenly ear, knowledge of other's thoughts and knowledge of past lives, you no longer need televisions, radios, radar, or sonar. One whose mind is free of idle thinking can miraculously perceive and penetrate events throughout the universe. Every cell of the body becomes a picture tube, and every hair a control knob."

At that time, I heard the Master shouting to one of the American monks who happened to be in the vicinity. Within a minute, the monk came running down the corridor toward me, excitedly waving a ten-dollar bill in the air. "Heng Ju! The Master wants to know if you have change for a ten!" I stood there for a moment unable to speak, my mind totally blown. Still in somewhat of a daze, I pulled out a couple of fives and handed them to him. He said, "Hey! You look like you've just seen a ghost!" "Yes," I replied, "My own."

A teacher who has spiritual penetrations can instruct on so many different levels that it is impossible to describe them all. The realms of thought and language are only an aspect of the teachings. One must realize that when the teacher's mind and disciple's mind are one, then literally everything can become a vehicle for teaching. The sudden slamming of a door, when done at the appropriate time with the proper measure of force, can be an excellent way of getting one's point across. Again, there are telephone ringings, coughing spasms, grins, ignorings, scoldings, undue praisings, difficult-to-answer questions, and many other subtle and mysterious methods, which, although they might seem quite normal in themselves, occur at such incredibly appropriate times that it becomes impossible to mistake the unobstructed nexus between Master and disciple.

24 October 1973. Heng Ju writes:

Cold and frosty as we bowed north from Olema into the relatively large town of Point Reyes Station. At 9 a.m. a reporter from the Point Reyes Light, a local newspaper, came out to interview us, and we answered his questions as best we could. Perhaps now more people will understand what we are doing. Once in town, I bowed along the sidewalk, while Yo kept close by. He reports hearing the following conversation as we passed the local hardware store.

"Hey Martha! Look at this! Shall we call the Sherriff?"

"No, George, leave him alone; he's not hurting anything."

After about fifteen energy-packed minutes, we reached the outskirts of town where we met a Buddhist laywoman named Katy Powell (Gwo Sying) who lives in Point Reyes with her two children. She wanted to get in on a little bowing, and followed about 20 feet behind, going almost a full mile in the sharp gravel before heading back home.

Gwo Dun Schweig and family arrived at noon with hot brown rice, vegetable soup, dark bread, oatmeal cookies, and apples.

Members of the Sino-American Buddhist Association Circumambulated Heng Ju and Heng Yo and recited the Great Compassion Mantra as they began their journey at the San Francisco Marina.

In the afternoon, Ben Williams and the Channel Five CBS News team from San Francisco arrived, and did a lot of filming as we worked our way along the rocky coastal cliffs. In the evening, just as a storm was coming over us, we found an abandoned little cabin nestled in the woods. I spent half an hour gathering deadwood and lit a fire, and now we are drying out our gear and boiling water for tea.

25 October 1973. Heng Yo writes:

Today Upsaka Gwo Jou Rounds,[3] editor of the *Napa County Record*, came by with supplies, and wrote a news item about the trip.

We started bowing by Tomales Bay, and toward the end of the day, discovered another abandoned, dilapidated cabin in which to stay out of the rain for the evening. But during the pitch-black night, we found that it was far from abandoned. There were raccoons, rats, squirrels, and other busy living beings in there along with us. Their sounds filled the blackness, amplified by the unfamiliar background of silence. For a moment, I felt genuinely scared—what if it was a bear? It is one thing to understand intellectually that the world is illusory, and quite another to actually live without fear. I recited the Buddha's name, trying to hold my mind still. A thought then replaced my irrational fear: All living beings are endowed with the capacity to become Buddhas, enlightened beings. During the course of the Venerable Xu Yun's life, there were many instances when wild animals came and actually bowed to him. His virtue was so powerful that it brought out this latent capacity even in tigers, wolves and foxes. He would explain and transmit the Three Refuges, accepting them as disciples, and then explain the moral precepts. Their improved behavior would then guarantee them a better rebirth, thus affording better opportunities to cultivate the Way.

After contemplating in this way, the night-noises in the shack ceased to alarm me, and I dozed off with the amusing thought that a thousand little Buddhas of the future are hard at work, gathering in their winter stores.

26 October 1973 Heng Ju writes:

Gwo Tung Almassy (Ya Ya), a Buddhist disciple who runs a health food store in Stinson Beach, brought us lunch today. Later in the afternoon a man on a motorcycle stopped to talk. He mentioned a couple of times that he thought what we were doing was "a work of God." Another man, who lives in Inverness, brought us some fresh fruit, and wanted to know how bowing works. We sat down in the grass alongside the highway, and I explained to him the possibilities. I told him that at first it is just a physical act. But after a while, when the body is fully accustomed to the work, it is possible to start bringing together a harmonious union between body and mind. The physical act of bowing and the mental exercise of reciting the Bodhisatva's name work together as a mantra, or method, for stopping the intellectual processes. The work lies in just trying to be aware of what's going on within me and around me, and not letting my mind wander off into the realms of past and future. It says in the *Shurangama Sutra* that when the mad mind stops, that very stopping is enlightenment. A person who has reached this stage has no thoughts of bowing, of peace, of separateness, or of wholeness. Instead, everything is of a single suchness. One directly perceives that the mind is simply Buddha.

The man, who had been listening intently, thought about it for a moment and then said that he thought it was definitely a very worthwhile goal that we were pursuing, but perhaps there might be a better way to go about it.

Today we bowed alongside Tomales Bay, past a large Synanon community, where a few hecklers yelled at us from the top of a hill. Then we bowed through the small village of Marshall, and finally set up camp on a rolling hill overlooking the bay.

27 October 1973. Heng Ju writes:

It was a beautiful Saturday morning as we worked our way into the little town of Tomales. Although it was only 8:00 a.m., over a hundred people were crowded along the main street. Something was strange here; there weren't even any cars on the street! In the very center of town, right at the main intersection, the crowd fell absolutely quiet. I could feel the energy of hundreds of eyes staring silently at me. It was a heavy scene. Suddenly from out of the crowd, an older woman with lots of lipstick and makeup on came running out and handed me a box of jelly-filled donuts (my favorite). "Will you take these?" she nervously asked. I stopped my bowing and slowly stood up.

I suppose that every person has a few events or moments in their lives that stick in the memory forever. This would be one for me. I had been bowing for over two hours, and as I stood up to receive the donuts I could feel the warm sun drenching the whole scene with its light. The feeling of warmth seemed to go all the way through my skin right to the very center of my being. I just felt really peaceful, and at that moment, I remembered the Master's oft-spoken words: "You have to learn to see all affairs as no affair." At least for this one time, I could see what he meant.

The lady and the silent crowd were waiting for me to respond. I nodded in the affirmative, accepted the donuts, and put them into a very large pocket that I had sewn onto my baggy pants. She ran back to the safety and anonymity of the ever-increasing crowd, and I heard her remark, "Well, at least he eats!" I continued bowing and Yo kept close by. As we reached the north end of town, we heard a shrill whistle and the staccato beat of big drums rolling out. I thought I must be imagining it, but then at the last intersection, we heard two big Harley Davidson motorcycles fire up. Off to our left down one of the side streets was an entire parade with marching units, horses, a big band, floats, and all kinds of things! It was the Tomales Homecoming parade, and they had held it up for half an hour to let us pass. What a fine bunch of people! Only in America could something like this happen. Yo and I stopped to rest and watched the parade. A lot of friendly folks stopped to chat with us.

Gwo Dzun, who makes a living by delivering organic beauty supplies to health food stores, came by with lunch. In the afternoon, we bowed uninterrupted, and after a total of five miles, made camp under a lone, giant oak in somebody's pasture. After evening meditation, Yo walked down to the nearest farmhouse and bought a gallon of fresh milk, while I put together a small fire. Now, sitting here bloated with hot milk, I write the log.

28 October 1973. Heng Ju writes:

Gwo Mien, a friend of Gwo Dzun's, brought us lunch today. (She has also come by a couple of other times.) She always brings a very balanced meal, cooked according to the strictest macrobiotic tradition. We pushed on through Valley Ford, a small town built around one main intersection, and then on out through the windy flatlands and over the Marin-Sonoma county line.

Country bowing goes pretty smoothly, but in the towns it's a different story. There is a real tendency to be self-conscious. This presents a real fine opportunity to contemplate the emptiness of self. The Chan school of Buddhism has a device called "Who?" At all times at all places, one simply asks just who it is that is aware. This is called reversing the light and illuminating within. The idea is to impartially observe thoughts as they arise and to try to trace them back to their source. One finds, though, that there is no source. The *Avatamsaka Sutra* [5] says, "There is no thinker nor that which is thought of; there is only the rising of karma-bound thought." This process of investigation is what the Chinese call *cān chán* 參禪 (literally, investigating Chan).

Melissa, a young woman from the Blue Mountain Meditation Center, brought us a loaf of bread. A young couple in a dilapidated old pickup stopped. They said that ten years ago, people around here would have thought us to be insane, but now they pretty much accept what we are doing, and some even think it's a great scheme!

29 October 1973. Heng Ju writes:

Gwo Dun Schweig and his wife, Gwo Chin, appeared on the horizon right after 12:00 in their beat up Ford van. Heng Yo and I had just finished lunch, and were just starting the afternoon's bowing when they pulled alongside, and said, "We've been looking all over for you; we've brought lunch." Well, they looked so sincere, and they had obviously gone to so much trouble to bring us the lunch, that Yo and I didn't have the heart to tell them we had just eaten. So just to be polite, we sat down and went through an entire lunch again, Gwo Dun making sure that we ate plenty. I even ate an entire jar of Gwo Dun's Deaf Smith peanut butter, as is my usual practice when he comes.

This afternoon, some more people stopped us to talk. We've noticed that people begin to fall into categories. Most people, we find, have made up their mind before they even talk to us. They are either for us or against us; it's just a question of intensity. People in this category themselves feel that every person must be categorized. They feel that you are either a Catholic, or a Jew, or a Buddhist, or whatever. It's one of those black-and-white, or right-or-wrong things. Despite all the movements of the new consciousness, it is surprising to see how many people still think this way.

30 October 1973. Heng Ju writes:

Now, as the thin snaking highway begins its descent back to the coast, we have met with disaster. We were just a mile short of the coastal town of Bodega Bay, when I felt a call to go to the bathroom. Needless to say, there were no bathrooms, so I crawled off the highway into a little clump of bushes to perform my daily duty. Unfortunately, there wasn't any toilet paper available, so I grabbed at the nearest bush and pulled off a handful of bright orange leaves. That was a costly mistake! I soon found out that those pretty little gems were, in fact, poison oak! (I had always thought poison oak was green.) Thinking didn't help at this point. We secured bowing, and by evening my entire body was itching something terrible. It kept me up all night; I didn't get a moment's sleep. I did, however, remember to recite the name of Avolokiteshvara Bodhisattva (in Chinese, Guan Shi Yin Pu Sa), and it helped keep my mind off the pain.

By morning, I could hardly move, much less bow, so Yo and I just sat down on a mound of dirt by the side of the road. We were both in total despair. Once again, I was overwhelmed with doubts and with a sense of impossibility and unreality of what we were doing. Here, with half of California, all of Oregon, and all of Washington left to bow through, and I don't even know how to wipe my own ass!

We sat there for several hours. We couldn't turn back (or could we?). We definitely couldn't go on. We sat and watched the cars pass by. There seemed to be no conceivable way to solve our problem. Suddenly, though, as if in magical response to our dilemma, two familiar-looking vans pulled to a stop before us. Out popped the whole group from Gold Mountain! And the Master, too! We moved to an empty parking lot in front of an abandoned cannery. They brought out food, clothing, medicine, everything we needed, even toilet paper! What a wonderful feeling in the air!

We all sat in a circle about fifteen feet in diameter. First Yo and I explained our experiences over the last few days; then one by one the monks and nuns gave short Dharma talks. While they spoke, the Master took my right hand and began rubbing it. He rubbed and rubbed, very softly, while he recited a mantra. Gradually, I could feel every bit of tension and pain leave my body. I couldn't hear what anyone else was saying. I could only feel the warmth of the afternoon sun. Nothing else mattered.

The meeting lasted about an hour, then they got in the vans to depart. The Master instructed us to put more mental energy into the bowing. He said that reciting the name of Guan Yin Bodhisattva is the best method (dharma) for this situation. He said that not only does Guan Yin have the power to help individuals, but this Bodhisattva can greatly help in the bringing of peace to the world, in ways that are inconceivable.

Just before they left, I asked the Master, "Last night I called for Guan Yin Bodhisattva to come and rescue me, and today you and the people of Gold Mountain have come to the rescue. Isn't this quite a coincidence?"

The Master immediately replied, "It's no big thing. Anytime you like, just give a call. I'll be there."

I learned a lot today. For one thing, I'll never forget what poison oak looks like as long as I live, and I'll do my best to save others from this painful experience. But more important, I got a

A delegation from Gold Mountain arrived "as if in magical response to our dilemma."

better understanding of what I call the Master's central philosophy, "Everything's OK." Those two words are the essence of his teaching; I have heard them spoken hundreds of times. "Everything's OK" doesn't mean that you can just run out and do whatever you please. No, "Everything's OK" is a very disciplined state of mind, wherein one observes the rise and fall of all conditioned things with complete detachment. It is a place of no-place. And yet, without leaving this detachment, one can be totally involved and lead a responsible and mature life. It is something that can be sought after and obtained. No matter how bad conditions may seem in the world of phenomena, ultimately "Everything's OK."

Before going back to Gold Mountain, the Master gave each of us his instructions. This is what he said:

On the Occasion of Seeing Off
Chan Cultivator Heng Ju,
Who Has Vowed to Bow Every Three Steps
Seeking for World Peace:

At Gold Mountain Dhyana Monastery, in the United States of America, the Sangha is young and numerous. They concentrate on safeguarding the proper Dharma, and each one has his particular good points. Now you have made a vow never made before, to practice sagely conduct which has never before been practiced, bowing every three steps to the Jewels, to the Buddha, Dharma, and Sangha throughout the ten directions.

Because your sincerity and earnestness in seeking for world peace is genuine, you will certainly evoke a magnificent response. Although your initial resolve came easily, however, it may be difficult to fulfill your vows. Don't give up; remain firm, sincere, and constant. The thousand miles over which you will pass is only one small step within the Dharma realm. Be resolved never to cease until you reach your goal. Raise up your spirits! I leave you with this verse of parting:

Practicing what is difficult to practice
  is the conduct of the Sage;

> Enduring what is hard to endure
>   is the genuine patience;
> All Buddhas throughout the ten directions
>   have walked down this road;
> The eighty thousand Bodhisattvas
>   have followed right along.
> Blow the magnificent Dharma conch,
>   and raise up the cry.
> Shake your precious pewter staff;
>   transform stingy greed.
> Your work complete and result full,
>   return midst songs to triumph.
> Then I'll give my disciple
>   a meal of berry pie.

Instructions to the Chan Cultivator Heng Yo
Who Protects and Aids Cultivator Ju
As He Fulfills His Resolve
To Bow to the Buddhas, Seeking for World Peace
For All Living Beings:

   From start to finish, don't waver; when meeting with difficulties, don't change. Acting as his protector, help him to realize the power of his vows. The ancient worthies most esteemed the ability to forget oneself and to safeguard others. In the present day, worthies are rare. Among the practices of a Bodhisattva, this is one practice. Among the doors into liberation, this is one door. Never, even for an instant, forget your initial intent; always maintain it single-mindedly right to the end. Be heroic and diligent, and defeat the demonic hordes. If gods or dragons come to pay their respects, don't be pleased. If you meet obstructing situations, even less should you become angry. Be without knowing and without attainment, and the wonderful function will be difficult to exhaust. When your studies are put into practice, you will have the translucence of fine jade. Remember these instructions, and don't turn your back on my heart.
   I leave you with this verse of parting:

> *In every step fiercely progress*
> 　*on to victory,*
> *Gwo Dao Heng Yo, act as*
> 　*his guardian and his aid!*
> *As Gwo Yu passes over*
> 　*fully three thousand li,*
> *He will cross, as would a car,*
> 　*eighty thousand steps.*
> *Here in the scientific age,*
> 　*you are practicing as of old;*
> *The evoked response from the Buddha's teaching*
> 　*will shake beings from confusion.*
> *Strive forward! Strive forward!*
> 　*Ever strive forward!*
> *Don't stop! Don't stop!*
> 　*Don't ever stop!*

31 October 1973. Heng Ju writes.

"Everything's OK" doesn't mean slopping around the beach with a can of beer in one hand, and a copy of the *Diamond Sutra* in the other. There are too many people now who live like heathen pigs and think they are enlightened. People who really understand Buddhism know that the single most important dharma is cutting off desire. Buddha himself said that the highest consciousness of all is simply no desire. The Master at Gold Mountain teaches it that way, too, but not many people really want to hear it, how much the less do it. Take me, for example. In the last line of the poem that the Master just gave me, there is a reference to a berry pie; I'll now tell the story it refers to.

When I first came to Gold Mountain, I carried with me habits which I had been gradually accumulating for twenty-five years, the heaviest of which were ten years of smoking, and six years of drinking. Now, to enter the monastery where discipline is quite real, it is necessary to cut off these habits point blank. Well, I managed to stop smoking and drinking, but my heavy greed energy then began to manifest in the realm of food. I quickly found that I could at least temporarily gratify my desires by eating a lot. However, when I took up the practice of eating only one meal a day, all my neurotic energy became confined to the forty-minute period allowed for lunch. What a tremendous challenge it was to turn all this bad energy into meditation and wholesome action!

There were occasions, though, when I couldn't handle it. And I used to slip out and head down to the local bakery to buy a bag of heavy pastries, which I found were capable of totally obliterating all my afflictions. To get to the point, one day I had gone out for pastries and had eaten the entire batch, except for one berry pie, which I simply couldn't find room for. So I carefully tucked it inside my coat and returned to the monastery. Now at Gold Mountain, everyone follows the rules of not eating after noon. Some people eat breakfast, but most people cultivate the ascetic practice of eating only once a day. That day during afternoon meditation, I began to get hungry again, and my thoughts turned to the pie. During the evening lecture, while the Master was speaking the Dharma, the pie was all I could think about. I decided I was going to eat it after the lecture. The hell with the rules!

It was about 10 p.m. and everyone had retired when I very quietly slipped out the third-floor bathroom window, carefully shutting it behind me, and climbed up the fire escape to the roof. I opened up the pie and sunk my teeth into that luscious sugary crust, biting down into those succulent juicy red berries. "Christ!" I thought to myself, "If this isn't Nirvana, what is?"

Just at that very moment, I looked over at the fire escape to see that someone else was climbing up onto the roof! I stood there terror-struck, with a mouthful of pie. There was no place I could run! It was the Master! I stood there unmoving for a moment while my brain began hemorrhaging. Then I began walking around in a circle on the rooftop as if in deep contemplation. The Master, too, began to circle the roof as if in deep contemplation, but he was going in the opposite direction. We passed each other twice without looking at each other, but on the third lap, I looked up and saw him grinning like a Cheshire cat. He said four words: "How does it feel?"

It was just too much. I knew there was no way he could have known that I was up there, without spiritual penetrations. We both erupted in laughter at the ridiculousness of the thing, the whole endless universal thing. Then he left me to finish my pie.

That's the berry pie story. The Master takes great delight in it, and has had me tell it several times. Now he's dangling another pie in front of me. We'll surely reach our goal.

Eric (Gwo Hwei[4]) Weber arrived in his van, just after we resumed bowing. He brought boots and a collapsible Chinese shopping cart that the Master had sent to Heng Yo. I bowed four miles, through the city of Bodega Bay, before the poison oak began to start itching again. By late afternoon, welts were rising up all over my body, and some of them were breaking open, spilling out clear sticky pus. We stopped bowing and sat by the roadside. It began to rain.

Fortunately, Gwo Dun Schweig came by, and, seeing my condition, insisted on taking us to his home in Inverness for a recuperation period. When we got there, I took a shower and applied ointment over most of my body. It looks like the problem will get worse before it gets better. We are now encamped in Gwo Dun's carport. The most vicious looking storm I have ever seen is now blowing in from the Pacific.

1 November 1973. Heng Ju writes:

Much despair. We are still in the garage. My body is one big rash. My mind is full of doubts, and there is a terrible storm outside. I dread the thought of going out there and getting drenched, and having people point and stare, asking questions that I really don't know how to answer.

There were times like this when I was on the submarine in the Navy, and my mind was filled with the fear of sinking. When we were down deep, I could hear the hull creaking and groaning under the tremendous pressure of the sea. I could imagine an immense wall of water coming to crush us, and I could see the ship imploding and falling to the ocean floor. It wasn't until after several months of contemplations such as these that I finally found how to pacify my mind.

First of all, I always made sure that I did my job right. I learned to act on every intuition, and checked every possibility for human shortcomings or failure of equipment. I would try to locate the fault before it did us in. Everyone on the sub was supposed to be like this. We all spent our first six months learning the systems of the ship, and were therefore capable of coping with any emergency. We watched each other like hawks. Thus, there was a certain amount of satisfaction and a sense of well-being derived from doing the job well.

Secondly, I learned how to divert my thoughts. When a submarine is running deep and all the work is under control, each person is pretty much left alone with his thoughts. The jovial atmosphere that may have been bubbling away at the surface subsides as the depth increases. By the time a sub reaches test depth (312 feet for our ship, The Rock) the imminent presence of death hangs in the stale air like a dragon in an incense cloud. Those who are not on watch usually occupy their minds by playing cards, reading, engaging in conversation, or going to sleep. There is not much sense in thinking about the possibilities of disaster: the hundreds of valves and pipes which could break at any moment, or the thin copper and nickel skin wrapped around the ship's frames which had been rusting out for the last twenty-six years. Thoughts like these could tear a person apart. And what a shame! The more sensitive, intelligent members of the crew seemed to be the most nervous, while the sluggish, doltish ones were the most relaxed. For once I realized the advantage of ignorance! But it was too late; I had already taken great pains to learn the intricate workings of that ancient vessel, and I was only too aware of the limitless possibilities for death. I knew that it took only one mistake of equipment failure to send seventy men to their watery graves.

Diverting the mind, however, is not ultimate. Scanning the past or dreaming about the future is a fickle way to face one's death. It's better to return to the present and offer up the mind to death. I used to sit back in the engine room, when all the machinery was quiet, and think to myself: "Well, this is it. The sewer pipe could burst any second that I realize. In the past, I did a lot bad things, and I wish that I hadn't done them, but it's too late now. If by some chance I should ever make it out of this predicament, I'm going to radically change my life, and start doing things to help the people of this very confused world. Now, I have done all that I can do; if it's time to die, then let it happen!" Then, I would get up and go about my business. As The Book of Job says, "The blessing of him that was ready to perish came upon me." It was no big deal; I was simply ready to go.

2 November 1973. Heng Ju writes:

We are still in the garage. My mind keeps entertaining thoughts of a full-scale retreat (not the religious variety). Resolving upon enlightenment is one thing. Keeping the resolution is another. One day you strike up vigorous resolves, but the next day, something comes along and you get spun around by it and go off on a sidetrack. Today I thought, "Well, we've bowed over fifty miles, and nobody has ever done that before in America. We could just quit right here; it wouldn't make any difference." I thought of all the things that I took for granted at the monastery, like the roof, the walls, the Chan hall, the lectures. My mind idled along, thinking of the alternatives. Perhaps I could flee to the mountains. With a bag of rice, I could probably get by for months.

3 November 1973. Heng Ju writes:

Still here. Itchy-itchy-itchy-super-itchy-super-itchy. Think I'll take a bath. Today my false thoughts have led me back to the submarine service. Been thinking of rejoining and becoming an undercover monk. I would be like everyone else, except I wouldn't smoke, drink, eat meat, or carry on. I could spend my wages on a big Norton motorcycle, get a nice little apartment, and …right! …

4 November 1973. Heng Ju writes:

Today we're back on the road! It's raining like crazy. I've still got welts all over my body, but I couldn't sit still any longer.

This morning Gwo Dun took us out to our spot, and we made a good five miles before setting up camp here on the beach near Jenner. At 10 a.m. we passed over the Russian River where it spills its muddy load into the Pacific. At noon, Gwo Jou Rounds and his wife Sue arrived, and fixed us a lunch of hot tomato soup and thick peanut butter and jelly sandwiches. There has been hardly any traffic at all; maybe two cars pass by every hour. This afternoon, I was working my way along beneath a heavy ceiling of ominous black thunderclouds. I looked up to see a flock of several hundred seagulls. I stopped bowing. They were putting on an air show for me! In tight formation, they ascended straight up into the heavens, and then, stalling out, they fell straight down to earth, only to recover at the last minute and then begin another ascent. They had formed a giant revolving mandala, like the wheel of birth of death. I watched them for several minutes. They seemed to be saying, "Strike up your spirit! Keep rolling along!"

5 November 1973. Heng Yo writes:

Last evening we camped on the beach in our new tent, but in the morning we awoke to the howling of a Sonoma Coast gale. It felt like the tent was about to become airborne. The Pacific Ocean, which last night peacefully lapped the sand, had become a violent, angry churning force. Large breakers were crashing not ten feet from the tent, so we quickly packed up the equipment, already heavy with rain, and managed to make some slow progress. It was rough going. After a couple of miles we decided to rest for a while out of the rain. There was a garage next to the road. It looked abandoned so we went in. Ju had a good idea: he propped our backpack in front of the garage to show others where we were. If anyone wanted to find us, they'd know where to look. We hung up some of our wet gear, but the air was so saturated that the stuff just hung limp and sad, without drying at all.

Later, while we were sitting in meditation, a car stopped out in front. My concentration gave way to a purr of joy from my stomach, which perhaps anticipated a hot meal offered by Gwo Dun and family. But to our surprise, the pack had attracted the attention of the garage's owner, and a county sheriff! Luckily, they had heard about us. The owner, a real estate broker named Mrs. Mitchell, took us to a laundromat to dry out the gear. She was rather surprised to hear the goal and methods of our trip, and a little amused at our predicament. She advised us to forget about traveling until spring, when the rains generally abate. So after another trying day, we camped out in Jenner. Our home is a leaking cowshed, but at least we are out of the wind.

6 November 1973. Heng Ju writes:

Still raining. The old cowshed didn't keep it out. Today we bowed through Jenner, which boasts only a few summer houses and a little store. Some eyes and noses pressed against windows, a dog following us down the bleak road; nothing much happening except the weather. Ah, the weather. Perhaps more important than the external weather of clouds, wind, and rain is the internal weather. The climate of a person's mind actually has more to do with his inner situation than the external environment. The storms of greed, hatred, and stupidity, known in Buddhism as the three poisons, are largely responsible for covering over the bright sun of our inherent wisdom. These negative energies all center around the view that "self" exists in a "world." Basically, there is neither self nor world, and so we waste energy catering to our greed, which rages like a fire. Every time we succumb to it, it's as if more fuel is poured directly on the flames. Anger is aroused when we don't attain the object of our desires. Our stupidity convinces us that we know and understand what we do not. If we can gain more control over our internal climate, the rain, the fog, and windstorms are child's play by comparison. We work to keep this in mind as the rain comes down. Today we bowed three miles along high windy cliffs.

7 November 1973. Heng Yo writes:

Unlike the weather patterns of the earth, which we cannot influence, the internal climate can be controlled to the finest degree. First we must be willing to look within, and acknowledge that the internal climate is perhaps not the way we would like it to be. For example, it is hard to admit that anger is frequently the basis of action. Until we recognize this fact, the climate of anger cannot be dispelled. Therefore, we must take time and look within, and complement the looking with proper behavior. The moral precepts set out by the Buddha are guidelines for our daily actions, as well as for specific situations. By adhering to these codes of behavior, we reduce our desires, and eventually eliminate them. When desires disappear, greed also vanishes. The energy we waste in anger or enmity can now be applied to the practice of concentration.

The development of concentration brings with it the ability to be patient in the face of provocation, insult, or bad weather. Moreover, concentration is the key to uncovering the inherent wisdom which gradually illuminates delusion. Therefore, in order to gain control over the internal climate, we must "reflect within, reverse the illumination," and develop morality, concentration, and wisdom, thus ending greed, hatred and stupidity. It's easy to learn about but hard to practice.

Heng Ju bowed more than three miles today according to the mileage posts which appear at culverts and bridges.

8 November 1973. Heng Yo writes:

We discussed the idea of taking an inland route to avoid some of this penetrating rain, but we agreed we're better off following the coast route. Since we are not out to break speed records, we decided to go forward when possible, and to hole up when it gets really bad.

The shoulder along Highway One is nearly non-existent, and making prostrations inches away from onrushing trucks—each one loaded with tons of logs—takes a bit of courage. At first I thought that most of the truck drivers tried to come as close to hitting us as they could, on purpose, because we appear to them as a couple of kooks creating a road hazard. Later I realized that more often than not, they have no choice in the matters since vehicles are always approaching from the other direction. The road is not wide enough to accommodate two cars and a bowing bhikshu. Whenever possible, we try to get off the road when traffic is coming.

I'm reminded of a story about the Venerable Master Xu Yun. On his bowing journey, he once met a bhikshu who had been repairing a road that was travelled by many Buddhist pilgrims. The monk had made an iron-clad resolve to keep the road in good repair; every day he carried rocks, spread sand, and so forth, and yet asked absolutely nothing for himself in return. He was over eighty years old, and he had worked on the road unceasingly for over forty of those years. To toil for the benefit of living beings and to expect no reward is the truly selfless conduct of a Bodhisattva.

We are camped on a cliff with grazing sheep, and can hear the sound of the surf pounding on the rocks far below when there is a lull in the high winds and rain by which we are being battered. But remembering the story of the old monk and the road somehow takes the sharp edge of the day.

9 November 1973. Heng Yo writes:

A man in a white pickup truck slowed down to observe the bowing. He drove down the road and then made a U-turn, and headed back toward me. Heng Ju was up ahead bowing. The truck pulled up on the shoulder of the road. The driver, roughly thirty years old, cut the engine and got out. I always feel a brief apprehension before the first words are spoken, before I know whether the encounter will be friendly or not. "Hi," he said. "Mind if I ask you a question?" The man seemed interested in our trip, and willing to stand in the cold drizzle to talk to me.

In the course of our discussion, he was surprised to learn, among other things, that Gold Mountain Monastery is located in the heart of the San Francisco Mission District. "I can't understand why you don't leave the polluted, noisy, crime-ridden city," he said. "I'm sure you've passed through a lot of beautiful quiet country up here which would be ideal for a monastery." He had a point. I thought: Here we've walked nearly 100 miles of highway as it twists along the Pacific cliffs. Even the drenching rain has a natural beauty which appears in many mysterious and subtle ways: it turns motor oil into rainbows; it makes the trees reach for the sky; it melts the snow that fills the rivers that carve out the valleys. I could almost, but not quite agree with the man. I explained that the practice of Buddhism takes place on the mind-ground. That is, one's physical location is not as important as what goes on in the mind. The object of cultivation, or religious work, is to rid the mind of extraneous and idle thoughts which flow like a fountain. This work can be done anywhere, at any time.

A man once asked the Master if it was advisable to discontinue the recitation of mantras while doing mundane clerical tasks. The Master answered that if he truly did the work he was doing at the time, the effect would be the same as holding the mantra. The same is true of meditation. If we are bothered by the noise of the city (which becomes astonishingly apparent when we leave the city), and if we can't meditate because of the noise, then we should learn to transcend the noise. If peace of mind depends on a silent environment, then we still have a "place of dwelling," an attachment. We should clean up the noise, pollution, and crime of our own minds; then wherever we go will be clear and pure, because the world is no more than a reflection of our minds.

The man was able to listen, a rare and valuable quality, and he left us with a good-luck wish. Later on, Gwo Dun came again and helped us locate an old garage at a dilapidated mill at Timber Cove. We stayed the night.

10 November 1973. Heng Yo writes:

Today the rain was like bullets penetrating our gear. After bowing by Fort Ross in the morning, Gwo Mien brought us a hot lunch. I am slowly adjusting to pulling the cart along as I walk, although to be perfectly frank, I wasn't too fond of the idea at first.

It will, however, enable us to carry more supplies and equipment as we travel between towns along the route. After bowing a good four miles, we walked back to the abandoned timber mill to spend the night again in the garage. The place is really depressing. The wind and rain constantly batter the ruined buildings; there are heaps of rusted machinery everywhere and a huge hulking conical skeleton of an incinerator—Desolation Row, indeed.

11 November 1973. Heng Yo writes:

Heng Ju has gone out alone this morning to bow since we plan to stay here in the garage again for the evening. He walked up ahead to the point where he had left off bowing last night. I've hung up some wet gear, but it hasn't dried much in the saturated air. I've been looking over previous log entries, sitting in meditation, and wondering what happened to Heng Ju. Later a car pulled up. It was Gwo Jou Rounds and his wife, who had rescued Heng Ju from the rain. They provided lunch, supplies and a supply of chocolate bars. Gwo Jou had heard about the poison oak incident and he compassionately donated two rolls of toilet paper. Today is Sunday, and the shoulderless road has more traffic than usual; the ditches are filled with poison oak, and yet old Ju chalked up another three and a half miles.

12 November 1973. Heng Yo Writes:

This highway has been cut through rocky, volcanic cliffs that jut straight up hundreds of feet above the beach. The view is awesome here, and so is the weather. Gale force winds blow in from the sea, and of course, the rain keeps us soaked to the bone.

Just for a pleasant diversion, we made a side trip today. Gwo Mien had earlier mentioned that we would be welcome at a small Indian reservation about four miles inland. So early in the afternoon, we secured the bowing and walked into Stewarts Point, bought a few supplies at the general store, and then proceeded inland on a little winding road. Darkness quickly fell, and the ferocious rain-bringing dragons started kicking up their heels. It became pitch black, the heavy cloud banks totally obscuring the moonlight. It got to the point where we actually couldn't even see our own hands, how much the less the road. The rain was hammering at us like millions of watery bullets. We stumbled up the mountain, with a raging creek to our left and a steep precipice on the right. I was walking in front and Yo was following, when I realized that he was no longer with me! "Yo," I cried out. No answer. Fear swelled inside me. "Yo, where are you?" The only sound was the relentless rain and the raging creek. Finally, I heard his voice and we began yelling at each other, until we could trace the sound out and find each other. I never did see him, I ran into him. He said that he had fallen off the road into the canyon, and had never been so scared in his life—rolling down, down a mountain, blind. Foolishly, we had left our flashlight back at the bowing spot, but we did have a little piece of rope with us. We fumbled around and finally tied ourselves together with a ten-foot space between us. Then we continued the ascent. I went first, gingerly feeling each step of the way, scraping my boot on the road ahead, while Yo followed behind, ready to stop me should I fall over the side. We proceeded like this for a couple of hours—cold, wet, and lost on our own planet. We had gone too far to turn back; our only hope was to go on. We were seriously wondering if we were going to live through this little trip.

It was some time after midnight when we stopped walking, and broke out a nylon tarp and huddled together under it in the middle of the road. We were shivering and wet, but we managed to light a candle, and broke out the map to see where we were. The way it looked, we had another mile to go. It would take all night at this rate. Suddenly we saw a flicker of light from down the mountain. A vehicle was coming; it was an old Indian in a truck. He picked us up and gave us a ride to the reservation. But when we inquired at the reservation, we were told that white men were not allowed.

We were too cold and wet to do anything else but turn around and keep moving. We headed down the mountain, and it was hell for a while, but then the moon began to shine through the clouds, and we made it back to Stewarts Point just before sunrise. We found an abandoned motel to sneak into, and despite the fact that there was a dead cat rotting away on one of the armchairs, it was like the Hilton to us.

13 November 1973. Heng Yo Writes:

Bowing along through rain and hail, we stopped at a sheep shed to eat our meal. We have been on the road about a month and have gone just over 100 miles. At the end of the day, we decided to spend $2.50 to stay in the dormitory at the Stillwater Cove Resort. The place used to be a school. The dorm, which we have to ourselves, is old: built of stone and rough-hewn cedar. Soon we had a fire blazing in the large fireplace and the rafters and chairs were adorned with our wet clothes, jackets and the tent. The fire hissed and popped, drying out our gear. Tomorrow is big Ju's birthday. It will be nice to start out the day fortified with dry clothes and a night's rest behind us.

"Stillwater"—that's a great name, not only because it conveys the peaceful feeling here of the tall hilltop pines that overlook the coast, but also because it reminds me of a verse which the Master often recites:

When the water of the mind is stilled,
The moon is reflected clearly.

Our minds are disturbed by many thoughts, emotions, and desires; it is like unsettled water, which reflects nothing. Only when the mind is stilled can it reflect the moon, our Buddha-nature. Still the mind's water at Stillwater Cove.

14 November 1973. Heng Yo writes:

For the last few days, a feeling has been growing within me, and only after the experience of groping through the black wetness for hours on that Indian mountain road has it become clear enough for me to express.

It isn't an emotion, nor is it a philosophical conclusion. Rather, it feels deeper than the plane on which my everyday mind functions. I suppose it would best be called "knowledge"—not of details, or even facts, but a feeling of absolute certainty that, despite everything, we are going to successfully complete our journey. It is no longer a question of whether we'll make it; the question is how to deal with the specific problems which will arise and how we will react to the events of the coming days.

We passed through Stewarts Point and stayed in an old shack. Mice ran over Heng Ju every few minutes, waking him up all night.

14 November 1973. Heng Ju writes:

My birthday is today, November 14. We have gone 100 miles, and are becoming accustomed to operating in the rain.

15 November 1973. Heng Ju writes:

More rain. According to the map, the highway runs alongside the ocean shore for eighty more miles and then turns inland at Rockport. Now and then we pass a home, but most of the time we are surrounded by open rolling hills and evergreens, and of course the ocean. Not much traffic.

This afternoon, I was bowing through Sea Ranch, a progressive ocean front community where there are dozens of homes constructed of natural materials and spaced in harmonious relation to the beautiful landscape. Yo had just gone up ahead to search for a campsite when an old Ford sedan came grinding to a halt beside me. There were five very drunk people in it. I kept bowing and concentrated on reciting "Na Mo Guan Shi Yin Pu Sa" (Praise to the Bodhisattva Who Regards the Sounds of the World) as the Master has instructed me. I could feel my adrenalin pump up and all systems shift into battle-ready. Then I recalled a poem that the Master occasionally speaks:

When the Way grows a foot,
  the demons grow ten.
When the Way grows ten feet,
  the demons are right on your head.

The car rolled along beside me while some of the men leaned out the windows and yelled obscenities. This went on for several minutes. Then seeing that they could get no response from me, they stopped the car and one person got out and started walking behind me. I didn't know if he was going to kick me or not. He was drunken crazy and yelling, "Hey! What the hell you trying to prove? What the _____ good do you think that's gonna do?" I paid him no attention but carefully observed my own mind. There was no fear and no anger; I felt very centered. This dharma really worked!

After a few minutes, I could tell that the guy was beginning to cool down. He said, "Hey! What are you doing, anyway? How long you been doing that?" Finally, I stopped bowing, stood up, and slowly walked over to him.

I answered his questions in a calm and friendly manner and watched his attitude flash from drunken arrogance to sober respect. He was basically a pretty nice guy. We talked for a few minutes, and then he went back to the car where his friends were anxiously awaiting the outcome. I heard someone exclaim as they drove out of sight: "A hundred miles! All the way from San Francisco!"

While all of this was taking place, a woman in a Volkswagen bus had been watching, ready to intervene in the event of violence. Afterward, she drove up and introduced herself as Judy Bruff, a Quaker who lived up in the hills. She said that we couldn't camp on Sea Ranch since it was all private. She offered us the use of her cabin for the night, while she went to stay with relatives.

16 November 1973. Heng Yo writes:

Bowed across the Sonoma-Mendocino County line. Outside of Gualala, a man in a late-model sedan pulled off the road and onto the shoulder. He studied Heng Ju as he bowed, then drove off and cruised by again for another look. He stopped the car on the shoulder, and waited for me to walk up. The man was about fifty years old with graying temples; he was nicely dressed. He had the air about him of a successful businessman. His manner was reserved. "May I ask what your friend is doing?" he asked.

I explained our pilgrimage briefly and answered affirmatively when he asked if I thought we would make it.

The man then said what was really on his mind, "Can't you prove the same thing some other way? I mean, why should you take all of this suffering on yourselves?"

Heng Ju bowed by without stopping, his boots and gloves scraping the pavement, punctuating the man's question. I replied that suffering and pleasure are merely names. What counts is how you see the world. If you put on red glasses, the world appears rosy. If you think that certain actions involve suffering, then they do. I don't consider what we're doing painful. We are often drenched with rain, but it doesn't necessarily entail suffering—it's just being wet.

I went on to say that the Master often uses a verse to explain this idea very well:

To undergo suffering is to end suffering;
To spend one's blessings is to end one's blessings.

As I was about to launch into a full-scale explanation of this verse, delving into the Law of Karma in order to answer the man's question, I saw that he was glancing sideways; he interrupted the conversation, and excused himself. He thanked me, said he was glad he stopped, got back into his car and drove off.

Perhaps I had said something to offend him; then again maybe the man heard as much as he wanted. Maybe he remembered an appointment. I'm beginning to realize that people are like vessels. some can hold quite a bit, others hold very little. When the vessel is nearly full, people can feel mentally uncomfortable; when the vessel starts to overflow, people usually change their lives. How much we can hold is directly related to how much we let go. When you let it all go, you'll have everything!

17 November 1973. Heng Ju writes:

Battered by another treacherous storm, we inched our way along the cliffs. The rain was extremely heavy as we came through the town of Gualala. No one was on the streets, but as we passed a yellow house on the south of town, a man who introduced himself as Greg invited us to come in. We told him that we wanted to keep bowing. He said that he would come pick us up at nightfall. After four miles of rain-soaked bowing, we passed through Anchor Bay. A man came running out of the town's only tavern and, wiping the beer from his chin, gave Yo two dollars. He said, "You gotta eat, don't you?" Then he ran back to the beckoning door of the tavern, and yelled to us from the porch, "If you thank me, you're crazy!"

When Greg located us in the evening, we loaded our cart into his truck and went back to his house. Power had just been blown out by the storm, so his house was lit by candles. It was a bachelor's house except for one girl who did the cooking and the astrology. I recognized her. She used to be my cousin Mike Kennedy's girlfriend in Seattle and had lived on the commune I lived on near Mt. Rainier. Strange coincidence! Yo and I talked with everyone for a while, but when the party started to gather up a little too much steam, when they began drinking and smoking dope, we went to our room and sat in meditation. In the morning Greg fixed us some hot chocolate and drove us out to the operating area.

18 November 1973. Heng Ju writes:

Bowing in the rain is like submerging in the ocean with scuba gear. It is a weightless, silent dream world where one is temporarily free from everything. Right here, there is another world, simply as near as sweeping out all thought. Here, there is no world, no peace, no strife, no liberation, no bondage. It is a place of no place. No one can really know it, much less own it. All that is seen has no real

Bowing in the rain is like submerging in the ocean with scuba gear. It is a weightless, silent dream world where one is temporarily free from everything.

substance or separate nature. All that is seen is like the fading dreams of yesterday. There's nothing to hang onto. Or like this highway: our future work is always ahead of us, and our past merit and virtue is behind us. Right here we have nothing, but within this nothing is something wonderful.

This evening we had nearly finished bowing—in fact it was the final bow of the day—I looked up to see a maroon Mercury sedan speeding toward us with several arms and heads hanging drunkenly from the windows. They must have been doing a hundred miles an hour when they whizzed past. Suddenly, a full can of beer flew through the air. It missed my head by a fraction of an inch and exploded on the ground, splashing Yo with beer. If it had hit us it would have killed us. We quickly headed for the woods and pitched camp. Only after settling down and sipping some tea did I begin to realize what a close call this was.

This called to mind something that the Master conveyed to us in a recent telephone call: "If you are sincere, and hold your precepts purely, then the gods, dragons, Buddhas and Bodhisattvas of the ten directions will guard and protect you, and there will be no way anyone can harm you."

19 November 1973. Heng Ju writes:

Gwo Dun Schweig came again today. He must have driven over ninety miles to bring us not only a balanced meal but hot water, towels, dry socks, and, of course, a jar of Deaf Smith (peanut butter).

A Mendocino County deputy sheriff, responding to the calls of some alarmed citizens, stopped us for questioning. He made a thorough radio check on us but could find nothing to arrest us for. He finally departed, shaking his head as if to say that we were totally nuts.

We stopped bowing just short of Point Arena, where Jo Ann, who is a friend of Gwo Dun's and proprietor of the local health food store, gave us a room for the night. According to the calculations, we have covered 130 miles so far. Heng Yo reminded me of the line in the Venerable Master Xu Yun's autobiography: Although his progress did not seem like much, it accumulated slowly, day by day.

20 November 1973. Heng Ju writes:

Down the main street of Point Arena, past the store fronts, along the gutters, we buff and scrape our way northward. After five miles of vigorous bowing, we reached Manchester, where we found an abandoned house with all the glass broken out, and blackberry vines growing through the filthy rooms. This house is basically not fit for hogs, but to us it is a castle.

I really look forward to the evening meditation period after a long day of bowing. Every day, in the tent, a barn, the beach, in fields, or on clifftops—it doesn't matter where, we always meditate. With the body wrapped in warm clothes, and the legs covered with a blanket, we sit alert and upright while the energy circulates freely. In full lotus for the length of one incense stick—about one hour—we recover, regenerate, relax, and become centered. This meditation is the rich reward of a day well spent. It soothes pain, calms cares, and levels all distractions. In the mystery of absorption, our little lives are like a dream, and all our troubles dissolve like the wet snaking road behind us. Just like in a dream, all of our yesterdays have gone, and tomorrows never come. In reality there is only the present moment, but how few are able to dwell in it!

In meditation, we seek to become what the Chinese call a man of the Way without a mind. Since he takes nothing to be his own mind, he clings to nothing; and yet because of this, everything is his. He never is out for his own benefit in any situation. He is in harmony with conditions, without grasping or thrusting himself forward. He sees all existence as a dream, an illusion, and therefore keeps his mind unattached, unobstructed, and liberated. Who could tie him up? He realizes that the whole universe is merely a manifestation of the Buddha-mind—pure, clear, and essentially unmoving. All the suffering of birth, old age, sickness, and death are no longer problems, because he has united with the self-nature. Even if an atomic bomb went off, it would be no great affair.

Occasionally I am coerced into telling a sea story, and go into a long rap about my days aboard the submarine USS Rock. The captain on that boat was bold and daring as a lion, and together we had many high adventures while crossing the Pacific. One of his favorite tricks was to run at full speed along the bottom when we were chased by surface craft. This is really quite dangerous, because a submarine travels blind underwater, and only relies on compass and charts. But it makes us hard to find. He would estimate where the bottom was and run at full speed just 5 feet above that estimate. Everyone's nerves would be on end, imagining us running into a large underwater mountain, but we never did. One day I asked him why he did that and he replied, "Don't think about death. If you are going to play this game, you play to win!" In fact, in all the fleet competition for battle efficiency, opposing two diesel subs and two nuclear subs, we came out first!

21 November 1973. Heng Yo writes:

"After reading 10,000 books, you should walk 10,000 miles." The principle expressed by this old Chinese proverb is an important one. The "10,000 books" refers to intellectual study, theories, and vicarious experience, while the "10,000 miles" refers to practical and actual experience. The verse means that a cultivator of the Way should be aware of both theory and practice; he should recognize the importance of their mutual relationship. To read 10,000 books is to investigate and study the written teachings of Buddhism: the scriptures (sutras), the moral rules (the *vinaya*), and the commentaries (the *shastras*), which discuss concentration, morality, and wisdom. Understanding without practice is not true understanding, and practical application without understanding is useless. If we really have understanding, we also apply that understanding because our knowledge is practical and our practice is well-informed.

One of the products of this trip is the chance to actually walk some of those 10,000 miles, after having read a few of the 10,000 books. When the walk is completed, the ideas in the books will be better applied, and the walk will be better understood in terms of the principles in the books. Out on the road, it becomes increasingly clear that the opportunities at hand should not slip by, or else we may find ourselves reading 10,000 wrong books or walking 10,000 miles in the wrong direction.

22 November 1973. Heng Ju writes:

Since we are getting out of range of the Monastery, the collapsible Chinese shopping cart, which the Master sent up after the Poison Oak Incident, is proving its usefulness. We are able to carry more supplies and gear.

The last time Kuo Yu came by, I told him to ask the Master a question, which had been bothering me. I said, "I've always wondered about these Krishna people. They seem very diligent in their practice; they are vegetarians and all day long they recite "Hare Krishna, Hare Krishna." Is that like the Pure Land School in Buddhism? Will they receive birth in Amitabha Buddha's Land of Ultimate Bliss because of their practice? Just what exactly is the difference between the two?" After several weeks the reply came back. "It's the same as the difference between reciting the name of Marilyn Monroe or Richard Nixon!"

Thanksgiving today. Gwo Dun and Gwo Rung Epstein and his family gathered with us in a roadside park. Kuo Tun, Kuo Mien, and Kuo Yu came too. We had a meal par excellence. It was finer than any meal I ever had back in the days when I still ate meat, fish, eggs, garlic, and onions. But most folks, as is the custom, are probably eating turkeys today. So after lunch I shared with everyone the following story.

A few years ago, when I was still a layman, we were preparing for a Liberating Life ceremony. During this annual event, Buddhist disciples purchase animals that were intended for slaughter. After reciting mantras for them, we set them free in the country. This particular year, Gwo Gwei Nicholson and I decided to drive fifty miles south of San Francisco to purchase twenty-one pigeons which were to be live targets for a gun club. We drove my 1951 Chevrolet hardtop down the coast on a most beautiful Saturday afternoon. It was the first time we had been outside the temple in several weeks. Once at the gun club, we realized we had no way to carry the birds, but the owner stuffed them into a burlap sack, saying that they would be all right for a while. It was late in the afternoon when we headed back to the temple. Had we gone straight back everything would have been all right. But we didn't. We were ambushed by greed as we passed the La Honda grocery store.

Ordinarily, Gwo Gwei and I don't eat in the afternoon, nor does anyone else at the monastery since abstaining is very conducive to good meditation. When we saw that store, we were overcome and broke discipline. After devouring several pounds of cheese, donuts, pop, candy, ice cream, and other atrocities such as these, we finally realized that we were late for the Master's evening lecture. We got back in the car and hurried back to the monastery only to discover that the Master had held up the lecture just for us! Guilt pangs... I quickly carried the gunny sack of birds to the second floor where a small empty room was waiting for them. I opened the bag and they all came flying out... all, that is, except for two dead ones! Thud! Thud! They rolled out onto the floor.

"Uh oh. If we hadn't gone on that selfish greed trip those birds would be alive now." I consoled myself, "Oh well, at least no one knows about it." I went down to the lecture hall and sat next to Gwo Gwei. I persuaded him to tell the Master that two of the birds had died, but told him not to mention anything about the store. At the end of the lecture, Gwo Gwei gingerly approached the Dharma seat, put his palms together and said, "Master, two birds died on the way back to the temple. What should we do with them?" There was a frightening moment of silence, then the Master slowly looked at Gwo Gwei, and spoke two words that cut through all the lies and half truths. "Eat them!" he roared.

Everyone else in the hall no doubt thought the Master was joking, but Gwo Gwei and I knew very well that he was on to us. We were filled with shame and remorse. By the next day, we had worked up enough courage to make a public confession. We didn't eat the birds. We buried them at sea. But we did undertake a three-day fast to somehow compensate for our offense. I'll never forget that. Gwo Dun, after hearing it, said that he didn't know whether to laugh or cry.

At night, there is the problem of finding a place to camp. Lately, we have been lucky to find a lot of abandoned shacks along the way, which we gladly share with the small animals who now inhabit them. Since just about all of the land along the highway is privately owned, we are forced to trespass at night—no one has minded so far.

We are now seven miles short of Elk, and have found a lean-to to live in. I took a bath in a nearby creek. Cold!

23 November 1973. Heng Yo writes:

Nothing much has happened today; a few people stopped to talk with us; there is intermittent rain. These uneventful days are hard to describe but they are just as important as any other. Their importance has to do with being vigorous. To perfect our vigor—which is the fourth of the Six Perfections—means that after we have selected an appropriate dharma door, or method of cultivation, we must be consistent in our work. For example, it is far more beneficial to sit in meditation every day for a set amount of time than to sit for a long time one day and then miss the next two or three days. The same is true while keeping a steady pace and rhythm when bowing. The progress you make is jeopardized when you stop, even for a short amount of time. Being vigorous does not imply that you should run around and scatter energy in a frenzy. Consistent effort is the key. If we keep the precepts, our vigor will increase all the time. We will require less sleep and will quickly learn how to control our new-found energy.

We ate lunch under trees. The road winds inland here because the Pacific cliffs are interrupted by a wide gap where Elk Creek meets the sea. After crossing the creek, the road twists back to the coast. We stopped about two and a half miles outside of Elk. We spotted a shack which has no front, but has a good roof, overlooking Elk Creek and cliffs of Pacific Ocean. We moved in for a dry evening, sharing house with a bird. Heng Ju and I gave each other short Dharma lectures. I spoke on cause and effect; Heng Ju spoke about the four marks of self, personality, living beings, and a lifespan and the *Diamond Sutra*.

24 November 1973. Heng Ju writes:

We passed through the town of Elk on a bright Saturday morning. A few people stopped to talk or say hello but there were no incidents. On the outside of town, however, my faithful shopping cart's aluminum and rubber wheels collapsed. The wheels can't take the heavy load or the rough terrain when we leave the road every day to make camp. I unloaded the cart, stashed the gear, and headed back to the Elk Garage, and instructed the man to install lawnmower wheels. Robert Matsen, the garage man, put two lawnmower wheels on the cart by welding extensions on the axle. He also brazed the broken hand-frame, and brazed on a place to tie our handle. The cart is now lower and has a wider wheelbase and wider wheels, which means better handling on and off the road.

The man commented that he had seen some strange pilgrimages in his time on Highway One. Once he repaired a beer barrel which some people rolled from San Francisco to Olympia, Washington, and now he was repairing our buggy. His garage is the other hangout in town besides the bar, and some people started to gather around to see our "happening." One man thought that what we're doing was terrific; another volunteered that Heng Ju's use of kneepads was in some way cheating. I politely told him that people have different ways of doing things, and that when he bows his 1,000 miles, he can do it any way he wishes.

The cart is now fixed and we are camped right next to a creek north of town. Tonight I bathed in the icy cold water. Yeeow!

25 November 1973. Heng Yo writes:

As we slowly push our way northward, I am becoming familiar with the laundromats and post offices of each little town, the former for drying out the rain-soaked gear and the latter for keeping in contact with Gold Mountain.

Today, Dharma Master Heng Shou and Upsakas Gwo Gwei and Gwo Hwei arrived at lunch time. About ten minutes later, so did the Klein family. A meal offering was made. Gwo Hwei stayed on for some bowing. It was good to see people from the Monastery and hear of the Master, and things in general.

Now I am studying the maps in order to take mental note of our position, and to survey what might be up ahead. The precepts which Buddhists hold are in many ways like a map. When we want to get to a certain place, we use a map to guide our travel along the most direct route. When we decide to set out for unsurpassed enlightenment, our conduct is likewise guided by the instructions of the ancient sages. These precepts, or "maps of conduct," show the most direct path to Buddhahood. By following them, we avoid confusion and wasted effort. The precepts are moral prohibitions which prevent one from acting in ways which can be harmful to oneself or to others. Precepts are the basis for the practice of concentration and the birth of wisdom, and are explained in the vinaya division of the Tripitaka, the three-fold Buddhist canon. The best way to learn the precepts is to receive them in a formal ceremony from a Master who has practiced them for twenty or thirty years and who has purified his conduct. He holds and follows all of the rules of pure conduct naturally, and yet makes no distinctions. The bhikshus in China usually spent a minimum of five years studying the precepts in great detail and applying them in their daily lives before they were even allowed to enter the meditation halls.

It is as if the first 100 miles of the trip were practice—finding the right gear and operating procedures. Not much progress was made today but certainly a rest was in order, especially since Heng Ju had developed a boil on the back of his knee. We stayed that night in an abandoned shack near the ocean.

26 November 1973. Heng Ju writes:

We were told that the Master had requested our presence at Gold Mountain for a day to help in the transmission of the novice precepts, so we returned with Heng Shou. Six people had their heads shaved and formally left the home life to cultivate the Buddha path. Heng Yo's old friends, the Leibmans, happened to come and visit on the one-day that we were there. "Now that you have shaved your heads, shave your minds," Heng Ju told the new shramaneras and shramanerikas.

Gwo Hwei and I bowed four miles. We quit when a sore broke out on my knee. We walked back to our little cabin, a rotten shell perched atop a 300-foot cliff which descends straight to the sandy beach. Yo had straightened out one of the rooms, but the rest was in shambles. There was a broken brass bed perched on blocks near the western window, where ancient lovers once watched the mighty ocean shore. Now slender green stickers snake their long fingers through broken windows. In the living room a double mattress silently rots on the floor, surrounded by broken plates, rusty silverware and empty cans. I cleared out an armchair and settled down while the night wind whistled through the house.

27 November 1973. Heng Ju writes:

Last night I dreamt that I was swimming across a deep river. When I reached the middle, I got caught in a whirlpool and was sucked down into the depths. I remember looking up and seeing the surface of the water getting farther and farther away as I sank hundreds of fathoms down. After a while, the thought occurred to me that I must be dead. It didn't matter; there was no pain, only quiet peace. Eventually, I began my slow ascent to the surface. I returned to where some people were gathered. The first thing that I realized was that I was different. I could see that they were still struggling along in the dreamworld of their own existence. I had returned from the deep after living out my own death. I was free. I awoke with this knowledge and found myself sitting in the cabin. The task of bowing a thousand miles now somehow seems like a very small affair.

Because of the storm, we spent today meditating in the cabin.

28 November 1973. Heng Ju writes:

The storm has us trapped in the cabin. Well, we certainly have learned to appreciate what a luxury four walls and a roof are.

29 November 1973. Heng Ju writes:

Gwo Hwei bowed three miles, then headed back to San Francisco. This evening, as Yo and I topped the crest coming into the little town of Albion, we were met by four young people who invited us to stay at their Christian commune up on Albion Ridge. It was just starting to rain, so we accepted the offer, but I felt doubts. When we reached the commune, which is about a mile east of the highway, we were warmly received and shown around the property. There were communal gardens, shops, and various farming activities going on. The men all wore beards, long hair and simple clothes. The women were quiet and humble. Nuclear families were sprinkled across the property, living in little huts and domes. We were shown to the men's dormitory, a large two-story wooden building where about thirty single men lived. After being assigned to our bunks, I hung up my wet clothes and sat down in meditation next to a wood-burning stove. That was a mistake. Soon I was surrounded by about eight of them, all out to convert me. Yo sat down by me and together we tried to talk with them, but they could not hear a word we were saying. They were like high-pressure salesmen; we couldn't even talk to them. They tried every angle of persuasion: sympathizing, arguing, consoling, bearing witness, etc. We withstood it for about two hours and finally had to be rude and went to sleep. Thanks to the rule that says lights out at 10 o'clock. We got up in the morning before everyone else and hit the road, the good old road.

30 November 1973. Heng Yo writes:

We bowed through the rain in the morning, and just before entering the village of Little River, we set about looking for a dry place to take our meal. There was an old shack on a side road, which looked okay, but a man came out of a nearby house and said that we could not use it because it was private property. We turned around and headed down the road to the highway. Suddenly the front door of the man's house opened, and a woman called out, "Where are you all goin'? C'mon back here for a cup of coffee! You can't go anywhere in this weather." This was Gert Dailey. She invited us in and made a lunch of Louisiana rice and beans. Later she and her husband Bill invited us to stay the night.

They had ten children who were captivated by the *gong fu* lesson Heng Ju gave them. Later some Buddhist friends of the Daileys came by, and a long discussion ensued. Too long. The Daileys filled our cart with provisions, and we're ready to depart early in the morning.

1 December 1973. Heng Yo writes:

Passing through Little River, we accepted an invitation to spend the evening at the Little River Zen Farm, which is located in the hills near the village of Mendocino. After a day's bowing, we walked a couple miles inland. The sun had set when we arrived. There were several young people at this small country *zendo*. It is set up in the Japanese-American tradition. Their meditation hall includes a large stereo phonograph.

Many people, when they think of Buddhism, think of Zen. Its popularity in the West is rapidly increasing. The full word is actually *Zenna*, which is the Japanese pronunciation of the Chinese words *chán nà* 禪那. *Chán nà*, or *Chan*, is in turn the Chinese transliteration of the Sanskrit word *dhyana*. Dhyana means making the mind still; it is the method of basic Buddhist meditation. Many people feel that Chan is the essential core, the potent nucleus of everything which is subsumed under the word Buddhism.

In brief, the origin of the Chan School is directly traceable to Shakymuni Buddha himself. Once the Buddha wordlessly held up a flower which had been given to him by the king of the Brahma Heaven, a smile crossed the lips of his disciple, the Venerable Mahakashyapa. Mahakashyapa's smile showed that he understood the Buddha's meaning. The essence of this silent, mind-to-mind communication was transmitted from generation to generation by each successive patriarch in India, to Bodhidharma, who was the twenty-eighth patriarch. He carried the teachings and the "mind-seal dharma" to China, and so became the first patriarch in China. That was approximately 1,500 years ago. Buddhism flourished in China, and the transmission of the Buddha's essential truth continued right up to the present day. Buddhism took root in other countries as foreign monks came to China to harvest the seeds of enlightenment and to transplant the Dharma to their own native soil.

The Chan school has survived despite the ravages of time because its essence is not found only in sacred images, scriptures, or monasteries; it dwells in the hearts of people. The Chan school does not really have any particular characteristics that can be defined. But in general, four descriptive statements are traditionally ascribed to it. According to this description, Chan is: (1) to directly point to the mind of man, (2) seeing the nature and becoming a Buddha, (3) a special transmission outside the teaching, and (4) not dependent on language. One of these days when things are quiet, I'll go into it again.

Several years ago the bhikshus and bhikshunis of Gold Mountain attended the formal Dharma transmission at a large Zen temple in the area. The old Roshi, in transmitting the Dharma, very solemnly pointed to the ceiling, then to the floor, and mysteriously traced a circle in the air with his finger. Later, upon our return, someone asked what this meant. Without a moment's hesitation another person answered, "Suddenly in the heavens, suddenly in the hells, see you on the turning wheel."

2 December 1973. Heng Ju writes:

The editor of the *Mendocino Beacon* interviewed us as we passed by the little town of Mendocino today. At noon, Gwo Dun Schweig drove up and presented us with a SVEA stove from Craig and Sunny Bach of San Francisco. We shared a quiet and sunny lunch atop a hundred-foot cliff.

My soul quivers as I watch the mighty waves roll in and crash against these ancient lava banks. I am constantly in awe of the infinite power and oneness of nature. Not just the ocean, but everywhere, limitless, endless power. I was raised in a society that taught me to see nature as something outside of me—a society that trains people to manipulate nature, and treat it as an object, separate from one's own being. But now, a major shift in consciousness is occurring in the West, and people are beginning to realize that the nature inside and the nature outside are one complete whole. People are less interested in manipulating external events. They want to stand on central ground.

To reach this ground, Buddhism has traditionally taught the three "non-outflow" studies: morality, *samadhi*, and wisdom. Morality is self-discipline. It's like damming up a river. When you hold back the flow of the river, its power immediately begins to rise up. The power which comes from cutting off dark habits is equally impressive. It can sometimes be quite neurotic at first, but through the cultivation of samadhi, the energy is transmuted into something subtle and wonderful.

Samadhi, or concentration, means keeping the mind from straying too far out the doors of the six consciousnesses: the eyes, ears, nose, tongue, body, and intellect. It is practiced at all times, but the best place is sitting in full lotus. No-outflow wisdom is achieved when one is no longer tangled up and confused by sensory objects, but constantly dwells in the unmoving ground of the self-nature.

3 December 1973. Heng Yo writes:

Making pilgrimages is a way of life for a Buddhist monk. The monasteries in Asia were set up to receive wandering monks, and it was expected that a monk would spend at least part of his life going from place to place, hearing the teachings explained by the high Masters. This was excellent training; not only did it afford the monk the opportunity to visit and pay his respects to the holy shrines, but it taught him how to survive on his own in a changing world. It is easy to stay in one place and become quite comfortable, but before very long impermanence takes over, and what you thought you had is gone. This can be unpleasant. By not growing fond of any one place, one can flow with the changes. The result is that one is prepared when events take an unexpected turn. One can develop stillness in the midst of movement.

A modern-day pilgrimage in America takes a different form than the pilgrimages made by monks in Asia. First of all, a matrix of monasteries and temples where a pilgrim would be welcome has not yet developed in the West. Therefore, we take advantage of technological devices—camping gear, which allows us to lodge practically anywhere. Second, the roads we take are walkable, although sometimes not quite wide enough for us alongside the automobile traffic. Compared to the pilgrimages made in Asia over narrow, rutted paths, perhaps we have an advantage. Third, since people here are unfamiliar with our tradition, we spend a lot of time explaining it to those who ask about it. Still, although the form of this pilgrimage differs from those made by monks in Asia, the reasons for undertaking it are the same.

In the Vajra Sutra there is a line that says: "Even the dharma must be given up, how much the more what is not dharma." This means that certain dharmas, that is, methods of practice, are used to take the common person into the realm of the sage. In order to arrive at this state of true understanding, one must not be attached to anything, including the methods used to get there. For example, after crossing the river, it would be useless to carry a canoe around at all times.

We've camped in a thicket, and have been meditating to the sound of a nearby lumber mill which runs constantly day and night.

4 December 1973. Heng Ju writes:

It was a big day today as we bowed through the city of Fort Bragg. Bus drivers, students, kids, old folks, hippies, young girls, all came out to see us. Some drunken motorcyclists stopped their big Triumphs and Harleys and began to hassle us, but today I felt really strong and didn't want to stop for anything, so I passed them off to Yo. They pestered him for a while asking him why the hell we were doing what we were doing. He asked them why they were doing what the hell they were doing, and that finally shut them up. In the heart of town, a Catholic priest walked up to me and said in a mournful voice, "Where are you going in such a slow and painful manner?" I tried to explain our trip, but I could see that he was only feeling sorry for me. After he left, I got to thinking about it. Actually, there is no pain at all. He's just projecting it. In fact it is quite invigorating work. Never before have I been in such good physical shape! The painfulness is his, not mine!

I think people fail to realize that bowing is not painful at all. In fact it is good exercise, both physical and mental. What is difficult is trying to explain it. Physically, we have never been in better shape. The muscles have become strong and flexible, and we haven't been sick, even with all this foul weather. We just bow at a steady pace, not so fast as to work up a sweat. Mentally, it is good discipline and an exercise in concentration.

I'm really delighted by these encounters. Sometimes I don't recognize what's happening at first, but usually after a little more bowing and reflection they become clear. I realize what I said that was right and what I should have said, and I store all this information for the next encounter. It's a way to learn the dharma of the "eight winds."

The "eight winds" are gain and loss, ridicule and flattery, praise and blame, and joy and sorrow. We all have these winds constantly blowing against us. The idea is to practice stillness in the face of them. If a person can learn to be calm and a still while these winds blow, then his samadhi power and wisdom will grow stronger every day. For example, there are many people who praise our work and call us holy men, sages, etc. Others call us neurotic idol-worshipping heathens. Moved by the former, we become more egotistical. Moved by the latter, we become sad and depressed. Therefore, we are learning to view all talk as so many empty words, and merely continue on our "slow and painful way."

Another good point in bowing is that it can help remove karmic obstacles. Karmic obstacles are those forces, which prevent one from making progress in cultivation of the Way, such as Old Black

Habit Energy. This energy of old habits is sometimes difficult to break, but if one can take all that energy and turn it around, then it can become highly beneficial. For example, when people are young, they have no fear of death; they romp and stomp and run around without the slightest care. Now if this energy can be turned into cultivation, with no fear of suffering or even death, then the Buddhas and Bodhisattvas will smile in approval, and the Way can be quickly accomplished.

Now, we're camped behind a slow and painful bulldozer in a gravel company lot just north of the city.

5 December 1973. Heng Ju writes:

Made five miles without incident. Now we are camped in a run-down water tower. It isn't the Hong Kong Hilton, but to us it's even better. Everything's relative.

Today Yo told me the story of the late Venerable Master Xu Yun, when he was traveling across China on his way to a Chan session. While trying to cross a river, he fell in, and sank and bobbed downstream for a whole day until finally a fisherman caught him in his net and pulled him out. The Master was very sick; blood was running out of his mouth and nose, but he continued on his way. When he arrived at the monastery where the session was to be held, he did not explain that he was sick. The Abbot asked him to take an administrative position for the session but the Master politely refused saying that he only wanted to participate in the session with the rest of the cultivators. He was ready to do some serious meditating! But because of his refusal, some of the monks took him aside and gave him a serious beating. He did not tell anyone that he was sick, but joined the session even though he was urinating blood and sperm. He worked hard day and night without rest, totally forgetting his mind and body.

Eventually, the Master's undivided concentration, his Chan samadhi, began to take hold. Late one evening, he opened his eyes and perceived that the entire monastery was glowing with brilliant light, just as if it were daytime. He could see right through the walls.

There were monks in the courtyard. There were boats out on the river. He experienced many subtle and wonderful states, until one day a server accidentally dropped a teacup on the floor. When it broke, the Master became completely enlightened.

The Venerable Master Xu Yun was considered to be among the highest of cultivators in China. His diligent perseverance in cultivation brought him great success. He died in 1959 at the age of 120.

6 December 1973. Heng Yo writes:

After bowing across the Ten Mile River bridge, we were invited to spend the evening at the Frazier Farm, a commune run by a group of people our age. Like many of the young people we've encountered, they are turning to forms of Eastern religion for various reasons.

We got into a rap about Buddhism, and Chan in particular. Someone asked what our bowing trip had to do with Chan Buddhism, and a man in the group immediately answered with a famous meditational topic, "Why did Bodhidharma come from the west?" Now, who knows? Maybe this man was a Chan Master, but there are many people who mistakenly feel that they understand what Chan is all about. This myth seems to be fostered by some of the "Zen centers" which have sprung up in this country in recent years, particularly on the West Coast. These centers are not monasteries in the manner of the strict Chan temples of the Asian past. Some people in America assume that since everyone is fundamentally the same as the Buddha, everyone can be lax and ignore the moral codes. In this view, since everyone is already enlightened, anyone can do quite as he pleases, and there is no distinction between the monks and the lay communities. This erroneous attitude seems to have been imported from places other than China, along with the more popular aspects of Chan. Thus we end up with the strange combination of Zen halls and loud rock music, meditation and marijuana, and "enlightened masters" with several wives.

The ultimate purpose of the Chan school is to "directly point to

the mind of man." This does not refer to the ordinary mind which we use for the tasks of our day-to-day mundane existence. The mind which a Chan Master points to is the true mind, which is like space; it pervades the universe, does not come or go, and contains everything within it. The aim, then, is to cultivate the path and to develop our inherent potential for the realization of this mind, which is Buddhahood. The phrase "directly point" is used because words are often not sufficient to convey the state of mind exactly. Short of defining it, it can be pointed to directly. A skilled master can help others to experience it directly. Sometimes very startling, impolite, or outrageous methods are used to help a cultivator over the last hurdle. Today in America, these stories have been overemphasized and blown out of proportion to their context in training. People may be unaware of the years or lifetimes of practice of morality, samadhi, and wisdom which are required to bring the adept to the brink of enlightenment. Only then will one small shove in the right place at the right time result in his reaching enlightenment and ending birth and death.

People tend to forget about the less sensational aspects of cultivation, the day-to-day diligence required to bring one to maturity. Zen Buddhism is often misrepresented as nothing more than a lot of fast-talking, wise-cracking antics. The Chinese call this "verbal" Chan, which refers to someone who has done little or no cultivation to back up his baseless and silly efforts to prove that he is enlightened.

7 December 1973. Heng Ju writes:

Bowed into Westport, a little town nestled on a sloping rock cliff that descends to the ocean. A young couple, Gary and Zida Bachelor, invited us to stay at their home. Saved again! Just as we arrived at their house a big black storm blew in from the West. The wind and rain hammered away at the house all night long. Gary entertained us with slides taken on a recent trip to Israel. He sang us folk songs, accompanying himself on guitar. Zida watched after their newborn child and fixed us hot chocolate. She sewed a bright yellow patch on my pants where my knee had worked through. I feel as if I've known these people forever.

At about 11:00 Yo and I retired to an enclosed front porch. I slept sitting up on an old couch, while Yo found a corner to lean against for the night. Sleeping sitting up, a practice common to most of the cultivators at Gold Mountain, makes for lighter sleep. It's like meditating all night. The real pros sleep all night in full lotus without any back support. They vow that their "ribs will never touch the mat." It will be a while before I can do that.

I had been sleeping for about two hours when I suddenly awoke and experienced the sensation of having no body. It's hard to explain. I opened my eyes just like always, but this time I was just sitting there in a state of undifferentiated awareness, without the usual flow of idle thinking. I had woken up, but I hadn't assumed the usual cloak of identity that I had spent so many years developing. It was like stepping outside the limited realm of intellect into another world. For the first time, I was aware of everything around me dwelling in a state of still purity. My body was sitting there like a healthy plant, just growing and breathing. It was wonderful beyond all imagination. My discriminating mind had not yet begun calculating, categorizing, organizing, and dividing. I had forgotten to plug in my intellect. It didn't last long, however, for soon I began to wonder what was going on. With that false thought, my mind started up, and I returned to being my ordinary self.

8 December 1973. Heng Ju writes:

Little progress today. Gwo Fa Olson, Gwo Gwei Nicholson, and Gwo Hwei Weber drove up from Gold Mountain and prepared a big lunch for us. In the evening Fa and Gwei returned, but Gwo Hwei remained; he wants to try some bowing. At nightfall we set up camp in a rickety old barn in the midst of Westport. It was a very creepy place, all three of us had very vivid dreams. Heng Yo dreamt that he was a janitor in a large hospital. He saw several transformation-bodies of the Master tending sick people in bed.

Hwei was propped up in a dark corner of the barn, also dreaming about the Master.

I had started out sleeping up in the sitting posture, but after a couple hours I lay down on my back (too much cheese). At about 2:00 a.m. I awoke with a start. The bright moon was shining into the barn through the cracks where the boards were missing. This was no dream! There were about 200 pounds of pressure weighing down on my body, arms, and legs. I couldn't see anything, but I had heard about these things. It was what is called a *kumbhanda* (wintermelon) ghost. They sometimes take the form of a big melon; at other times they are invisible. I didn't really believe they existed when I read about them, but now there was no question about it! I panicked. During the past five years I had learned all kinds of mantras and magic spells which can be used to combat and subdue demons and ghosts. But there was only one word I could think of: "Hellllllllllpppppp!" I screamed with all my might. "Hellllllllllpppppp!"

The sound filled the barn and echoed down the foggy streets of Westport. I lay terrified for what seemed like five minutes. Yo and Hwei had long submerged to the safety of the bottom of their sleeping bags. I was on my own, unable to move. Finally it went away. A couple of hours later, I had a very clear dream in which I saw my late grandmother, Mrs. Testu, strolling through empty space with the Master.

We got up early and began bowing north along the misty cliffs.

9 December 1973. Heng Ju writes:

This morning we made a routine phone call to the monastery to report our progress. When the Master came on the line, I told him about the ghost. He immediately replied, "If you hadn't gotten so close to those women a couple of nights ago, you wouldn't have gotten the ghost." I almost dropped the phone. My mind raced back to when we stayed at Frazier Farm on the sixth. I remembered that there were three attractive young ladies who had shown us around the farm. They talked with us for a long time, and gave us some food for making soup. Who could have told him? We hadn't told anybody about this.

The Master said that it was definitely a kumbhanda ghost; they really enjoy sitting on people. He cautioned me to be more careful in my relationships with young women. He also mentioned that we were bowing too fast. He said that bowing slowly would be more conducive to samadhi. He gave us a contemplation to make while bowing. He said to envision the world as becoming more and more peaceful as we go along. He said that if we were really sincere, the Buddhas and Bodhisattvas would help us out.

Five miles north of Westport we found a cabin with a roof partially collapsed. Tomorrow we will leave the coast and head inland.

10 December 1973. Heng Ju writes:

The thermometer on the buggy read 28 degrees this morning! Exhilarating! We bowed along narrow twisting Highway One as it turns eastward and heads up over the coastal hills and down into the canyon town of Rockport, a small stopover surrounded by hills and green trees. We have set up camp in a cement building which used to be the town school.

During the bowing today, a contemplation from the Great Compassion Repentance kept running through my mind: "The worshipper and worshipped are empty and still in nature. The response and the Way are intertwined and difficult to conceive of. This body is like a great temple; all Buddhas manifest within it." Stated otherwise, the person who is bowing and all Buddhas to whom he is bowing are together in the state of undifferentiated thusness. The Buddhas (or Reality, Nirvana, Truth, Enlightenment, whatever name one wishes to use) are just right before one's face. If one is truly concentrated on the act of bowing, and the mind is steadily holding its mantra, then the Buddha is just everywhere. It is often said, "Buddha is just mind, mind is just Buddha." But if one has false thoughts, fantasies, and worries, then there is no Buddha. It is said, "The highest form of offering, the greatest good, is to work at making the mind pure, concentrated, and unattached."

11 December 1973. Heng Yo writes:

Highway One has turned inland now, and the logging rigs speed by more frequently. We are camped on a logging road about ten miles from the town of Leggett; the elevation here is probably one or two thousand feet. The mountain air is crisp and delicious; the sky is almost white with stars. There is something different about being here, away from the sea. The smells are different; the sound of the surf is replaced by the loud whispering of wind and trees. Confucius expressed this feeling very well:

The wise find pleasure in water; the virtuous find pleasure in hills.
The wise are active; the virtuous are tranquil.
The wise are joyful; the virtuous long-lived. [6]

Wisdom and virtue are two of many qualities which the Buddha has perfected. His actions reflect his wisdom, joy, and skill in helping others. His virtue reflects his unmoving presence, which is like an imposing mountain.

"Seeing the nature, becoming a Buddha" is the second description of Chan. "Nature" refers to the innate wisdom which lies dormant in all living beings; it is called the "Buddha-nature." "Buddha" is a Sanskrit word which means "the enlightened one." Anyone who develops the Buddha-nature is one who has awakened. This is, however, easier said than done, for the Buddha-nature lies buried under layers of covering which have been allowed for countless eons to obscure its natural purity and brilliance. The work of cultivation is not only to stop adding to the coverings, but to start vigorously drilling through them to reveal the source of wisdom.

Greed, anger, stupidity, arrogance, pride, and doubt accumulated during countless lifetimes past—all leave a sediment which must be gotten rid of. The process by which this is done is cultivation of the Way. One need not be a monk to undertake this work, nor does one have to be a certain age, sex, color, or creed for there are no such distinctions in the Buddha-nature. The only requirements are a pure and sincere heart, and a desire to end birth and death and save all living beings. Whoever cultivates successfully sees the nature, and becomes a Buddha.

12 December 1973. Heng Ju writes:

We are in the woods just five miles short of Legett where the Coast Highway intersects and ends at U.S. 101. Last night Gwo Hwei, who is still bowing with us, chose the campsite. It was a beautiful spot. The ground was somehow already cleared, and there were plenty of trees surrounding us. But there was something funny about the place. Nevertheless, we set up two tents, meditated for a while, and then scalded a pot of hot chocolate. Then it hit, the heaviest rainstorm of the year! We quickly got into the tents and battened down the hatches. The rain battered down on us like machine gun bullets, and soon water was seeping in everywhere. It was like being lost on the ocean in a storm. We sat up all night bailing out water. Finally at dawn it started to let up a little, and I ventured outside the tent to survey the scene. Good Lord! We were camped in a creek bed! The water was six inches deep in places. We packed up all our soaking wet gear and headed down to a local laundromat. One thing we learned, Gwo Hwei would never be allowed to choose a campsite again.

13 December 1973. Heng Yo writes:

Because of the continued heavy storm, we spent a day in Leggett, a town which pretty much owes its existence to the fact that it's located where State Highway One ends, and meets U.S. 101. We've had the whole day to repair broken gear and meditate.
"A special transmission outside the teaching." This third description about Chan refers to the mind-to-mind certification of the patriarchs from generation to generation up to the present. Since language can fall short of representing the essence of the wonderful Dharma—that is, the state of existence of a Buddha—the mind-to-mind method is used. It is much like the signal of a radio transmitter, which can only be received by a receiver which has

been carefully tuned to the correct frequency. If a person cultivates vigorously and holds to the moral codes, he will naturally become tuned to the right frequency and will be capable of receiving the transmission from an enlightened sage.

"Not dependent on language." In the *Shurangama Sutra*, the Buddha says that in his efforts to describe the true mind, he is like someone who wishes to show a friend the full moon. He points to the moon with his finger, but the friend misunderstands and thinks that the finger is the object of attention. He is doubly deluded, for not only does he not see the real moon, he doesn't see the finger for what it really is. Just as the pointing finger is not the moon, the language which is used to refer to or point out our inherent enlightenment is not itself enlightenment. One must be careful not to seize on language as ultimately true or real, for it is transcended by the fundamentally pure, clear Buddha-nature. Thus the fourth traditional statement about the Chan School is that it is "not dependent on language."

The storm has broken up. We are camped up on a hill on a logging road, under a bright full moon. Let us hope that we all see the real moon, and not mistake the pointing finger as our own original bright light. It's hard to believe that we've made over 225 miles so far!

14 December 1973. Heng Yo writes:

A lot of traffic on 101! We were sitting by the side of the road under a tree today, resting. The cars and trucks were speeding by, their tires spinning off water from the slick blacktop. All this water makes a lot of mud for us to bow through.

Mud reminds me of the first lesson I remember about greed, and how it is related to stupidity and hatred. I was about nine years old; it was my first summer away from home at camp in Maine. One day I noticed a group of boys who had gathered in front of a cabin. They were laughing, shouting, and pointing into the crawlspace under the building. I approached, wondering what was going on. "There's a quarter under there!" said a boy with big teeth. "See it right there?"

Now in those days, twenty-five cents would buy five large candy bars when the candyman came around after lunch. "Yes," I lied.

My greed was aroused, and I hardly needed the instigation of others. I found myself crawling under the building to get the money. I could hear a few stifled laughs as I slowly made my way through the darkness to where the quarter was supposed to be, but I ignored the giggles, seeing only visions of candy. Suddenly my hands slipped, and SPLASH! I fell flat on my face into a mud puddle which was hidden by pine needles. Upon hearing the pent-up laughter erupt, I knew I had been tricked. I emerged from under the cabin to face a laughing, jeering, dancing, pointing group. I was covered with mud from head to toe and started swinging blindly at anyone who approached, but it made matters only worse. Finally, I just sat down and cried.

It was my first lesson in greed, stupidity, and hatred, and I never will forget it.

"Hey Yo" said Ju, bringing me out of the past. "Why don't you go up ahead and see if you can find a dry place to drop anchor?"

15 December 1973. Heng Ju writes:

Highway 101 at this point is carved out of the steep cliffs of a deep canyon, which the Eel River has formed over the centuries. The river snakes through hundreds of miles of redwood wonderland, just like the eel it was named after. The highway is narrow, twisting and has much more traffic than Highway One.

Hwei, whose name means "the returner," returned to San Francisco yesterday. Yo and I made another routine call to the temple to report our progress. The Master advised us not to waste our energy staying up late and rapping with people when we are invited to stay in their homes. He also said that if we bowed sincerely, no rain would fall on us. Now that is something to think about!

We did five miles today, and now are camped in a remote clearing high above the roadway. There is a gurgling creek nearby, and a big pile of split cedar which was left here by some kind soul. Yo is meditating in the tent. The sun is setting. I am bundled in warm robes, with legs up in full lotus, sitting by the campfire. At this time, if I were doing what most Americans are doing, I would be sitting down to a large meal after a long day on the job. Maybe later I would put the kids to bed, pour myself a couple glasses of beer, and entertain myself in front of the television until it was time to go to bed. Then after a long night's sleep, I would rise and do it all again. But no, I am here sitting on the slope of an unknown forest. Below, the distant rumble of a lone Kenworth echoes through the quiet canyon. Above, the dim glow of a winter moon illumines the sleeping earth. The campfire has dwindled to a few coals, but I feel the heat from my legs rising, crawling up my spine. My stomach is empty, but there is no hunger. I feel my flushed cheeks brushed by the night wind.

16 December 1973. Heng Yo writes:

We passed by Hoffman's Restaurant, where Mr. and Mrs. Hoffman gave us hot tea and a block of cheese to carry with us. It's raining again; in the morning the temperature was in the twenties, but our bodies have adjusted to the weather. This road is quite a contrast to Highway One, the coast route. Highway One is mostly a two-lane winding ribbon which makes its way along the cliffs and over the rivers. It is Main Street of a hundred small towns, and is subject to frequent washouts and mudslides. There is not much traffic, especially during the winter. U.S. 101, however, is more of a highway, with stretches of freeway, and is a main transportation artery between California, Oregon, and Washington. There are numerous logging rigs, tractor-trailers, buses, campers, and passenger-cars. This section is known as the Redwood Highway, since it passes through diminishing acres of this giant and unique tree. Large billboards proclaim the virtue of this or that resort, and there are many tree-oriented tourist attractions, such as a tree you can drive through, and a house made of a single redwood log.

I am reminded of a verse written by a Chinese monk hundreds of years ago:

Deep in the mountains, I live in an aranya.
Alone on this distant peak, under tall pines,
Roaming around and sitting in stillness.
Here is the home of this bucolic monk.
Filled with stillness, I peacefully and ethereally remain.

An aranya is a still and silent place set aside for cultivation of the Way. Alone in the forest of a distant mountain, living off the land; this does not necessarily mean that he was physically there, but can be understood to represent a state of mind. Having cultivated successfully he now dwells in a still and quiet place, which is simply his mind. He remains unaffected by the vicissitudes of fate; he is in total control of his life and death.

As we slowly make our way along the rushing river, this description of the state of mind of the enlightened man takes on a new clarity to me.

At the end of a wet day, we are camped in Smith Redwood Grove. The sign says no camping, but there isn't anyone around to kick us out. It's too wet for a fire.

17 December 1973. Heng Ju writes:

The storm continues to howl, and the Eel River is steadily rising. If this weather doesn't let up, there is going to be serious trouble. We are now traversing the most dangerous part of the trip. The road is narrower than ever, with giant redwood trees protruding where the shoulder should be. Yo has rolled the buggy several times in order to avoid being hit by speeding trucks. When confronted by these difficult times, I often think about a poem that the Master occasionally recites:

Mind fixed, demons vanquished, everywhere happy;
The false stopped, heart empty, everywhere peace.

"Mind fixed" means samadhi, the ability to remain centered, aware, and alert in all situations. It can be developed to infinite degrees. "Fixed" does not mean fixed on a particular object; it means the mind is in a state of dynamic concentration. It accords with conditions, yet remains fundamentally unchanging.

As to demons, they can be either internal or external. Anyone can become a demon. Demonic forces manifest in thousands of ways to challenge a cultivator. Demons don't like to see people cultivate. Even best friends can be demons. There are many demonic teachers in the world nowadays. Some are fairly decent; some are really upside-down. They use their talent to twist around Buddhist terminology and conceal their own deviant views and practices. Although they themselves are confused about karma and principle, they still lead many a faithful follower down the road of ghosts, animals, and the hells.

"The false stopped": most forms of meditation now being taught in the West help one to relax and better cope with the world, but do not lead to ultimate liberation. The highest goal of meditation should be to end the cycle of birth and death, to end the flow of false thinking and emotional attachments.

"Heart empty": when the mind is free of afflictions, attachments, false thoughts, and selfish views, one can truly say that the heart is empty. The word "empty" often used in Buddhism follows from the Sanskrit word "shunyata." It does not mean like an empty can. It means the heart is empty of all restrictions and limitations. It means the heart is actually full without obstruction. The true substance is manifest. So when the false is stopped, and the heart is empty, everywhere is peaceful.

At nightfall, we found an empty cabin just north of Piercy, right on the river bank. We built a fire to dry out our wet gear, and scalded some milk. We are now sitting quietly, listening to the ominous sound of driving rain.

18 December 1973. Heng Yo writes:

Lately the temperature has been in the twenties, but the refrigerating effect of the wind makes it seem even colder.

When one has been practicing meditation for a while, one may notice a radiant heat which develops in the area of the abdomen, and spreads to the limbs of the body. This is known as "psychic heat." Many years ago, our teacher had been developing his meditational skill, and thus was producing this psychic heat. He would go for walks barefoot through the snow in Manchuria, and once rode for several hours in zero-degree weather in the back of a horse-drawn carriage while wearing only three thin layers of cotton cloth. One day another young monk, having seen him walk through the snow barefoot, tried it. As a result, he could not walk for six months.

In ancient China, there was a cultivator who went to visit a fellow cultivator named Liu Chang Chun. When the latter offered him some tea, the first cultivator said, "Tea! How luxurious! Where I live in the mountains, there is sometimes not even any water to drink!" Whereupon the host, Liu, took a pot of cold water, put it on his stomach, and boiled it. The visiting cultivator was ashamed of his lack of success in his practice, and resolved to do better and not be so critical of others.

It must be said that one does not cultivate the Way for the express purpose of developing psychic heat, or any of the other side effects which may result. But if, in the course of cultivation, these powers do develop, we should use them only to aid both ourselves and others. To set out on the path with the sole intention of developing powers such as these is to mistake the branches for the root.

Tomorrow we will cross the Mendocino-Humboldt County line.

19 December 1973. Heng Ju writes:

The storm continues. Once again, it is like diving along the ocean floor. At times like this, there is no use for words; better to just behold the awesome spectacle of it all.

When I was on the submarine "Rock," our squadron Submarine Squadron Five had a motto: "detect, attack, destroy." This slogan could well be applied to self-cultivation. In that seemingly never-ending interior battle, we must vanquish all enemies. This emphasis on personal victory cannot be overstated. In Buddhist literature, the character *shèng* 勝 appears thousands of times. It means superior victory. In our quest for spiritual growth, we must meticulously detect, attack, and destroy the seeds of evil karma, and arrest the flow of false thinking. We must defeat our tendencies to get attached to all outside conditions. We should have control over our own minds at all times, and not be turned around by every little thing that blows along. We should be able to see everything without grasping, rejecting, calculating, categorizing, theorizing, or dramatizing. In this manner, reality remains undefiled, and we do not overlay it with the falseness of our own projections. Life returns to being a miracle.

In the morning we passed a truck-stop cafe. I overheard two truckers talking. One of them said, "Yeah, Ken, he's praying for a damn truck to run him over! Yuk, Yuk, Yuk!" We ate lunch in the pouring rain at a roadside picnic area. The few motorists that drove by looked at us as if we were nuts. We had a heck of a day bowing in the rain, and dodging the giant logging trucks. Finally we set up the tent in Richardson Grove Campground.

20 December 1973. Heng Ju writes:

We're just five miles short of Garberville now and have encountered an unavoidable stretch of freeway. There is no alternate route, so we have been bowing right out on the freeway. The Sheriff and the State Highway Patrol must understand, because they haven't stopped us. It's amazing to note that the freeway is the safest place to bow that we have so far encountered. There is a great big paved shoulder that gives plenty of distance from the traffic.

This morning a lady in a big Lincoln rolled up and stopped next to me. She was of the variety that doesn't like to get out of their cars but like to just drive up to wherever they are going, and roll down their power windows and do business. So I obliged her. She looked at me as if I were a denizen from the deep (not far off), and after a short interchange issued me a Bible. She asked me, "What bowing has to do with reality as it is today?" I said, "Bowing is reality as it is today." I explained to her that one of the purposes of bowing was to contemplate reality as it really is. I think she was more interested in the everyday realities like where the next meal is coming from, and where to live, but I was talking about ultimate reality. Why not?

The lady resembled Elizabeth Taylor in wealth and size, and she seemed interested in the welfare of this sojourning Scorpionic soul. I told her a story about the television tube. Now in a television set, all the actors and their environment are the phenomena. They come and go like images in a dream. The picture tube itself is the noumenon; it remains perfectly still despite the thousands of comings and goings that take place every day. The human mind is the same way. If we are caught up in the phenomenal aspect of it, then it's just drama after drama, life after life, in endless succession. But through cultivation of the Way, we return to identifying with the noumenal source, and from that point we transcend the world, yet remain in it. We link up with the four qualities of Nirvana: permanence, truth, purity, and our own true home. Our minds are like that tube, able to encompass the myriad images, yet fundamentally still and unmoving.

The woman listened respectfully, and when I was done, she motioned for her driver to take her away.

Gwo Kwei and Gwo Dzung Bach and their daughter Gwo Fong arrived from San Francisco and cooked us a Mexican lunch by the roadside. In the afternoon, Yo and I put in five miles, and then the Bachs picked us up and took us to their little cabin which they had just rented. We gave a little lecture before hitting the sack.

21 December 1973. Heng Ju writes:

We hit the road real early this morning. At noon the Bachs came back and made lunch, then headed off to San Francisco. By the time we came bowing into Garberville, the temperature had dropped to 20 degrees. A few days ago when we had talked to the Master on the phone, he invited us to return to the monastery for the two-week winter meditation session. Basically we had wanted to continue bowing, but the invitation was too much to resist. We have decided to catch a Greyhound south to attend the session, and will then return here to Garberville to continue the journey when the session is over. It's a rare privilege to attend a Chan session, especially when one receives a personal invitation from a sage. Also, we will have an opportunity to make some much needed repairs to our buggy and other camping equipment. Tonight we will stay here in this abandoned house in the heart of town, then tomorrow we will get on the bus back to the city. The crisp winter air adds to the excitement of returning.

II. Garberville to Coos Bay

7 January 1974. Heng Yo writes:

The two-week Chan sit is now over, and we are on the bus back to Garberville.

The monks of ancient India were also wandering mendicants. They would roam from place to place with not much more than their begging bowl and a razor. They paid their respects at the shrines, and heard the teachings explained by the eminent teachers of the day. But during the monsoon (the rainy season), the roadways and paths were impassable. It was the swarming season for insects and so it was easy for travelers to inadvertently step on them. For these reasons, the Buddha said that monks should gather together in retreats, so that study and meditation could effectively take place. Through the ages, these conclaves became what we now call monasteries. The tradition of gathering together for a period of concentrated practice is the basis of the meditation session. Nowadays, these sessions, lasting seven days or more, take place at monasteries at various times throughout the year. All the activities in the monastery come to a halt, and only meditation is done. In the meditation halls of China, a person would be severely reprimanded if even a single sutra was seen in his possession, because this showed that he was not fully concentrated on meditation and on meditation alone. Daily instructional talks were given, and the environment was perfect for those who really wanted to break through ignorance.

We are especially glad to have taken time out from the bowing to participate in the Chan session.

8 January 1974. Heng Ju writes:

Garberville: The New Year has begun and the trip is off to a fresh start. The two weeks of meditation, plus all of the Dharma talks, have left us in an exalted state. It feels totally exhilarating being out here. It seems as if we have encountered and linked up with some awesome kind of spiritual power that keeps multiplying. We are a mere part of it. It comes from the Master; it comes from within us; it comes from the people we meet. More and more am I beginning to appreciate the truth of the Master's statement, "You must learn to turn the world, and not be turned by it." Who knows what wonders or hardships lie ahead? I feel ready to meet them with a level and equal mind.

Not only our spirits, but our equipment is also in excellent shape. Gwo Gwei Nicholson, on the night before we left the monastery, stayed up all night working in his wood shop at the Blue Peter Company, totally rebuilding our buggy. He used steel and welding rod to reinforce all the weak spots. He added roll bars to protect the spoke wheels when the cart overturns. He installed an adjustable handle which allows for perfect weight distribution.

We have now traveled over 200 miles, and have 135 miles to go, as the crow flies, to the Oregon line. To avoid the freeway, we will be traversing the scenic Avenue of the Giants, a long winding stretch that runs on the east side of the Eel River.

9 January 1974. Heng Yo writes:

About 250 miles north of San Francisco we passed through

Garberville, and then took the old road through Redway. A ten-year-old who had just gotten off a school bus asked with wide eyes, "You mean you've done that all the way from Garberville?" (about one and one half miles) In the late afternoon a green school bus of the California Ecology Corps rolled slowly by and came to a stop on the shoulder. Two men in well-worn working clothes got out. "Hello. We heard about your trip. Did you really come all the way from Los Angeles?"

"No, San Francisco."

One of the men, who had long hair, asked where we stay, what we eat, and our destination. The other man, older and less outgoing, looked absorbed in thought, and then asked, "Why are you doing this?"

I replied that pilgrimages were a way of life for Buddhist monks in other lands, and that we are a modern part of that tradition. There are not yet any monasteries to receive wandering monks, so we stay in our tent.

"But," he said, "I have seen you and your friend bowing up and down. Do you have to make your pilgrimage like that?"

I talked about the significance of the act of bowing, both as a gesture of reverence, and as a meditational device. He listened with one hand cupping his elbow, the other on his chin. I felt he was about to voice an objection of some sort, but the bus driver beeped the horn, and motioned them to get in. After a good luck wish and a "Hope you make it!" the bus disappeared down the road.

When the day was nearly over, I set up the tent near the intersection of the old road and the freeway. Tomorrow we'll have a short distance of freeway bowing and then take the Avenue of the Giants.

10 January 1974. Heng Yo writes:

When we rose this morning, the condensation on the inside of the tent had frozen; we were in a dark blue ice cavern. Heng Ju put on his gloves and went ahead to the bowing area, while I disassembled the tent and stowed all the gear, making a mental note to dry out the tent at meal time if there was sun. I have made it my daily practice to recite the Shurangama Mantra between the time everything is packed up and when I catch up to Heng Ju. A single recitation takes about 15 minutes. At first I tried to recite it while I was engaged in breaking camp, but it was impossible: the flow of the mantra would be interrupted by discriminative thoughts about stowing the gear and so forth. But while walking along the deserted highway early in the morning, the mantra seems to say itself.

The practice of holding mantras belongs to the Secret School of Buddhism, and involves the recitation of certain syllables which have been passed down for centuries by eminent masters. This practice functions on several different levels at once. Like Chan meditation, the effect of its continued application is to still the mind. There is a definite force or power which comes from doing this, linking the mundane tasks of daily life with the realm of the spiritual. One begins to see relationships and connections between events and thus to get an inkling of the vast power within oneself which is waiting to be tapped. There are many different sets of mantras to be learned. The longest and most powerful is the Shurangama Mantra.

The *Shurangama Sutra* tells how the Buddha spoke the mantra in order to rescue his disciple and cousin Ananda, who, under the influence of an evil spell, was about to break his vow of chastity. The Buddha sent Manjushri Bodhisattva to the scene to repeat the mantra and bring the young woman and a contrite Ananda before the Buddha. The Buddha then spoke the *Shurangama Sutra* to instruct Ananda in the powers and methods of samadhi (mental concentration).

The *Shurangama Sutra* was explained by the Master during the first summer session at the Buddhist Lecture Hall in 1968. The English translation of the Sutra, with the Master's lectures as commentary, is being prepared for publication by the Buddhist Text Translation Society. The first volume will be published in the fall of 1977.[7]

About quitting time, Connie and Mark Piehl invited us to spend the night at their house in Phillipsville.

11 January 1974. Heng Yo writes:

Today we bowed a long five and one half miles, passing through Phillipsville. It looks like it is about to rain again. We are camped in a dump. The proprietor of the small grocery store in town asked how we managed to get enough food along our way. I replied that many people, both Buddhist and non-Buddhist, have on many occasions donated bread, fruit, vegetables, and peanut butter to keep us going. Whether the donors are aware of it or not, the practice of accepting alms has been the fundamental means of survival of Buddhist monks since the time of the Buddha, two thousand six hundred years ago.

The Buddha taught five contemplations to be made while eating, so that the monks would never forget how their food was given, and the purpose of eating. Meals are taken in silence so that everyone can keep his mind on the contemplations, which are as follows:

1. *Consider the amount of work involved to bring the food to where it is eaten.*
2. *Consider whether one's virtuous conduct is sufficient to enable one to accept the offering.*
3. *Guard the mind from violations, of which greed is the principle cause.*
4. *Properly taken, the food is like medicine, to keep the body from wasting away.*
5. *The food is accepted only in order to accomplish the Way.*

It is easy to forget that someone had to grow the food that we consume in our daily meals—especially since the advent of the supermarket. After being grown and harvested, the food must be transported, marketed, prepared, and served. Briefly in this first contemplation, we reflect on all the labor which results in having this food before us: all the way from seed, to crate, to finished dish.

Second, we examine our conduct and decide whether it merits our taking food on this day. We should honestly ask ourselves what cultivation we've done to justify eating the fruits of other people's labor. Cultivation of the Way is aimed at saving all living beings, and if we only put on an appearance, we will incur bad retribution, for we are then actually stealing from others. Therefore, a verse says:

> *One grain of rice is as heavy as Mt. Sumeru.*
> *If you do not cultivate after eating,*
> *You are bound to end up with fur and antlers.*

That is, you'll be reborn in the realm of animals, who know only greed.

The third contemplation is to make it one's principal concern to avoid greed and other faults. Greed is one of the fundamental defilements. If we do not get rid of our greed, we'll never accomplish the Buddha way. Desire and greed cover over the potential bright wisdom within us. When eating, we should be mindful of how much we are eating in relation to actual need. Going overboard is the result of greed, like a fire that blazes when more fuel is added on, and diminishes when not fed. Therefore, we should not let our minds wander when eating, but should consider these contemplations.

The fourth contemplation is to consider the food as good medicine for the body. In order for us to function, we must have proper proportions of nourishment. This is important especially now when commercially processed food is mercilessly subject to a profusion of chemical additives, refining processes, and other incredible technical "advances." It is wise not to eat junk; however, when one has attained the Way, it no longer matters what one eats, or if one eats at all. The Patriarch Bodhidharma was poisoned on six occasions when he was in China, but was not affected in the least.

The reason for accepting the food which is offered is to provide us with the strength to cultivate the Way. This is the fifth and final contemplation. Instead of letting the mind wander, resolve that the energy and strength which this food yields will not be misdirected, squandered, or lost.

12 January 1974. Heng Ju writes:

Battered by torrential rain, we nevertheless made five and a half miles. We are still alongside the raging Eel River on the Avenue of the Giants. We are camped in a roadside Redwood grove. The tent is doing fine except for some seepage in the bottom. Next time I'll put more effort into digging the trench.

The river is really getting out of hand. I remember the Master often saying, "The whole world is constantly speaking the Buddhadharma; you just have to learn to recognize it." To the poor inhabitants of Weott, Myers Flat, and Pepperwood, it speaks the law of cause and effect. From this awesome spectacle, these poor people are learning of karma, retribution, suffering, and impermanence. As they helplessly observe their worldly treasures wash down across the state and into the sea, they have an opportunity to see the Buddha, disguised as a turbid river, turning the Dharma wheel. He spoke it so clearly thousands of years ago, "All worldly things are like a lightning flash, an illusion, a dream, a magic show."

To me, the river is a reminder of the ever-flowing stream of thought that runs in the mind. In Chinese, this flow is called *wàng xiǎng* 妄想 (false thinking). This superfluous cogitation is constantly making discriminations: dividing and categorizing, breaking up a fundamentally undifferentiated reality into myriads of pieces. Of course the pieces seem to be reality, too, but we become confused by these false projections, and greedily seek what we think is "good" and reject what is "bad." The superficial boundaries of "mine" and "others" are falsely established. From this arises quarrelling and all manner of afflictions, up to and including world wars, and it's all simply because we are confused by this river of thought.

13 January 1974. Heng Ju writes:

Passing through Myers Flat, I had an encounter with a man in a fire-engine-red pickup truck. He was parked outside of town waiting; there was no one around except me and him. Heng Yo was at the laundromat, drying out the gear. As I passed near his truck, he started yelling at me. He was drunk and really angry. "What the hell are you trying to prove? What do you think you are doing?" he yelled over a public address system mounted on the top of his cab. I wasn't sure how to respond to him, so I just kept bowing. He began driving right alongside of me, sparing no words, cursing and shouting obscenities. He was truly a fireman with much fire.

This weird scene continued for several minutes, during which time I still hadn't said a word. Finally, after thoroughly emptying himself of his rage, he began to break down and cry. "Why won't you talk to me?" he wailed. "What kind of religion is this that won't permit you to talk to me?"

I stopped bowing and finally spoke, "Basically, I am not doing any harm. Why are you upset?"

"Why can't you pray alone?" he said.

"I've prayed alone for several years," I said. "I need some fresh air."

"Look," he said, "Why can't you do good, like me. I'm a fireman, I save people's lives. Now that has a real use. Listen, I'm sorry that I got mad, but there's a lot of mean loggers up north of here, and they're not going to like this bowing along the road business."

"Well," I said, "I'm sorry also, but this is what I do; it's very meaningful to me; I'm sorry I upset you."

"Well," he said, "I've been drinking, and I get angry real easy. Let's forget the whole thing, OK?"

"OK."

14 January 1974. Heng Yo writes:

Since it is winter, there are not many people who come to see the giant trees, and thus there is not much traffic. It's almost as if the entire Redwood Empire is our own.

When we first saw the Eel River, it was a smooth, broad, green stripe, flowing through the rocks and trees. Now, because of the constant rain which melts the snow, the river has become a dark, churning force which is rising daily. If the rain does not let up, there is going to be trouble. Someone mentioned that already there has been three times the amount of rain of last winter.

Through Phillipsville and Miranda, I overheard a few remarks. "They came all the way from Frisco doin' THAT?"

"Well, it takes all kinds, don't it, Maggie. You know, I told the minister he should go out and counsel them."

The trees impinge on the already narrow road, and constantly let fall huge drops of water, whether it's raining or not. Toward the end of the afternoon today, the rain still hadn't stopped, and the tent was still drenched from last night. As I was looking for a place to camp for the evening, I spotted a giant redwood which was conveniently hollow at the base of the trunk. There was room enough for Big Ju and me both, so we spent a dry night inside it. The rain continued, and the thundering river was not far away.

15 January 1974. Heng Yo writes:

We decided not to try to do any bowing today due to the heavy rains. My first reaction to this delay was disappointment, because I have yet to let go of the notions of "progress" and "stagnation." After a while, however, I saw that if we are to be successful, we must be in accord with the conditions at hand, and not force the issue, like the man from Sung in ancient China.

Tradition relates that people from the state of Sung were noted for their stupidity. Once there was a Sung farmer who was disappointed about the slow progress of his growing corn. He decided to do something about it, and at the end of a long, backbreaking day in the fields, he returned home, sat down, and said, "I certainly am tired." His wife and son asked why, and he answered that he'd been hard at work all day helping the crops grow. The son went to the fields to look, and to his great surprise, saw that all the crops were dead. Why? Because this impatient farmer from Sung had helped each little plant grow by pulling it up a couple of inches! Since then, the expression "helping them grow" has become a common idiom in China.

Sometimes, it is better not to do anything at all.

16 January 1974. Heng Yo writes:

It finally has happened: the river has exceeded the flood level (at present it is at 43 feet), causing widespread damage to the string of towns along the banks. We heard that Pepperwood was completely wiped out. Other rivers in the area have also flooded, and Governor Reagan and President Nixon have declared this part of the state a disaster area. As we approached the town of Weott, we found that the main street was under a good six feet of water, and the level was rising. Some people who were smart enough to settle in mobile homes after the last big flood have been able to move them to higher ground. Others, not so fortunate, were being evacuated by boat by the National Guard. A house and its occupants were found crushed by a giant mud slide near Myers Flat.

Today we telephoned the monastery, and the Master repeated emphatically that if we are sincere in our efforts, it will not rain. Looking from the phone booth, I saw water flowing everywhere, huge trees being swept along by the swift current in the river, and the rain still coming down. I must not have been sincere enough. We holed up in an old shed on high ground, waiting for the water to recede and the road to surface.

17 January 1974. Heng Yo writes:

Some of these redwoods are extremely tall and imposing, with diameters of twelve or more feet, and circumferences of forty feet. Although they are 2,000 to 3,000 years old, and around 300 foot tall, they have extremely shallow, spreading root systems, perhaps five or six feet deep. So when the flooding river washes away soil, the trees are left with no support. Lately, they have been crashing down quite frequently, making loud explosions, sometimes taking other trees down with them as they fall. Millions of dollars worth of lumber have gone rampaging down the river, threatening the bridge pilings.

It's like the cultivation of morality, concentration, and wisdom. If one were to base one's cultivation on a moral practice with shallow roots, then when the going gets tough, as it usually does, one will be easily washed out.

Today the water receded almost as fast as it jumped the banks, and the mud which it deposited has leveled off all the undulations in the ground. We are standing in the middle of a vast expanse of what looks like the smooth surface of a just-opened jar of Skippy peanut butter. The mud had been ploughed off the road, leaving a thin, slippery layer on which to bow. Truly a strange journey through a strange land.

18 January 1974. Heng Ju writes:

Last night we slept in an abandoned horse trailer. It had no top, but we tied a sheet of clear plastic over it just before the big storm came in. It was like being in a small boat in a raging sea. It was great to sit there and watch the wind and rain come down, and yet still be comfortable and dry. I hated to leave that sweet-smelling abode, but bright and early we were up and away.

By the time the morning sun dawned on the horizon, I was half mile ahead. Yo was still at the trailer packing up when a clean-shaven man in his early forties walked up to him. He said that he had known about us for a long time, and had been observing us closely for the last two weeks. He told Yo that he felt that we could read minds. After some polite conversation, he got to the point. He said that he had been happily married for about sixteen years, and had a good family with two teenage boys. Recently, however, he discovered that his wife was cheating on him. She was having an affair with another woman! When he asked her about it, she admitted it, but said that she couldn't change. She said that she loved both her husband and her girlfriend. In any case, the guy was at the end of his rope. He was ready to jump in the river and end it all. He was too proud and embarrassed to discuss it with any of his friends, but he somehow felt that he could trust old Yo. Yo talked with the man for about two hours straight, while I bowed ahead wondering where Yo was. Just before lunch time, Yo appeared and explained what had happened. We worked our way north toward Redcrest. Just before dark, the man Heng Yo had counseled came back with his wife in hand. It seemed that Yo's talk had had quite a beneficial effect on them both. They offered him some money, but he politely refused.

We bowed until it was too dark to see, and then took shelter behind a giant lumber mill in Redcrest.

19 January 1974. Heng Yo writes:

The Master has insisted that if we bow sincerely, it will not rain within a quarter-mile radius of where we are bowing. We are trying to do so as we move slowly northward along the river, and the rain seems to be slacking off somewhat. We are now camped away from the road, with nothing but trees for miles around us. It is pitch black and silent.

A few minutes ago, while we were sitting in meditation, there were heavy footfalls and breathing just outside the tent. Heng Ju and I sat staring at each other for ten minutes of thundering silence before we dared to move. The still blackness provided the impetus for the imagination to create all kinds of frightening images. Was it a bear? Or a Bigfoot? Its breath seemed five times the volume of any man's; and after a few moments, it gave a snort and went away. Whew!

The mind is like a movie projector which can create thousands of images. Sometimes we are fooled by them and mistake them for real. Actions based on this fundamental misunderstanding are not effective, for like the dancing images on a movie screen, their reality is here for a moment, and gone in a flash.

In Buddhism, the mind is understood to have eight different consciousnesses. The first five are the consciousnesses of the eye, ear, nose, tongue, and body, which arise from the interaction of the sense objects (sight, sounds, smells, tastes, and tangible objects) and the sense organs (eye, ear, nose, tongue, and body). True reality transcends the closed realm of the consciousness created by the interaction of the sense organ and the sense object. The mind which thinks is considered a sense organ as well. In the same way that the eye sees sights, the mind thinks thoughts. Although these objects of mind, thoughts, are not commonly conceived of as objects in the same sense as trees and rocks, they are nonetheless what the mind-organ interacts with to create mind-consciousness, which is the sixth consciousness. This consciousness has various functions, among them the coordination of data received from the first five consciousnesses and the production of dreams. But all of these sense perceptions and mental perceptions are illusions; they are impermanent, empty, without solid foundation, like a phantom breathing outside our tent.

20 January 1974. Heng Yo writes:

Today we bowed a long six and one half miles, right up to the bridge at Rio Dell. The huge trees that have crashed into the furious river rush along in the current, and are a serious danger to the bridges. The pilings cannot stand up to their repeated blows. Yesterday, a log jam which endangered this particular bridge had to be dynamited by some courageous lumber-jacks.

We are camped on a hill just south of the town of Rio Dell, where a new freeway and bridge are being constructed. Shortly after Heng Ju arrived, a local police officer pulled up in his cruiser, got out, and started to walk up to us. From his obvious youth, he was clearly a rookie on the force. As he approached, he sunk up to his shins in mud. It was all we could do to keep straight faces. Although he had come out to sternly warn us that he'd tolerate no more complaints that we were bowing in the middle of the road, his demeanor was deflated as he became more concerned with the mud on his fresh pants and shiny boots than with us.

21 January 1974. Heng Yo writes:

We are camped in a dump in a place called Alton, after having bowed through Rio Dell in the frosty morning, where we received a lot of flack. People were racing their engines, blowing their horns, pointing, and shouting. Several people stopped to ask questions, among them a police officer who ran a radio-computer check on us. He thought we were rather crazy, and asked Heng Ju if it was messy bowing through all of that dog shit in the gutters. Heng Ju replied that this was not a problem. The officer then asked him if he'd ever spent any time in any institutions—mental institutions. After Ju explained the purpose of our trip, the cop no longer thought we were so crazy, but was still skeptical about the effectiveness of our efforts.

Later in the day, Heng Ju told me that a man who professed to follow the teachings of Christ tried to convert him on the spot. After the man lost his temper, and as Heng Ju bowed up the road, the man walked alongside, screaming and yelling things like, "Not by works! You want everyone to see you come on spiritual, but none are righteous! You are going to go to Hell!"

22 January 1974. Heng Ju writes:

It was a chilly 28 degrees this morning, but the sun came out early to make it a beautiful day. We spent most of the time making the long passage through the town of Fortuna. From the very beginning, there was energy kicking up everywhere. The whole town was wired! High-powered cars were strafing us, racing their engines. Kids were yelling, lots of old folks were asking questions, many people were on the street. Ordinarily after a day like this, I would be a nervous wreck, but today something happened, and although I can't quite put a handle on it, I feel it is important.

As I mentioned earlier, when bowing through these heavily populated areas, I focus my attention on various contemplations. This, I find, offsets the overwhelming tendency to be self-conscious. It helps shatter the illusion that there is a self. Many people are familiar with this Buddhist concept, but it is the intensity of the city passage that gives real power to the investigation.

"Who is it that is bowing? Who are they yelling at?" These are the questions that I deeply ponder as the action intensifies around me.

One of my favorite contemplations is from the *Avatamsaka Sutra*: "There is no doer, and nothing that is done; there is only the arisal of karma-bound thoughts. Beyond this there is nothing." When I get into this one, my sufferings seem to melt away. I can't find anyone to whom they belong. It is said: "Having no view of self, one is always peaceful." There is no worry, fear or affliction. Even if people want to poison you or take your life, it's all okay.

Why? Because there is no 'knowing' that you exist in the first place. In the Chan school it is said that "you don t even wear one thread of clothing; you don't eat a single grain of rice." Well, I've a long ways to go before I reach that stage. Nevertheless, holding in mind these contemplations, I feel a change occurring. Bowing through Fortuna today, I felt a deep trust in the teachings that were guiding me. I felt a certainty that no matter what happened, everything would be all right; and it was.

At the heart of town, I saw Yo up ahead with a small crowd around him. He was answering questions left and right. I had gone pretty much non-stop to this point, but after I passed him and reached the main intersection, a big school bus came rolling to a stop next to me. I looked up and saw the doors open, and suddenly I was surrounded by a crowd of high school boys, leather jackets and all. For one instant I felt a surge of panic, but it passed and I found myself calmly standing on the main intersection of this California town explaining the whys and wherefores of a bowing monk. When I was done, and they had respectfully listened to every word, I slowly got down on my knees and commenced to crawl out of town. There was no problem whatsoever.

Nightfall. We are now camped across the railroad tracks from a cement company at the north end of town.

23 January 1974. Heng Yo writes:

After bowing for a while this morning, we chanced to meet Marge Rauum, who was on her way to work. She is a Buddhist disciple of Dharma Master Mao Jui, of Hong Kong, and is the guidance counselor at the local high school. After putting us up for the night, she filled our cart with provisions, and called ahead to her friends up north to be on the lookout for us.

We have emerged from an area where the major industry of logging seems to affect the residents' life-styles, the way they see themselves, and even their religious beliefs. The logger image is aptly represented by the legendary Paul Bunyan: a giant and powerful man with a flannel shirt, black beard, and a large chainsaw. Babe is his one-ton blue Chevy pick-up, equipped with a CB radio and a shotgun which is displayed across the cab's back window. He is a good Christian, but has been known to have a few beers on Saturday night.

Fortuna is located in the valley where the Van Duzen river meets the sea. Flat and fertile, the land is ideal for the many dairy farms in the area. The contrast from the logging world to this world is so sharp it can almost be tasted. The Fortunans seem more refined than their logging neighbors. Doctors, lawyers, and teachers came out to watch us pass through. Even in this country, the type of land people inhabit has a great deal to do with who they are.

24 January 1974. Heng Yo writes:

There was a mild stir as we passed by the College of the Redwoods where people watched intently as Heng Ju took three steps and bowed, got up, and repeated the process over and over again. A bearded man handed Ju a letter and quickly left without speaking.

It reads:

Sir:

I first ask that you read all that I have written and then that you seriously contemplate it. Because I have asked these things of you, I know that you will do them.

I have seen you walking now about three times. The last, a few minutes ago, as I was driving home from town. I studied you as you knelt and bowed and then stood. As I watched, I noticed that you never wavered in what you were doing. I saw the intent purpose in your eyes, and in the manner in which you carried yourself. I then thought about the reason for your journey. As I drove on, my Lord spoke to my heart, and said God sees this man, and he loves this man also. Take him the message of My salvation. As I then drove on, my Lord who lives in my heart, showed forth his love, and his concern for you to me. I felt it come up from my innermost being, tears came to my eyes, I could hardly contain myself. I then in my weakness said, "Lord, I fear that he would not listen to me. I cannot stop and tell him." My Lord then showed forth His love again, "I died for him also tell him." I then said, "Oh Lord, I cannot, what am I to do?" "Write a letter, and leave it with his servant."

In much agony, and humbleness of soul, I give you this letter, my compromise with Christ, in hopes of your salvation.

With Christian love and best wishes,

Monte McKee

Romans, 3:23:24
For all have sinned, and come short of the glory of God. Being justified freely by his grace through the redemption that is in Christ Jesus.

John, 3:16
For God so loved the world, that he gave his only begotten son, that whosoever believeth in him should not perish but have everlasting life.

We had no choice but to bow on the freeway between Fortuna and Eureka. In California, it is against the law for a pedestrian to use the freeways, but Sgt. Williams of the Highway Patrol told us, "Go ahead on the freeway. You've come a long way. I'll take the blame if there's any problem."

The Tetrault family, whom Marge Rauum called, put us up for the evening, and we had a lively discussion of the Buddhadharma. Jerry Tetrault confirmed his thoughts that the Bible only represented a small period of time in the universe. He felt that there had to be more to it. We explained that the teachings of Buddhism envelop all world systems of the past, present, and future. Anyone can ascend the path and become a Buddha, an enlightened being of inconceivable great vision, wisdom, and compassion. It was one of the best discussions so far.

25 January 1974. Heng Yo writes:

As we entered the outskirts of Eureka, a city of about 25,000 people, we were interviewed by television, radio, and newspaper reporters. We've learned to be careful in speaking to reporters because one can't be sure that their faithfulness to the simple facts of our journey will not be overshadowed by their desire for a sensational story. Some reporters seem interested in finding out the facts as they are, and others, in varying degrees, are out to get the facts as they aren't.

Eureka is a city which combines a paper mill, a port, a nuclear power plant, lumber industries, a small financial world, supermarkets, gas stations, downtown businesses and stores, and little wooden houses. As we passed Tetrault's tire shop, Jerry took our cart in and had a couple of his employees fix up the ailing wheels, while we had some hot chocolate. Later on, at the end of a drizzly day, Mike and John, college students at Humboldt State, gave us a room for the night. That evening, in their kitchen, we got into a rap about Buddhism and non-violence.

26 January 1974. Heng Ju writes:

Bowed through Eureka today. A few Baptists came out to convert us, but not much else happened. John and Eileen Barstow brought us food and wished us luck. At nightfall, Mrs. Young, an old friend of Marge Rauum, took us into her home. She has two healthy boys, aged eleven and twelve, and a pair of huge Saint Bernards which inhabits the kitchen. It was an unusual evening for us as we spent most of the time watching the boys fight. Such vigor I have never seen! Their mother, unable to stop them from fighting, had at least managed to post a bulletin which regulated the conditions for it. It reads:

Rules for Fighting
1. Do it on the porch
2. No sticks or clubs
3. Settle own arguments (no running to Mom)

They fought and carried on all evening until big brother finally squelched little brother for the night, bringing him to tears. When they found out that I knew some gong fu, they pleaded to see an exhibition. I finally consented to show them a little if they promised to clean their rooms, which were a real mess. After a little demonstration of a simple tai chi chuan set, I explained to them the old Daoist principle that the best gong fu is the gong fu that is never used. But I don't think that they were listening. Good night, boys!

27 January 1973. Heng Ju writes:

Between Eureka and Arcata we made good time. We responded to questions from a lot of very interesting people. They cause us to constantly re-evaluate what we are doing. It is most stimulating. As T.S. Eliot once wrote: "Approach to the meaning restores the experience, but in a different form." It's quite true! The more we try to verbalize what we are doing, the more meaningful it becomes.

Now most of the people we encounter are from Christian backgrounds. We find that the scope of their religious understanding runs from paper thin to most profound. An example of the former are the young "Jesus Freaks." When they approach us, they want us to decide right then. "It's either Jesus or eternity in hell." On the other hand, many of the devout Christians are very impressive. A man named Dennis Dingus and his wife rode out on their motorcycle to have a discussion with us, and it proved to be quite fruitful for all. Although Dingus is a solid Christian, he keeps his mind open and makes it his business to look into and consider other philosophies. He was surprised to hear that I had spent eleven years in parochial schools, the last three of which were under the guidance of the Christian Brothers of Ireland at O'Dea High School in Seattle. I explained that I hadn't forgotten my good roots, but I felt that what I was doing now was helping those roots mature. As a young Christian I was trained to "know, love, and serve God," but I never learned what God was. Now I'm learning that, strangely enough, within Buddhism. People should be encouraged to investigate all religions, to seek the highest principles, and to get away from oversimplifications like "We're right and they're wrong." To me, the names Buddhist and Christian are only labels that have no real substance. All religions should be used to reach the goals of enlightenment, liberation, and freedom from suffering. Even the highest teachings of Buddhism are said to be like a raft: only for the purpose of getting people across the sea of suffering to the other shore of enlightenment is the Dharma spoken. We and the Dinguses agreed that religions are to be used, not merely followed. Too many people of all religions put in minimal performances and leave the rest up to the founder.

Some exciting news! Yesterday when we phoned the monastery, we found out that a Buddhist layman named Pong has given a forty-acre tract of land to the Sino-American Buddhist Association for the purpose of building a monastery. The land is located 130 miles northeast of Seattle, on the Skagit River at Marblemount, Washington. Heng Yo and I are planning to extend the trip, and bow all the way up to the monastery site.

28 January 1974. Heng Ju writes:

We bowed past Arcata and California State University at Humboldt today. A young law student came out, introduced himself as Larry Marks, and asked Yo what the basic tenets of Buddhism are. Yo replied without a moment's hesitation, "Don't be attached to Marks." Some fine humor there, but perhaps I should explain. "Marks" is a common translation of the Chinese character *xiàng* 相. It could also be translated as characteristics, appearances, externals, phenomena, particulars, labels, etc. It is another key word found thousands of times in Buddhist texts. A verse from the *Avatamsaka Sutra* can illustrate:

> *The Dharma nature is fundamentally pure,*
> *Like empty space which has no marks.*
> *There is no way it can be spoken of.*
> *Wise people should contemplate this well.*

Another verse says:

When one relies on the dharma which is beyond confusion,
Reality can manifest and be attained.
Far apart from the entanglement of marks (xiàng),
One is called supremely enlightened.

The human mind is basically boundless. Its substance is pure and eternal. But because for so long we have been calculating, making discriminations, and thinking, we have lost sight of this limitless nature. We allow ourselves to be turned and confused by the impermanent phenomena (marks) of the world. Our society has trained us to identify ourselves with our physical bodies and intellectual minds, but this is not right. It's a real identity crisis. Our true nature, or true body, is all pervasive. It is beyond all marks, and yet at the same time it is within marks. There is nowhere that it is, and yet there is nowhere that it isn't. It's just a question of awakening.

So that's why Yo told Larry not to be attached to marks.

29 January 1974. Heng Yo writes:

Just north of Arcata, the road turns into freeway again, and there are no other roads to take. It seems that traveling on the freeway is safer than on other roads, because the freeways are broad and level. The hills are graded, and there is always a bowing lane which keeps us away from the traffic. The drivers can see us clearly, and we can see their cars clearly. It's just one of those funny inconsistencies that freeways are only for automobiles.

I have begun to see that the principles of meditation do not apply only to the period of time when one sits motionless in body and mind. They are universal principles. There really should be no time when meditating starts or stops. For this reason, I like to term this journey a meditational pilgrimage—whether we are bowing, resting, sitting, or whatever, the basic principles of meditation can and should be practiced.

We are camped now on the banks of the well-named Mad River, where evidence of the recent flooding is abundantly present. Our tent is a wonderful portable meditation hall, although it is a mite too low for Big Ju's head to clear when he sits up straight. The wind in the trees, the rush of the river, and the whoosh of cars on the road blend into the cold blackness of night. Tomorrow is already here.

30 January 1974. Heng Yo writes:

We were having our daily meal by the roadside about 11:00 a.m. today when a little man of about 45 years walked over and stopped in obvious amazement. He introduced himself as Robert Alexander. It turned out that his old clothes and slouch hat were complemented by a quick wit. He was just appalled by what he saw us eat—not so much because of the content of the meal, but because we were combining foods which he said did not go together at all. He himself eats only one kind of food at each meal, and raw food at that. He either eats nuts, fruit, or grain which was soaked in water overnight.

He seemed to dance around as he spoke, a veritable barrel of energy, with a mind which always seemed to be trying to catch up with itself. He talked about building an eclectic religious center or monastery on his twelve acres of land near Trinidad, a small town north of here. He invited us to stay when we are in that area. After a while, he said goodbye, stuck out his thumb, and caught a ride with some college students from Arcata. In the silence which followed his departure, the whole encounter seemed slightly unreal. After our lunch, Heng Ju started bowing again, while I washed the dishes, and packed up the cart.

Because so many folks have been stopping to ask us the same questions, we had some cards printed up in Arcata:

We are two Buddhist Monks from Gold Mountain Temple, 1731 15th St., San Francisco. During the next few months we will be traversing the 1,000 miles between San Francisco and Marblemount, Washington, a small town about 130 miles northeast of Seattle. In

At Robert Alexander's (he is standing at Heng Ju's right).

the near future a Buddhist Monastery will be established there. Heng Ju has vowed to bow every third step of the way, and Heng Yo has vowed to handle the equipment. He also bows. We hope that by doing this, the Lords and Spirits who watch over the world will be moved to maintain peace. We pray that the people of the world will each work to get rid of the greed, anger, and delusion in their own hearts. We believe that this is the only way for a real and lasting peace.

    Sincerely,

    Heng Ju Heng Yo

We handed out several hundreds of these cards, but later on, we decided not to use them. We just answered all the questions personally.

31 January 1974. Heng Ju Writes:

Bowed past McKinleyville, where the freeway again draws near to the sea. Late in the afternoon, while bowing up a long hill, the thought kept arising how thirsty I was. Yo wasn't nearby, since he was having troubles with the wheels of the cart. Suddenly in front of me, I saw a van stop, and a young woman got out and began walking toward me. She handed me a large steaming mug of herb tea laced with honey. I accepted it without speaking and gratefully began to drink. Then she took a handful of dried green leaves and began rubbing them on my forehead. She said they were sage leaves and that they were very soothing. They were. I wanted to say something, but it didn't seem necessary. I didn't know what to say anyway. We stood in silence as I sipped the tea. When I gave her the empty mug back, she wished us luck, and said that she was really glad that we were bowing for world peace. Then she was gone.

  Yo finally caught up and we made a good six miles. Now we are camped on a rocky ledge about a hundred feet above the beach. Our trusty five-pound tent is proving itself again as another storm blows in from the southwest.

1 February 1974. Heng Yo Writes:

We are now at Robert Alexander's place, which seems to reflect the qualities of the man himself. Strewn haphazardly among the trees are about ten converted school buses which house college students, a dozen and a half junked Corvairs, and several uprooted buildings of an old motel. There is a spring with cool, pure water, and Robert's telephone is tacked to a nearby handy tree.

During the day's bowing, we passed by the road to Crannell, a town built by one of the large lumber companies to house its loggers and their families. For some reason, the prefabricated town didn't work out, and the place is now a modern ghost town in the forest.

Later on, a carful of Christian evangelists pulled over and told Heng Ju that he was a sinner, and that "none are righteous before the Lord." Ju said to them that he was neither righteous nor unrighteous. I don't think they allowed themselves to accept the fact that such an alternative exists. In fact, this seems to be a characteristic of many people who try very hard to convert us on the spot. If you are not saved, you are damned; you are eternally sentenced to either heaven or hell. If you are not one of them, you automatically belong to the retinue of the Devil. In their view, there are no alternatives.

But actually, if you think about it, there is no good without bad; no dark without light. Relative things define each other, and dualities have no meaning without their opposite. In Buddhism, the goal is to attain a state of being which is beyond all dualities. Even the very basic duality of birth and death must be transcended in order to be successful. Personally, I have yet to transcend the duality of being tired and not being tired, so this discussion will have to be continued tomorrow, so I can get some rest.

2 February 1974. Heng Ju writes:

Cold and windy as we made our approach into Trinidad today. At about 9:00 a.m. a car full of old friends arrived unexpectedly with a large feast and lots of good vibes. Professor Ron Epstein (Gwo Rung), a philosophy instructor at San Francisco State, had come out to see us once again. With him were Gwo Jou and Gwo Tsai Rounds and Steve Berman. Steve invited us to stay at his house in Trinidad when we pass through tomorrow.

Gwo Jou Rounds, a Harvard graduate like Gwo Rung, is another of those rare individuals who not only believes in the principles of Buddhism, but also practices them. Even though he lives seventy-five miles north of San Francisco, he still spends one day of every week working and meditating at the monastery. His cultivation is about to bear fruit, as he readies his first major novel, Celebrisi's Journey, for publication. The book is a fast-moving account of a man from New Jersey who begins to experience the opening of his mind. It tells of his adventures as he feels his way through a very sleepy and naive America in search of proper spiritual guidance. Gwo Jou's wife, Gwo Tsai, who is an educator at Berkeley, prepared us a hot lunch with vegetables from her own garden.

Now it is dark. We are still camped at the strange estate of Robert Alexander.

3 February 1974. Heng Yo writes:

Bowing past Trinidad, a big family, the Whittenbergs, introduced themselves and brought us tea and food. They told us they are going to visit the monastery in San Francisco. In the evening, Steve Berman and his wife Felicia took us in. Steve sang an old Buddhist song in Chinese, accompanying himself on the lute. In the song, one of the Buddha's disciples, Maudgalyayana, who had just opened his heavenly eye so that he was able to see anywhere in the universe, saw his mother burning in one of the hells. He asked the Buddha how to save her. "How many roads to the Magic Mountain?" The Buddha replied, "There are tens of thousands, and even more. Tens of thousands. Amitabha, Amitabha."

There is a passage which expresses very well what I was trying to say the other day:

The fault of rejecting existence while becoming attached to emptiness is like jumping into a fire to avoid drowning. Some reject the false mind to strive for the principle of truth, but these thoughts of rejecting and striving are just a clever ruse.

This is a prose translation of one of the verses of the *Song of Enlightenment*, which was written by Dharma Master Yung Chia, an eminent Chinese master. "To reject existence while becoming attached to emptiness" is to favor one relative thing over another. It is like saying blue is better than green. This error "is like jumping into a fire to avoid drowning." If you insist on clinging to one side, and do not allow for the validity of the other, you are making a fatal spiritual mistake. The way to avoid it is to understand that both sides of the coin make up its true existence.

"Some reject the false mind to strive for the principle of truth." This reminds me of those who say, "We are right, we represent the truth, and therefore you are wrong." It seems that in talking with evangelistic people we encounter this attitude often, because their teachings imply this dualistic system. "But thoughts of rejecting or striving are just a clever ruse." This means that all opposites come basically from a single source, and when we have attained it, we realize that all efforts at grasping the "true" and rejecting the "false" are illusory and unreal.

That is not to say that one can travel the path with reckless abandon and make excuses on the grounds that one shouldn't be attached to right and wrong. It means rather that when one limits one's spiritual realm to dualistic ideas of right and wrong, true and false, one will never be able to embody the single source of phenomenal existence, which is the gate to the realms beyond.

4 February 1974. Heng Ju writes:

North of Trinidad, old Highway 101 runs along the cliffs, while the freeway goes inland a bit. We took the old highway because it is much safer—there is hardly any traffic—and the scenery is stupendous. As we bow, we constantly see the surf smashing in blue and white profusion over large volcanic rocks that jut up like little islands. The roar of the ocean and the wet, misty air keep us invigorated and mindful.

After lunch a couple of middle-aged Irish men in a small Volvo stopped to talk. They were quite philosophically inclined, and only a little drunk, so we had a very interesting exchange. They wanted to know if I had ever had any "unusual" experiences in relation to my teacher. Well, I could have talked at length on that one, but as it was, I told them the first incident that came to mind.

Years ago, when I had first come to the monastery, my job was to wash the dishes. Now on this particular Sunday, since it was a big holiday, there were a lot of extra dishes, and I was stuck with all of them. After lunch everyone else was gathering around in little groups, talking and drinking tea, but I began to sink into a state of despair. "No one wants to help. No one cares," I thought to myself. I looked at the stacks of dirty dishes, and began to entertain thoughts of going upstairs to pack my backpack. So there I was, standing at the sink deeply submerged in self-pity, when I happened to look up, and there was the Master! He was standing about five feet from me on my right side with a big smile on his face. Then quite suddenly he began to rant and rave for no apparent reason whatsoever, yelling: "You break too many dishes!" he said in broken English. "Too many dishes go to blinking!" (breaking).

I was shocked. I didn't say anything, but my mind quickly shifted from despair to my own defense. "What?" I thought, "I haven't broken a single dish in over a month. What in the world is he talking about?" But I didn't say anything. "Heh, heh, heh, heh, heh." was the best reply I could think of. Then just as suddenly as he appeared, he was gone. I tried to figure just what the heck was going on, but couldn't make any sense of it. After a few minutes I had forgotten the incident, and was busily washing dishes, when I looked over to my right to see the most incredible thing occur.

Someone had been piling up dishes inside a large, round-bottomed wok. They were piled so high that the last dish set on top had made the whole pile start wobbling, and just as I looked in that direction, the whole bloody mess toppled over. When they hit the cement floor, pieces flew all over the place. There must have been over thirty dollars worth of dishes broken. Since I was closest to the pile, it looked as if I had done it. Everyone in the vicinity came running in to see what had happened. Then it dawned on me what the Master had just said.

Now there may have been doubts before, but now there was no question about it. I realized that I had been given a demonstration of the kind of powerful vision that was far beyond any average person's scope. I became aware then, and have been aware of ever since, that the Master is constantly watching over his disciples. There have been other incidents as well, far too numerous to count, which clearly indicate that he is "with us." I know this must sound preposterous, but it is almost taken for granted by everyone who has spent any length of time at the monastery. The Master calls this kind of teaching "teaching from the inside out."

The philosophers were really tickled with the story and departed still in high spirits.

Now we are camped at Patrick's Point State Park, a lush green forest campground, perched on the jagged coastal cliffs. Besides the rangers, we have the whole park to ourselves.

5 February 1974. Heng Ju writes:

Since it is such a nasty day out, we didn't leave the park today. We spent most of the day reading, meditating, walking along the cliffs, and relaxing. At sunset we gave each other a Dharma talk, and drilled each other on Chinese vocabulary. I have a pocket Chinese dictionary I have been using to drill Yo during rest periods. His Chinese is excellent. In fact, Yo is a remarkable person in many ways. He is a Pisces, with Aries moon and Gemini rising. Vigorous, industrious, enthusiastic, meticulous, responsible, intelligent, and sensitive—that's what he is. Whether installing plumbing, developing film, translating scriptures, baking bread, sitting in full lotus, or setting up the five-pound tent on a rocky cliff, he does it clearly and precisely, as if he were being well paid for it. He concentrates on the work before him and gets it done.

Now of course it wouldn't be a fair appraisal if I just mentioned his good points, so I must add, and mind you this is not a big fault, that he does at times take things a little too personally. He can upon occasion fall into a state which I call the Deep Pisces Blues and more often than not manages to pull me into it also. When he gets "that" look on his face, I know that somewhere, somehow, I have done something wrong.

At that point, it's up to me to figure out what I did wrong, and reconcile the differences. Often I say, "Hey Yo! Let's stop for a while and have some hot chocolate." The hot chocolate dharma has solved more problems on this trip for both of us than any other method we could think of. Usually I find that I, in fact, actually was inconsiderate in some form or another, and when the roots of the incident are dug up, Yo returns to being his cheerful, vigorous self. And I return to being my sometimes obnoxious self, and we're off down the road.

6 February 1974. Heng Ju writes:

We made five miles and are now camped right on a sandy beach. We have a roaring bonfire going. Today we passed Big Lagoon. It was a strange passage. As I bowed alongside the lagoon I began to lose my sense of time and distance. There was a heavy wind with lots of mist blowing in from the sea. I experienced the sensation that I was standing in one place bowing, absolutely still while all the world was moving past me. Perhaps it wasn't so much an exalted state of consciousness as it was the optics of the situation. The immense vastness of the scene and this long narrow highway disappearing like an endless thread over the horizon helped create the effect. In any case I must have set some kind of record for myself as I bowed over a mile and a quarter without once breaking pace. The energy just kept coming, and it felt good.

7 February 1974. Heng Ju writes:

Made only two miles before being forced to seek shelter from a heavy storm. We are now set up in the lot of a big lumber mill.

It sometimes feels really creepy being adrift like this. We are leaves blown by the autumn winds across an unknown planet, constantly in quiet motion, not involved in anything, just silently drifting and watching.

8 February 1974. Heng Ju writes:

It's still raining and we are still camped in the same wet place. There is a tendency to despair at times like this, but there is nothing we can do but wait. Fortunately we can always meditate. There is a line in the *Avatamsaka Sutra*: "The nature empty is itself the Buddha." Most people grasp at things and thus don't return to their basic nature, which has four distinct qualities: it is pure, still, genuine, and blissful. This spiritual heritage is covered over by karmic-bound thoughts, and so most of us are not aware of it. On rainy days in the tent, we have a good opportunity to meditate on this.

9 February 1974. Heng Ju writes:

Despite the rain, we got out on the road today. It's better to be wet with progress than dry without.
"Manifesting but uniting nowhere, coming and going in rapid profusion, all things are beyond characterization. This is the Buddha's true substance." These words from the *Avatamsaka* really bring home my feelings about this whole experience. Since Yo and I are constantly in motion, it is easy to understand that there is really nothing to hang on to. I think it is really good to set aside a time of life where you can temporarily put everything down and simply work on being unattached. It is a real lesson in values. One discovers that a lot of things one thought were important don't really matter at all. I suppose it could be said that at the deepest level, nothing really matters at all. Things are simply just the way they are. This is an ultimate truth which people should strive to be grounded in. Once one realizes that there is basically nothing at all, one can re-enter the world and really make a stand. One can clearly define what one's reality will be and then struggle to give it value. For in

this world false and true are mixed together. It just depends on how one looks at things. It is said that all dharmas are false and empty, but then again, these very same dharmas are a manifestation of reality. In either case, it is good to build a foundation, an unmoving center, from which all the various manifestations of life and death can be observed and worked with.

10 February 1974. Heng Yo writes:

We are camped out on the beach some forty miles south of Crescent City, and I can hear the pounding surf, the hissing, popping, crackling fire, and a chorus of 84,000 frogs in the lagoon behind us. There is something wonderful about a fire on a cold black night; I could sit watching and listening to it for hours. It's great for drying our wet clothes, heating water for tea, and even cooking tomorrow's beans, but there is something else which makes the campfire very welcome at the day's end. I can't seem to put my finger on it though.

According to my latest calculations, we've now completed 379 miles of bowing along our coastal route, although we are only 308 miles from San Francisco by the shorter inland route. Heng Ju is running on retreaded knee pads, the cart is on its fourth set of wheels, and we've consumed many pounds of Dharma Master Ching's famous granola. There have been only four or five days of rain since the big flood; otherwise the weather has been fairly good. Since leaving the Humboldt Bay area, we have been making our way among some magnificent stands of Redwood and Douglas fir toward Redwood National Park, which is the newest of the National Parks.

11 February 1974. Heng Yo writes:

Again we are camped on the beach just south of the town of Orick, the "Gateway to the National Park", as it calls itself. After setting up the tent, I gathered a big pile of driftwood, and just as the blaze got going, a county deputy sheriff arrived. I thought for sure we were going to be busted for camping on the beach, and lighting a fire to boot. To my surprise, the officer said, "Hi! Beautiful place to camp!" It was Officer James Kennedy, who had come by to chat and see if we needed anything.

During the day's bowing, three county road workers watched Heng Ju buff and scrape his way past their big orange dump truck. As I passed by a few moments later, the driver said hello, and asked a couple of questions about our trip. They were obviously a little uptight about talking with me, but this is understandable in light of some of the fantastic stories about us which sometimes find their way back to us. One of them asked if we made progress every day, and I said yes. It was a great opportunity to tell the Poison Oak Incident of Bodega Bay, which has by now become a great and humorous story, although it was far from that at the time it happened. It really cracks people up when they hear someone used poison oak in place of toilet paper. As if I had told them a great joke, the road workers roared with laughter. They praised our goal, wished us luck, and drove off.

I suspect the force of the Poison Oak Incident is that it lets others know that we are just as human as they are and thus make mistakes like anyone else. This story helps bridge the communication gap which sometimes appears.

12 February 1974. Heng Ju writes:

Bowed into Orick through a light rain. A few cars roared past us as we entered town, probably the local high school gang, but there was no problem. One middle-aged housewife tried to convert me to her fundamentalist religion. In the heart of town we passed Ima's Hamburger stand (I'm a hamburger?). A few truckers were gathered around in front, and they stopped us to ask a few questions. They didn't understand much about Buddhism, but they sure understood miles. When we told them that we had already bowed over 300 miles, they were really moved.

At nightfall, we met Tom Carter and his wife Sunny, and they offered us their living room for the night. We bought some flour at the grocery store where Tom works, and made bread; three loaves for them, three for us. We spent the evening drinking tea and talking Buddhism.

13 February 1974. Heng Ju writes:

As we passed the Mosely Motel on Dawson Road, Mrs. Mosely herself came out and invited us in for coffee. Her motel is full of vacancies because of the gasoline shortage. She offered us a room for the night but we decided to keep going, and eventually found a beautiful campsite way off the highway. Now it is dark and quiet out. I can hear only the sounds of the crickets and frogs. Yo is tending a small fire and cooking some pinto beans for tomorrow's lunch.

> *The nature of fire is one;*
> *It's able to consume all things.*
> *Flames burn without discriminations;*
> *All dharmas are the same way.*

This verse from the *Avatamsaka* reveals the selfless nature of the mind. "Flames burn without discriminations;" flames do not have a mind, yet they function perfectly well. They are simply a result of the right causes and conditions coming together. The mind has no self either. Without a sense of self it would function perfectly well, always in harmony with the environment, and there would be no problems. All dharmas are this way, that is, everything follows this principle whether the "self" arises or not.

14 February 1974. Heng Ju writes:

North of Orick we are inland and in the midst of Redwood National Park. We've got the whole place to ourselves, and these trees: some of them are 3,000 years old. They were on this planet even before the Buddha's time! It's quite peaceful here.

The mail truck stopped on the highway today, and the mailman popped out of the truck and came walking up to Yo, who was bowing by the side of the road. It was a special delivery from Bob Olson of the Olson Electric Company in San Francisco: a giant box of nuts. There was also a letter from Gold Mountain saying that everyone was really enjoying our trip from the log entries we've been sending. We are now camped in the woods just north of Prairie Creek Redwoods State Park, where a large herd of elk are grazing in an open field.

15 February 1974. Heng Ju writes:

We made three miles before Gwo Gwei Nicholson and his cousin Margaret arrived with lunch. They brought two rip-stop nylon robes for us made from parachute material. Since another big storm was on top of us, they drove us to an abandoned house, high above the banks of the Klamath River, and left us off. Now it is night, and there is a ghostly wind howling through broken windows. Loose boards are creaking and little animals are making sounds.

The *Avatamsaka Sutra* say:

The nature of wind is one;
Its breeze is felt on all things.
But the wind has no mind,
All dharmas are the same way.

The forces which sustain the wind and all of nature are inconceivable. There is no person or personality making them perform. The events of nature are empty of self. Strangely enough, people are the same way. In the last analysis, they have no minds or anything that they can really call their own. In Buddhism this is called the truth of no-self.

The Chan school for centuries has used a meditational device which helps lead the cultivator to this truth. It is the question "Who?" By invoking this question while witnessing behavior of body and mind, one can realize that one's nature is basically infinite. It is like the wind: boundless, beginningless, and selfless. Everything in the universe is without a self. To put it more positively: people are already complete; they are already Buddhas. Eternity is going on right now; there is nothing more that can be done to make eternity more eternal. Right now, the absolutely true and the completely false are simultaneously manifesting before us in perfect accordance with karmic law.

16 February 1974. Heng Yo writes:

Today we bowed along a narrow section of road, and made about four and a half miles before camping in a redwood grove. It has been raining most of the day, but this time we rigged up our plastic tarp over the tent as a rainfly. It is very effective in keeping out the rain, and reduces the condensation inside. Why didn't we think of it before?

Heng Ju and I have just finished meditating for an hour or so. It is pitch black out there, and silent. There seems to be a certain feeling of joy which follows a good period of meditation after a long day. It just might be the false sense of freedom which comes from traveling all day and camping at night wherever it's convenient. On the other hand, it is said that Chan bliss may be one of the effects of continued meditation. The feeling I've been experiencing is not an intense, emotional one, but it is rather a contentment, a feeling of fulfillment: I am finally in the right place, doing the right things for the right reasons. My worldly and spiritual destinations may be a long way off, or I may arrive in an instant, but the quiet joy of knowing I'm on the right path must be the beginning of Chan bliss.

The crickets weave a net of sound to set off the black silence. Have I really tasted Chan bliss, or have I succeeded in convincing myself that I have? What is the difference?

17 February 1974. Heng Ju writes:

We bowed down a long hill and over a long bridge. Two gold-colored cement bears stand at the end of the bridge. As we crossed the Humboldt-Del Norte county line, two deputy sheriffs stopped to check me out. There were two cars; one deputy stayed a safe distance away in his car, while the other cautiously approached and asked who I was and what I was doing. Every time I moved, he jumped. I've never seen such a frightened law enforcement officer. There was no problem, though: he was just curious.

We bowed into the south end of Klamath, and pitched tent on the spot where the old town used to be. It had been completely washed out by the big flood of 1964. The new town of Klamath is built on higher ground. It's interesting how people learn from their mistakes.

18 February 1974. Heng Yo writes:

We should have known better than to pitch the tent on such low ground so close to the river. We knew a whole town was wiped out right here by the Klamath River ten years ago, and why should a tent be able to stay where buildings couldn't? It has been pouring for fourteen hours straight. The rain kept us from bowing today, and by noon the water was three inches deep all around us. We packed everything up and made a scramble for better shelter. Luckily, we found an abandoned cabin overlooking the river. So much water I've never seen!

19 February 1974. Heng Yo writes:

Since we are over a mile from the bowing spot, Ju suggested that there was no need for me to haul all the gear out. So I stayed in this old skeleton of a house, while Ju went out in the rain to "get some miles in." I did some reading, meditating, made some repairs on the gear, and later, when it stopped raining, took a walk.

In the Navy, Ju spent five years in the confines of a conventional submarine, and thus he has little trouble getting along with others for long periods of time in small spaces. In terms of practicing the Way, Ju has shown me that everyone has psychic or spiritual space as well as physical space. People set up boundaries within which cultivation takes place, and sometimes we feel wronged if these boundaries are not respected. Getting attached to ideas of ourselves and how things should be done can prevent the very success we hope to gain. An occasional day when I am free to redefine and roam freely in my psychic space is most welcome. It is a great relief for tensions which occasionally build up between Ju and myself.

Ju returned. During the day's bowing, he reported that someone yelled at him, "Hey, man, got any more of that opium?" Later on, an older woman named Gracie Knight invited us to stay at her house when we pass by there tomorrow.

The wind is playing this old house like some strange instrument, and the weird rhythm and tune last into the night.

20 February 1974. Heng Ju writes:

North of Klamath, Jack, the owner of the Pines Motel, poured us a cup of coffee, introduced us to his dog, and told us a little local history. He said that the reason those cement bears on the Klamath bridge were golden-colored was that he and his friends got drunk one night and went out and painted them. They did this many years ago, and since then it has become a tradition.

After five miles of progress, Gracie Knight arrived in her car to take us in for the night. We marked the spot, and returned to her home on a little hillside north of Klamath. Gracie and her husband "Daddy Ray." are a couple of real characters. Gracie, although she is almost 70 years old, jogs five miles a day. She also holds a Thursday night meditation club, in which she and her friends investigate the principles of religion. Daddy Ray, a retired logger, is from Arkansas, and he showed us some splendid southern hospitality by specially preparing a guest room for us, complete with a roaring fire in the stove.

Gracie told us that in all of the forty-odd years she and Daddy have been married, they have never had a serious fight. She said: "Whenever trouble started brewin' up, me and Daddy Ray would sit right down on the floor and face each other and talk it over. Sometimes we'd talk for several hours, but we'd always settle it." Gracie also explained how she had experienced leaving her body while in meditation. She says that she is now going to investigate the dharma of sleeping sitting up, and cut down on her chicken consumption. What a fine couple of people!

21 February 1974. Heng Ju writes:

Gracie insisted that we stay another night, so we left the cart and pack at their home, and she drove us out to the bowing area. Yo, although he had no kneepads, bowed along about a hundred yards behind me. We broke all records this morning, bowing along the high cliffs for two miles without stopping. We passed an old coastal Indian camp; nothing left now but thousands of logs washed in by the tide. We then started a long climb up a hill where the road clings to the rocky cliffs like a caterpillar to a tree.

We made three and a half miles before Gracie appeared in her old Plymouth to take us back for lunch. She had prepared a formal vegetarian meal offering, and Yo and I used the hand bell to say the grace before and after meals. After lunch, Gracie invited her neighbors over for tea, and we all sat in the living room, and had a little seminar on Buddhism while the wind and rain pounded down on the roof.

22 February 1974. Heng Ju writes:

The Knights, Gracie and Daddy Ray, took us to the spot, and dropped us off for the last time. Gracie pulled out five dollars and tried to give it to Yo, but Yo refused. "Take it!" Gracie said, "And don't go defying your elders!"

We bowed along the ridge of a large hill, in the midst of Jedediah Smith Redwoods State Park. Tomorrow or the next day we will begin our descent into Crescent City, the last major town in California. The weather was most strange today. We encountered snow, rain, hail, and a brilliant sun, all within the same hour.

Toward day's end, a car stopped and a long-haired man got out and came running toward me, yelling: "Tim! Tim!" It was Dane from the old commune in Mineral, Washington. He was quite surprised to see me bowing, but quickly recovered and invited us to stop at his house for pancakes when we pass by.

23 February 1974. Heng Ju writes:

There was a lot of action as we made our passage through Crescent City today. Three ladies; Mrs. Extine, Mrs. Crites, and Mrs. Ross, brought us presents. Yo and I decided to open a bank account and use the money people offer us for the construction of a new monastery.

While in Arcata, we picked up a transistor radio for twenty-five cents at a thrift store. All it needed was a new battery. Since then, every night after meditation we have been listening to the news and weather reports. As we approached Crescent City this morning, Yo tuned in and heard Bill Stamps, of Radio KPOD, giving a step by step account of our progress. Bill is a real bright personality who takes pride in keeping his audience "well-informed." He sounds something like this: "Well, the last time I saw them two monks, they were bowing along the ocean front getting ready to make the turn into town. If any of you all have seen them, call me and let me know where they are. Yes, folks, this is really something! You should see that big Heng Ju move out! He's about six and a half feet tall, and when he takes a step he covers about seven feet of ground! This is really quite the undertaking! And his friend Heng Joe, or is it Hang Hoe? Well in any case, whatever his name is, the shorter one is always right there with the cart. What a fine guy he is! I tell you folks, I've never seen anything like it. Let's all of us try to show these two boys that Crescent City really appreciates what they are doing!"

I kept fairly close to Yo as we went through the city, and we both listened to the little radio which was taped to the outside of the cart. Bill was well-informed. He talked a lot about various aspects of Buddhism, he even knew about Master Xu Yun's trip across China. In the afternoon Bill himself appeared with a portable tape recorder and taped an interview with us. Bill looked like an overgrown leprechaun, with his pointed shoes, plaid pants, red blazer, fuzzy beard and devilish eyes.

At the end of town, we met Mr. Long, the city's only blacksmith. He did a good deal of free welding on the buggy. Last of all, we met Howard Cronk, owner of the Totem Hotel, who gave us a room for the night.

29 February 1974. Heng Ju writes:

One of the things that I've always wanted to do is make a pilgrimage to a holy mountain. And up in this neck of the woods, Mt. Shasta is the holiest one around. It is due east of Crescent City, and so on the 24th, Yo and I decided to take a couple of days off to climb Shasta. We left our buggy at the Cronks' motel. Taking just our sleeping bags and some food, we hitchhiked through the drizzling rain over the pass to Shasta.

It was a mistake from the very beginning. As T.S. Eliot said, "Distracted from distraction by distraction." Because of severe weather, the mountain was socked in with clouds and invisible, and the temperature just halfway up the mountain was a bone-chilling 18 below zero. I felt very disappointed with myself for leaving the highway. I knew that because of all the news coverage, there would probably be a lot of people out there looking for us. It was a wrong decision, but it was something that I had wanted to do for a long time. Perhaps in the future when conditions are right, there will be an opportunity to climb Shasta.

But right now, it feels great to be back on Highway 101.

1 March 1974. Heng Yo writes:

We finally got back to Crescent City by late afternoon today, and when we went to pick up our gear, Howard Cronk insisted that we stay the night at his place. There weren't many votes for bowing through the rain for the remaining hour of daylight, so we accepted. We'll be off to a good start tomorrow.

We are all travelers along a path—some are slow and inattentive; others reckless and fast. Some move backward, and some make steady progress every day; others are stuck in the mud. Some know they are stagnating or going in the wrong direction, but lack the concentration to change. Some take the time and trouble to lead others. It is a grand feeling to be back on the right road once again.

2 March 1974. Heng Ju writes:

Howard Cronk took us out to the bowing area. We certainly haven't made much mileage these last few days, but at least we haven't retreated.

There is a stage of spiritual development along the Bodhisattva path which is called *avaivartika*, Sanskrit for irreversible. At this stage, one's thoughts, position, and practice do not turn back toward confusion. A few years ago when I was a cook at the monastery, I had just taken up the practice of eating only one meal a day. It's really a difficult practice when working with all that food as the cook. I was doing really well for several days, but one morning I couldn't stand it any longer, and decided to have some breakfast. I remember it clearly: I was heading for the icebox, in fact I had my hand on the icebox door, when I looked out in the hallway to see the Master walking by. He was smiling as he walked down the hall. Then suddenly he stopped, and began walking backward, retracing his steps back down the hall, around the corner and out of sight. Not a word was spoken, but I got the message.

Today, Gene Hicks, an architect from Seattle, and Joe Collins, who lives in Crescent City, both came by to talk with us about Eastern religions.

3 March 1974. Heng Ju writes:

Frost on the ground this morning. Ruth Brewer, a reporter from the *Portland Oregonian*, did an article on us. She was seriously concerned about the poison oak incident, and consequently brought us a whole bag of toilet paper. Dale Parson, a Del Norte County deputy sheriff, stopped his patrol car next to me. I thought it was going to be another identification hassle, but he turned out to be really interested in the trip. He said that he was born and raised in

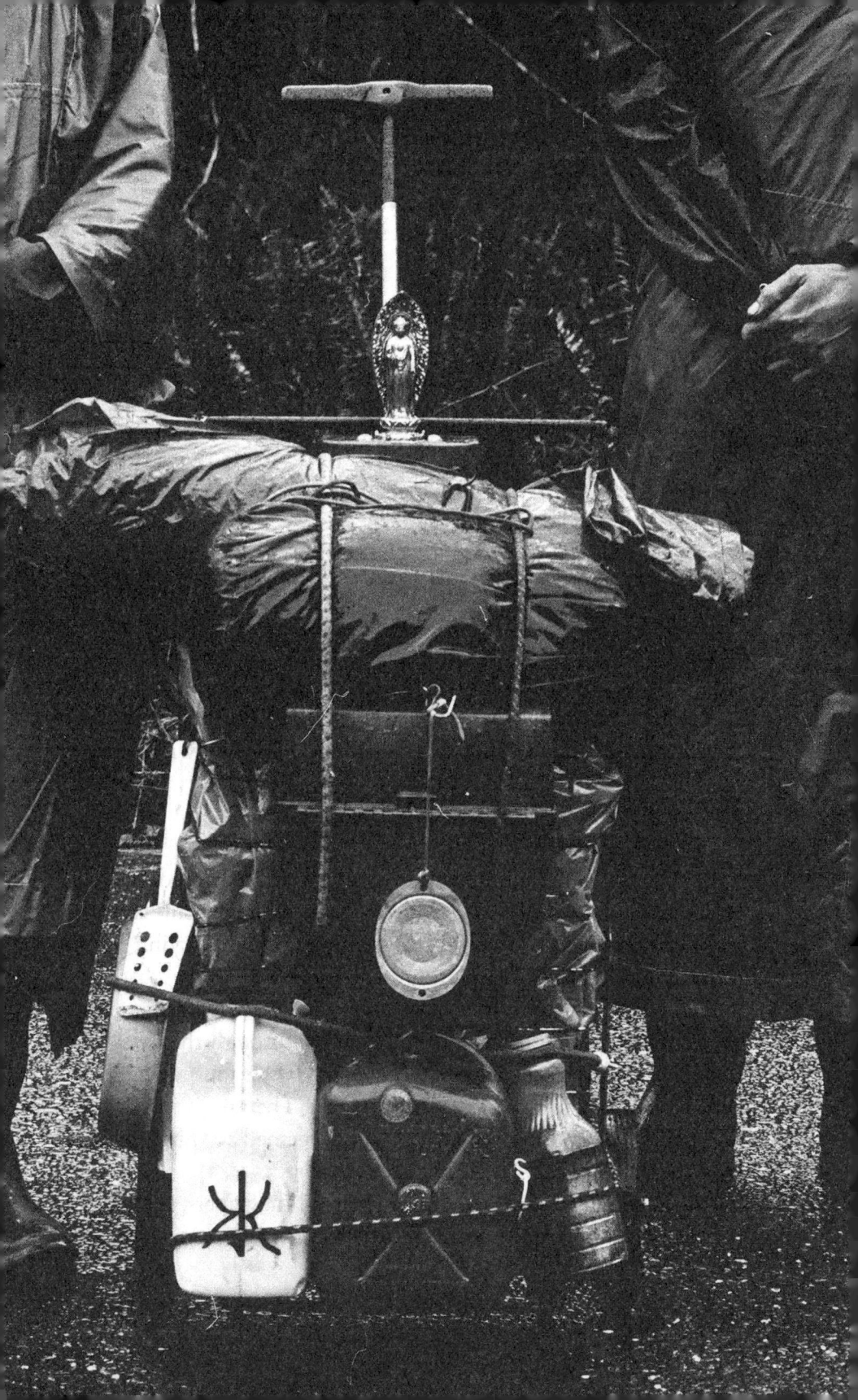

Marblemount, Washington, the site of the future monastery, and that he was "tempted to lay down his gun and follow along!

After a seven-mile bow, Howard Cronk appeared and drove us all the way back to the Totem Motel for the night.

4 March 1974. Heng Ju writes:

Mr. and Mrs. LaRue, eighty-year-old reporters for the local Brookings paper interviewed Yo this afternoon. Harold Howard, an old friend of Marge Rauum's, picked us up and brought us back to his home in Crescent City. He and his wife are the Del Norte County representatives for Eckankar, an organization of people who are into soul travel. Their "Living Master" resides in Las Vegas, and teaches that the best way to go is to liberate the soul from the body, and follow the living master back to God. The Howards both went out of their way to be hospitable to us. Yo and I were amazed to see that they had dug up their front and back lawns, and had the whole place turned into a vegetable garden.

In the morning, when the Howards had finished their soul traveling exercises, we were given a ride out to the bowing area.

5 March 1974. Heng Yo writes:

Today the rain continued to fall, but toward the end of the day, Nugget Marcus, a very kind and charming woman who is in the real estate business, took us in for the night. We are drying out in front of the fireplace after putting in about five miles.

As we approached the state line today, there was a large "Welcome to Oregon" sign grinning at us through the rain. The Cronks drove by to say farewell. A chapter in this journey has been ended, even as a new one begins: Oregon! The rain is just as wet, the road is just as long: what was it that seemed so different after crossing that arbitrary point of distinction?

With so many stories about our trip in the papers, a lot more people stop to question us or offer their best wishes. An incredible number of people have been taking pictures of us. At times like these, Ju does most of the bowing, while I do most of the talking.

An older woman gave us some pumpkin pie wrapped in tinfoil and said, "I commended you to the Blessed Mother this morning."

6 March 1974. Heng Yo writes:

Passing through Brookings, Oregon, was quite an experience. We bowed as far as possible into town without stopping, but finally a crowd of people in the middle of town stopped us, and we answered their questions for about twenty minutes.

Later on, we were invited to stay at the home of the town elder, Leo Lucas. He lives in the very building in which he attended grade school some sixty years ago. "Never got out of grade school," he says. He invited some of his friends over to meet us among whom were a local priest and Gerry Ross, an insurance man, and his family. Leo was very respectful to us and explained some of our practices to his friends. He was especially interested in the fact that we sleep sitting up. His age doesn't stop him from being very vigorous and open-minded.

7 March 1974. Heng Ju writes:

Today as we bowed along the cliffs, a big school bus came grinding to a halt. Mrs. Worlton and Mrs. Patterson had brought out the entire Brookings third grade, forty kids in all. We talked outside the bus for a while, but then it got a little too chilly, so we all went inside the bus. The teachers asked Yo and me to give a little talk, so Yo told them how it was to study hard, and I told them to take care of their parents. Then we opened it up for questions. They asked such things as "Why do you carry all of that stuff?", "What do you eat?", "Were you scared the first night out?"

In the afternoon Leo Lucas drove out and said that his friends whom we had talked to the night before had thought at first that we were kind of nuts, but after talking with us for a while, they had really become interested in Buddhism. Leo left, but not more than an hour passed when a big black Cadillac stopped beside us. "Uh-oh! The FBI!" said Yo. But nope, it was Gerry Ross and three of his business associates. Gerry said, "Please tell my friends what you were saying last night about meditation and liberation, as the Buddhists see it." We talked for a while atop a windy cliff, and then we left.

In the evening, we stayed with the Jim Stalcup family in Brookings. Jim is a Rosicrucian, and lives in a home that he built himself at the cliff edge. We spent part of the night in his shop installing full size bicycle-balloon tires on the buggy. Just before we turned in, some friendly raccoons wandered up to the living room and ate some dog food right out of our hands.

8 March 1974. Heng Yo writes:

After bowing all day, we are staying with Daryll and Jan Whirry, a young couple from Brookings. They invited several of their friends over, and once again we talked about the Dharma. They told us about some rumors currently going around. One story has it that we are the vanguard of some four hundred monks who are all bowing up the coast. Another is that people are dumping garbage cans over us. We have been called everything from saints to brothers of the Devil, and from Martians to Tibetan lamas. One completely cynical fellow named Norman said that his boss had designed a counter-weight for Ju so that when he bows down, he won't have to work so hard to get up. One woman said that it was "a real experience for Brookings to have us pass through."

It works both ways.

9 March 1976. Heng Ju writes:

Mrs. Witherspoon, a retired East Coast newspaper owner and widow, shared her home with us for the night. She plied us with hot milk and we spent the evening talking about Buddhism. But just before we turned in 11:00 p.m., she said that she was planning to take us to church in the morning. Yo and I slept for five hours, and then long before the sun came up, slipped out of the house and hit the road. In Buddhism, the whole world is our church, and every thought a prayer.

10 March 1974. Heng Yo writes:

Today a car went by and lobbed a rolled-up newspaper to us. It was the *Coos Bay World*. Marge Barret had written an article about us which appeared on the first page. There was only one mistake in it. Heng Ju had told her about the flying beer can incident in California, and said that when it happened, it was the final bow of the day. The newspaper read: "Someone threw a full can of beer at them—it was the final blow of the day." Close enough.

We pitched the tent in a small grove. Lots of rain is coming down. Some young boys came by and watched us do *taiji chuan*. That evening, one of them returned. His name was Chip, and he wanted to become a monk. Ju asked if he wanted to be a chipmonk. It was raining again. Chip was crouched outside the tent asking some very sincere questions about cultivation of the Way and about Buddhism. Finally, we invited him in and he related an experience he'd had while alone in the woods deer hunting: "I stopped for a while to rest, and ... and ...well, I might as well not lie, I had a cigarette. Then I looked up and there was a giant buck about twenty feet away staring at me. I grabbed my rifle, and aimed right at him, but I just couldn't shoot him." Later, Chip repeated that he wanted to become a monk. I told him that this is a decision which each person makes for himself and that we would not say what he should do. He acted much more mature than his fourteen years.

11 March 1974. Heng Ju writes:

Mr. and Mrs. Simon, a retired couple from Wisconsin, have stopped to give us water and food every day now for the last week. They are living on the coast in a trailer for a couple of months. They spend part of their days traveling around looking at things.

We see them every day around 10:00 a.m. Mr. Simon reports that we are just about 40 miles short of the halfway mark between San Francisco and Seattle.

Yo reports that the new bicycle tires on the buggy are infinitely better than the little eight-inchers we had on before. We have a little tool that I use to tune the spokes with. I tighten the spokes until they all emit the same tone. That way, I know they are all doing their proper share of the work.

12 March 1974. Heng Yo writes:

As we approached Pistol River, a man got out of his car and got down on his knees and held my hand, offering a prayer. He was on his way to his father's funeral, and he prayed that his father might go to heaven instead of hell. I told him that it all depended on what kind of life his father had lived. The man seemed relieved, got into his van, and drove off.

Nina Stansell and Trudy Reid stopped. Nina is the radio dispatcher for the Curry County Sheriff Department. They got our mail for us and brought us hot tea. Nina said that she's been hearing talk about us crackling over the radio and telephone for weeks. She said our trip makes people stop and think and reflect on their own lives and religious pursuits. Nina gave us her house for the night, and she stayed at her friend Trudy's.

13 March 1974. Heng Ju writes:

Nina and Trudy picked us up again and brought us back to Pistol River. They had gathered a group of ten friends at their house and we spent a couple of hours discussing the philosophy of Buddhism with them. One of the ladies there was named Mercedes. She said that when she first drove past us on the highway she thought it was Superman.

14 March 1974. Heng Ju writes:

It takes a lot of concentration to keep the mind from wandering. It is very easy to let the body fall into a routine, while the mind drifts away to other places. Right now, we have pretty much mastered the physical aspects of bowing. Our bodies are really in good shape, and we have learned how to deal with the various types of people. But now, the real work lies in truly hanging on to our chants and mantras.

Heng Yo is working with the Shurangama Mantra. The word "mantra" comes from the Sanskrit word *manas* which means mind. Mantras are also referred to as *dharanis*, which comes from the Sanskrit word *dhri*, which means "to hold." We can say that a mantra or *dharani* "holds" the mind. The Shurangama Mantra is the longest and most powerful of all mantras. It takes about twenty minutes to recite. Its functions are to divert calamities, to chase away ghosts and spirits, and to quiet the mind. Most importantly, it has the potential of opening the mind of the sincere aspirant to the wisdom of all Buddhas.

I have been chanting the name of Avolokiteshvara Bodhisattva. I do it in Chinese: "Na Mo Da Bei Guan Shi Yin Pu Sa." The meaning is "Homage to the Greatly Compassionate Bodhisattva Who Observes the World's Sounds." This chant works well for me. Whether holding a mantra or reciting the name of a Buddha or Bodhisattva, the idea is to get rid of extraneous thoughts, and become single-mindedly concentrated.

15 March 1974. Heng Yo writes:

We've been making very steady progress every day, and the miles are adding up. Today coming into Gold Beach, Oregon, groups of high school students came out to greet us. Cars were lined up like in a drive-in movie to watch the slow, ridiculous spectacle. In town we met Nina Stansell again who gave us a guided tour of the county jail. Charles Wykoff, a seventeen-year-old high school senior, gave us a place to stay for the night. We made it halfway through town before quitting for the day.

16 March 1974. Heng Ju writes:

The president of the Gold Beach Ladies Auxiliary and her retinue stopped for a group picture with us. We gave them ten dollars for their cause. Passing through the town itself we saw a big electric sign on a sporting goods store which read: "WELCOME HENG JU AND HENG YO! HAVE A NICE TRIP!" Gwo Fa and Gwo Hwei appeared from San Francisco and prepared lunch for us. In the evening, we accepted the invitation of Mr. and Mrs. Starr of Gold Beach to spend the night at their home.

According to the latest calculations, we have gone 475 miles so far.

17 March 1974. Heng Ju writes:

Father Welch of the Episcopal Church came by and wished us a peaceful journey. A lot of people have been coming out to talk with us these days. We can't remember all their names. Several times now, I have been having the sensation of standing in one place while the whole world goes marching by me.

John Andall, a Gold Beach resident, offered us lodging for the night. He related how in the past he used to do a lot of hunting and fishing; but after he witnessed his first wife suffer an unexpected death on the surgery table, he decided that he was never again going to have anything to do with taking life. We told him that this was in accordance with the very first Buddhist precept, to not kill.

In the evening, we unloaded the cart, sanded it down to remove all the heavily rusted spots, and gave it a fresh coat of paint.

18 March 1974. Heng Yo writes:

With all of our various stops, we are averaging four miles a day. We now project that we may reach Marblemount by September. Today a Pentacostal Christian tried to convert us to her faith. She talked to us nonstop for half an hour, while we were trying to eat lunch. She was intent on converting us on the spot. When she told us that she wanted to give us a Bible, I told her that we already had three, but her mind was made up, so we accepted it and then she left.

Dale Erickson, a local television repairman, and the only known

Buddhist in the area, stopped to chat. He studies the Theravada teachings, but does not accept the theory of reincarnation. In the evening, Dick Turnow and his family put us up for the night. Dick lost an arm in a logging accident, but that hardly stops him from working, driving, and being a good father. He showed us home movies of the local logging industry. The Turnows are Christians who study the principles of the faith and put them into practice.

19 March 1974. Heng Yo writes:

As we bowed along the beautiful Oregon coast, Nina and Trudy from Pistol River came by with a donation of new socks. Nina told us she is keeping a pair of our old worn-out boots as a souvenir. Ju told her they would make good flower pots.

Toward the end of the day, Mr. and Mrs. Braun, a retired couple from back east now living in Port Orford, stopped to talk. Mr. Braun's hobby is communicating with people all over the world by means of cassette tapes. He asked us to explain some Buddhist principles on tape so he could send it to his blind friend in Great Britain. It was a pleasant encounter.

We are camped on the beach in front of a blazing fire and have just finished a good hour of meditation. All of the logs on this beach are spotted with raw petroleum. The Master has often said that because people's minds are polluted, the world becomes polluted.

20 March 1974. Heng Yo writes:

Bowed past Humbug Mountain, and then up a long hill beside the ocean cliffs. We were buffeted by high winds off the ocean, but it is not raining. We've been in Oregon a couple of weeks now, and the giant redwoods have been replaced by myrtlewood as the area's most important tree. In the afternoon it became very hot, and the sun began to roast our skin. Ju's neck was as red as a cooked lobster, but some kind folks who had stopped to talk left us with a bottle of sunburn lotion. We are camped off the road in a small clearing.

21 March 1974. Heng Ju writes:

It was late in the evening and we had already bowed over five miles when we entered Port Orford today, but the energy was flowing strong and so we kept going. At the city limits, a crowd of about thirty people stopped us for a twenty-minute interview.

Halfway through town, there is a tavern on the coastal side of the highway. As I drew closer to it, I could see that there were a few people hanging around outside, and I could even hear some of their conversation. One guy was saying, "Quick, come here! Here they come!" It was too late to change to the other side of the street, so I decided to bow right past the front of the tavern. As I got closer, I could see people running around like crazy in front of the tavern door. I could feel all systems inside of me tensing up and preparing for action. Voices from the past raced through my mind: "Man battle station torpedo! Man battle station torpedo!"

I started concentrating hard on the Bodhisattva's name and headed directly toward the men in front of the tavern. About seven or eight drinkers had emerged from the tavern and from their midst, came a most foul, drunken, and enraged man. He began running at me, passing just inches away, and yelling, "Well, a bald-headed Jesus! What the hell do you think you're doing?" He threatened to kick me and continued yelling profanities which I won't repeat, while his comrades looked on.

I was most surprised at my own reaction to the whole scene. I'd spent six years of my life doing the tavern trip, and so I could understand what this guy was doing. I knew there wasn't any substance to it. My faith in the protective powers was strong, and so I didn't experience any fear during the entire encounter. I bowed right through the crowd without speeding up or slowing down, and at the very last minute they moved out of the way. It was as if they weren't there at all. The man continued to rant and rave, but there was basically nothing happening.

Mr. and Mrs. Tubb, good Christians from Port Orford, took us in at nightfall.

22 March 1974. Heng Yo writes:

Today a young boy asked us on behalf of his mother, Mrs. Kilpatrick, to bless their home. We stopped bowing and went there to see what was happening. The mother was at work, so we offered incense and recited the Great Compassion Mantra several times. Explaining to the people there that a pure house is just a pure mind, we said that if they could keep their minds free from desire and anger and if they didn't smoke or drink, then gradually everywhere they went would become pure.

As we bowed along later, a lady came out to talk to us. She started crying because it turned out she was extremely worried about our health and safety.

A lot of big logging rigs are beginning to stop and their drivers are quite friendly. One man has been stopping with his big rig for the last three days to give us sandwiches his wife has prepared.

The Brauns, whom we met a couple of days ago, picked us up at the end of the day and took us to their house in Port Orford. Unable to resist the call of the kitchen, we made a batch of bagels which we split with them. In the evening, Mr. Braun asked us to give a talk on the practice of Chan meditation, and he taped it. It has been quite an experience for us to talk to so many thousands of people along our way. We are able to explain some of the principles of meditation a little better than when we began bowing a few months ago.

23 March 1974. Heng Ju writes:

A large mobile home passed us today at about sixty miles per hour, and a loud voice filled the area, saying, "Have a nice day!" He must have had a public address system on board.

We passed an Indian museum, and the proprietors invited us in to take a look around. One of the exhibits was an Indian ceremonial club that was used to beat people who sang out of tune. According to legend, they even beat them to death.

Beating someone to death is taking it too far. But Buddhism is not averse to using a heavy hand now and then—psychologically speaking—if it will help someone along the path. I remember an incident that really shook up the old Buddhist Lecture Hall in Chinatown. This was in 1970, before I became a monk. Most of us had found living in a temple conducive to keeping precepts, but it was more difficult to keep the precepts on the outside, especially for those of us with heavy habit-energy. People would come to the temple, cultivate for a little while, and build up their energy, but when they went back out into the world, they would usually blow it. Well, there was a young fellow who had been living at the Buddhist Lecture Hall for several months. He had taken the five precepts, the fifth of which prohibits intoxicants, including tobacco. But one night he couldn't stand it any longer, and he snuck out on the town. He climbed down the fire escape and was gone for about three or four hours. He returned while everyone was still asleep, and was absolutely sure that no one had seen him. But later that morning, while we were all up meditating, the Master approached him, and the following exchange took place.

The Master: "Where did you go last night?"

Disciple: "Wh, Wh, What?"

The Master: "Where did you go last night?"

Disciple: "Ahh, Ahh, I, I, I, I just went for a little walk."

The Master: "Oh? Well then who gave you the cigarettes?"

Disciple: "Ahh, Ahh, I got them at a gas station. I just wanted to walk around and have a smoke."

The Master: "Just walking and smoking, eh? Well, then, how come you got on the bus?

Disciple (trembling with fear): "I, I, I wanted to go to Golden Gate Park, and it was too far to walk."

The Master (with ear piercing volume): "What about that woman on the bus? Why did you offer her a cigarette?"

Disciple (by this time blubbering and whimpering like a dog): "I didn't do nothing, I got off the bus after that. Who told you, anyway?"

The Master: "Nobody."

Disciple: "Well, then, how did you know?"

The Master: "Did you know?"

Disciple: "Yes."

The Master: "Then you told me!"

At this point, the Master smiled, playfully honked the kid over the head three times, and returned to his room. Everyone who witnessed this was sweating profusely.

24 March 1974. Heng Yo writes:

We were bowing along the narrow road when a driver's attention wandered off the road, and his fast-moving car almost followed along. This has happened several times when drivers see us slowly moving along, but there have been no accidents yet. I certainly hope we can make it all the way with a clean slate.

Late in the afternoon, Mr. and Mrs. Dahl and their son Tom picked us up, and took us to their place for the night. Mr. Dahl is now retired, and their house is in the middle of several large cranberry bogs. I always thought Cape Cod in Massachusetts, where I spent many summers, was the only place where cranberries were produced in great quantity, so I was surprised to learn that we have just entered the largest cranberry producing area in the world. The Dahls gave us food and supplies, and Ju remarked that this was the first time he'd ever slept in a Dahl house.

25 March 1974. Heng Yo writes:

The Reverend and Mrs. Augsburger invited us to have lunch at their old folks' home near Bandon. Reverend Augsburger was out making calls on his BMW motorcycle, and his wife gave us a tour of the old folks' home. She admitted that there is a "conspiracy" among the Pentecostals in the area to convert us: a representative from every town in the area has been telephoned to come out and pressure us. We've lost count of how many Bibles have been given us; we've been donating them to the libraries along the way. Mrs. Augsburger, although a strong Episcopalian herself, said she feels that what we are doing has value, and doesn't think we need to be converted.

26 March 1974. Heng Ju writes:

Students, housewives, loggers, cranberry growers, all kinds of people talked with us today as we passed through the town of Bandon, one of the cranberry growing centers. In the evening we accepted the invitation of the Erdman family to spend the night at their home. Mike and Marylyn Erdman are Christians but they happened to have a statue of Maitreya Bodhisattva in their living room. Marylyn asked me if we knew anything about the statue, and so I told her the story of Maitreya, the cloth-sack monk.

Once upon a time, a fat old monk roamed around China. He always carried with him a big cloth sack in which he kept all his belongings. He was always gleeful and happy, and whenever he met up with people, he would either ask them for something or give them something. In Buddhism this is a way of creating affinities (the Chinese phrase for it literally means "to tie up conditions"). It was believed that this fat monk was an incarnation of Maitreya Bodhisattva.

One day an official who had heard much about the old monk met him on a country road. The official was delighted and he wasted no time in asking the monk some questions about Buddhism. The official said, "Could you explain to me the essence of the Buddha's teachings?"

The fat old monk said not a word, but smiling, happily dropped his sack on the ground. The official stood there for a while and then said. "Oh, come on now, there must be more to it than that! I want to know the ultimate teaching!"

At that point, the monk slowly bent over and picked up the bag and, without uttering a word, went walking down the road. This then was the ultimate teaching of Buddhism.

27 March 1974. Heng Yo writes:

North of Bandon, Mr. and Mrs. Bates, retired cranberry growers, took us to a store for footgear which was paid for by Dr. Soper, the town dentist. We crossed the Coquille River in a heavy rainstorm.

The road now takes an inland course to the port city of Coos Bay, which can't be more than twenty miles away.

Don Hultin, another cranberry grower, came out in his pickup truck and hauled us two wet bhikshus back to his home. After we dried off and sat in meditation, some of Don's neighbors came over and we talked about the journey. For some reason or other, Ju sang them the song about Ullambana, in Chinese no less. They didn't know quite what to make of it, but really listened to what Ju was saying after the song, for he had captured their attention.

I showed them some of the books that Gold Mountain has published. One of the ladies was gazing at a picture of the Buddha seated serenely in full lotus. At the moment I saw her looking at the picture, I was overcome by a wonderful feeling. I could almost see seeds being planted in her mind for her future enlightenment. I wondered how many eons a person passes through before these seeds begin to flourish. Just for an instant, it seemed to me that past, present, and future became fused, and the karmic condition of this lady became clear to me. Someday, she will become a Buddha.

28 March 1974. Heng Yo writes:

The days seem to pass rapidly as we are making steady progress. We have developed a successful routine.

In the evening, a friend of Don Hultin's named Jimmy Olson picked us up after the day's bowing. He farms an almost unbelievable fifty acres of cranberries. After meditating for an hour or so, we had a lively Dharma discussion. It became clear that Jimmy was well-read in Western philosophy, and it was said that he enjoys getting into debates with local clergymen.

29 March 1974. Heng Ju writes:

This morning was one of those times when affliction and bitterness was in the air and it seemed as if nothing could make them go away. I was mad at Yo for some silly reason or another, and I knew that I shouldn't be, but I couldn't seem to get rid of it. I began really reciting Gwan Yin Bodhisattva's name with vigor, hoping that somehow this compassionate being who is capable of doing miraculous things would help me out. Having made this thought, I looked up ahead to see an old Chevy panel truck stopping on the side of the road. Two men got out and helped a woman out of the truck. She was blind.

The three of them approached me, and Yo came over too. The woman, who looked like she was in her early thirties, asked if I was the bowing monk that she had heard so much about. "Yes," I said. She held my hand for several minutes, and we all stood there in silence. I could feel my afflictions rapidly dissolving. The sun felt warm and good. After a while she said, "You are a really peaceful person, I can feel it." Then she told us how happy she was that we were doing this thing, and that there were a lot of people with us and thinking about us every step of the way. By the time they left, my afflictions were totally gone.

At nightfall, Jimmy Olson picked us up and took us back to his farm.

30 March 1974. Heng Yo writes:

We bowed in the rain all morning, and Mrs. Dahl brought us a freshly baked lemon pie for lunch. This is one of the friendliest areas we've passed through. I remember a television news team from San Francisco interviewing me when we had been on the road only two weeks. I was uncomfortably vague in my answers to such questions as "What are you doing?" and "Why?" But now, after talking to so many people every day, it is easier to explain what we are doing and why. This certainly makes a difference in the way people react to us. If they can't "get a handle on" what we are about, we remain a couple of crazies among many. However, if we succeed in communicating our motivation for this trip even to a small degree, the welcome is warm and meaningful.

Don Hultin came out in his truck and took us in again. He's been reading up on Buddhism, and we answered his many questions as best we could. In turn, Don told us about the fine art of growing cranberries.

31 March 1974. Heng Yo writes:

We bowed into the port city of Coos Bay on this wet day, past miles of the Weyerhauser logging complex along the bay. This is said to be the largest lumber port in the world, and ships from all over load and unload here; but today is Sunday, and it is relatively quiet. A few people stopped to talk while many others just watched. As Ju bowed by a restaurant, 100 wide eyes followed his movements. We totaled seven miles today, passing through Coos Bay and North Bend both.

The man who had stopped to offer a prayer for his father a couple of weeks ago had given us his phone number, and said to call him when we got to Coos Bay. When I called him on the phone, the man said, "Who is this?"

I replied, "This is Heng Yo."

The man was a little drunk and had apparently forgotten who I was. "Yeah, right," he said, "and thish ish Fooey Louis."

We have reached the halfway point of the trip, and on this occasion are going to take the Greyhound back to Gold Mountain to attend the spring meditation sessions. We will be off the road for an entire month.

III. Coos Bay to Marblemount

1 May 1974. Heng Ju writes:

We are back in Coos Bay today after a month at Gold Mountain. During this time, we attended the meditation weeks, gave speeches on Buddha's Birthday and talks at San Francisco State University, welded up the buggy, and had plenty of time to get ourselves ready for the second half of the trip. We decided that this half we are going to stick closer to the highway and not make so many side trips. During the meditation sessions I could hardly keep my mind off of the highway. After getting rid of many fears, and being in the best physical shape I've ever been, I feel really excited about this second half.

> Chan Session Poem
>
> *Nature pure, heart free:*
> *Ten Thousand practices,*
> *Yet nothing lost or gained.*
> *Faith in the teacher, the initial cause,*

Walk it to the end.
A thousand are called.
Who won't follow his mind?
Stand straight, want nothing,
Transcend chaos, strife, and delusion.
Faces, places, thoughts, and feelings,
All the systems of salvation,
All the paths to hell
Only from the mind arise.

2 May 1974. Heng Ju writes:

Two American missionaries from China have come out to convert us within the last week. They were both surprised to discover that Yo has an impeccable command of Mandarin Chinese. One of them, an ex Marine, has invited us to stay at his home in Reedsport when we pass through. That should be interesting.

Today I bowed along the sand dunes within a half mile of the ocean shore and got in a solid seven miles. Just before quitting time, a young Jehovah's Witness about age 19 appeared and made a gallant attempt to save me. He had with him pamphlets that were to be spread all over the world, telling of the coming Judgment Day, which apparently is due to arrive any moment. He went into his wellpracticed pitch at a rate of speed that allowed no interruptions. I patiently stood there for several minutes as he rattled on, "Those who believe will be rewarded with eternity in Paradise. Those who don't will forever burn in hell." It was starting to sound like a broken record, so I picked up a twig from the roadside and began examining it very closely. He, too, began to look at it. He talked faster and faster, but his eyes were glued to the twig. Right then, I knew I had him. Finally he paused for breath, and I said, "Do you know what this is?"

"It's a stick," he replied.

"This is God," I said, and gently tossed the stick high into the air. His mouth dropped open, and his eyes followed the stick as it sailed off into the bushes. I didn't say another word, but immediately

began bowing. I went about a hundred feet and then glanced back to see him standing there like a piece of shattered glass. Finally he put himself back together, and ran up along side of me, hopping along like an overgrown rabbit. "But, but, but, God is alive. He, he, he, he, has intelligence, and you've just got to believe." I didn't pay any more attention to him, and he eventually faded away, mumbling to himself.

3 May 1974. Heng Yo writes:

We are now passing through the Oregon Dunes National Recreation Area, which extends at least forty miles up the coast. Wildlife within the area is protected, and there are paths for the very popular dune buggies. The dunes themselves are vast mounds of ever-shifting sand, set off by an occasional tidal pool, and dotted with salal, manzanita, and madrona. We are seeing the beginning of what promises to be a large army of camper-trucks filled with families on vacation.

Today we were greeted by two county deputy sheriffs, who said they'd been watching out for us. This is quite a contrast to other occasions, on which we sat in police cars while the officer checked to see if we were wanted for any crimes. It seems like the farther we go, the more legitimate our trip becomes in the eyes of others.

After seven miles of bowing, we are camped in one of the numerous state parks along the Oregon coast. Usually, when we quit bowing, it is also the end of our public availability for the day, because no one really knows where we are after we leave the road to camp for the night. But tonight the word is out, and several groups of people have stopped by to chat: offerings, kids, pictures, lemonade, endless questions; divine chaos.

Now it is late, and the day's events echo in my head, arising and disappearing like bubbles on the ocean. But who is observing this cosmic sea? Isn't the viewer part of the whole thing? Is there really any difference between what happens and what I think has happened?

4 May 1974. Heng Yo writes:

We stopped by the side of the road today, and quite a few people came by to talk with us. Most of them would not get out of their cars, however, so they formed a line, as if they were at a drive-up window; they'd wait their turn, then drive up, roll down the window, and talk. Really strange.

After lunch, we bowed through the town of Reedsport, where both of us talked to many people. A platoon of kids on bikes collected around Heng Ju and followed him all the way down Main Street, circling and making noise. I found myself answering questions from groups of people every time I stopped.

At the end of the day, when I sat down to rest, the images of what has happened seem to float by. They are more than memories, but less than reality: more than memories because they shape what happens in the future in the same way that melon seeds will bear melons and not beans; but less than reality because the total does not equal the sum of its parts. Even when all the parts are reconstructed, there is something mysteriously missing, which had lent legitimacy to an instance, event, or thought. Call it the spark of life; call it Buddha, reality or divinity: it has as many names as there are attempts to define it. As an old Chan master once remarked: "You can't stand in the same stream twice." Come to think of it, you can't stand in the same stream once!

5 May 1974. Heng Ju writes:

Last night we took up the invitation of the ex-Marine, the former missionary to China, and stayed in his home. It was a mistake. Although he and his family were extremely hospitable to us, beneath it all was an intense desire to convert and save us. All night long, first in English, then in Chinese, he never let up. He had found everlasting life, and wasn't going to be happy until we too had found it. There wasn't any real problem during the evening, but in the morning, when he took us out to the bowing area, a little friction arose. By this time he was concentrating his efforts mostly on Heng Yo; I think he'd pretty much written me off as a lost cause. We had just gotten out of the car on the north end of Reedsport at the Smith River bridge when he said to Yo, "I hope you boys will give up your paganistic idol worshipping and accept the Lord. Especially you, Heng Yo, being a chosen one." Yo quickly replied, "We're all chosen ones." The scene ended with all of us getting upset and yelling at each other, until finally he jumped in his car and roared off. It was too bad, because, I know he really meant well.

This morning we found a bag of fresh fruit in our path. On it a note reads, "May the long-time sun shine upon you, and all love surround you, and the pure light within you guide your way on." (A quote from a song by the Incredible String Band). In the evening, Deputy Sheriff Richard Knack brought us a gallon of pure water and showed us a good place to set up camp. Now we are sitting beside the tent, simmering beans over a fire for tomorrow's lunch. A warm breeze is coming off the ocean, and a small brook is gurgling away. The moon is full and thousands of stars are out.

6 May 1974. Heng Yo writes:

The Venerable Master Xu Yun once came upon a giant fish which had washed up out of the sea. The local people cut it open and found inside a small boat and some personal belongings. I mention this because tonight as I sat in meditation I could hear the sounds of drunken fishermen echoing off the foggy mists of Carter Lake near where we are camped. The dipping of the oars, the spinning of their reels, and the booming of their voices filled my mind with imagery. Who knows? Maybe this life a fisherman, next life a fish.

7 May 1974. Heng Ju writes:

The Coast Highway
(A Close-Up View)

Highway surrounded by tall green pines,
Douglas firs and rhododendrons fine,

Flowers, bushes, stickers, and berries,
Scotch broom, salal, and good eatin' cherries.
The heavens adorned with myriad clouds,
Fleecy cirrus and nimbuses proud.
The air with whistling birds is alive,
Honey bees buzz back and forth from their hives.
The roadside is littered with dented cans,
Broken glass and busted fans.
Hunks of retreads and bustling ants,
Animal bones and worn out pants.
For countless miles it rolls along,
Like an endless dream, an endless song.
And the human traffic shuttles all day,
In their Pontiacs, Lincolns, and Chevrolets.
A slick young surfer in his Baja Volks,
Somber faces of older folks,
Crying babies in rusted vans,
Truckloads of empty soda cans.
There's a lone angel on his horse of chrome
Riding low on the beach near the ocean foam.
It's a world of life and death and dung,
Bowing the coast Highway 101.

8 May 1974. Heng Yo writes:

Activity is picking up as we enter the town of Florence. Father Maxwell of St. Mary of the Dunes stopped for a short visit; at first he thought we were Trappist monks. A Mr. Harris helped us weld up our ever-ailing supply cart. With each repair, it becomes a little heavier. In the midst of town, a group of local businessmen welcomed us. They took pictures and asked us many questions. On the way out of town, a motorcycle cop pulled up and asked scornfully, "What's with you guys, anyway?" I explained to him where we had come from and why we were doing what we were doing, and he had a visible change of heart. "Well, for Chris sake, be careful!" he said. Just after that, a man in a pickup motioned Ju to come over to him. Ju didn't go, so the man angrily squealed his tires, and drove over to where Ju was bowing, and yelled that he wished Ju would do his praying somewhere else.

We are camped on a sand dune near Heceta Beach with a comfortable campfire burning. Two little kids appeared with some food for us and asked about meditation. One of them, Gary Jenkins, asked Ju what our plans were after the trip. Ju said, "We may go to the Far East." "Oh!" he replied, perking up. "Minnesota?"

9 May 1974. Heng Ju writes:

Bowed six miles in the scorching sun. Yo figures that we're about halfway through Oregon. Today we had lunch near a botanical garden, which is the home of Darlingtonia Californica, a tall plant that eats bugs. Bugs fly into its cobra-shaped flower petal, then it closes up and digests them. I've heard of people who eat vegetables, but I've never heard of vegetables that eat meat!

Gary Jenkins brought us apples,
Nellie gave a buck;
Mr. Ball found us a place to camp,
and everyone wished us luck.

Later in the evening, however, an irate property owner asked us to move off his property. This is only the second time in the whole trip that we have had to move camp on account of trespassing. It's not that we like to trespass; it's just that sometimes it's impossible to find a place that isn't owned by somebody.

10 May 1974. Heng Yo writes:

As we passed the old Coast Guard station at Heceta Head, Harry Tammen invited us in to spend the night. He and his wife are the sole caretakers of this lighthouse and ancient home. The large house was built in sections, which were floated up here from San Francisco one hundred years ago. It's an ornate and amazing place.

After we talked about Buddhism with the Tammens over several pots of tea, I took my pad and walked alone out the half mile or so to the big lighthouse. I climbed up the cliff and found a spot to sit at the very same level as the light. I put the pad down, and pulled my legs up into the full lotus posture. A stiff breeze blew in from the sea, and soon after the sun set it was very dark. After about half an hour, I could feel a lot of pain in my legs because of the position that I was in, but I was determined not to move them until at least a full hour had lapsed, as is my usual custom. Somehow I felt that the beam from the lighthouse was giving me a boost of energy, and before long I had transcended the pain. In fact, I forgot about my body. After the hour had passed, I slowly put out my legs, and suddenly realized that it was terribly windy and cold. I hustled back to the shelter of the big house, where Ju was reading.

One of the sciences of ancient China which is still practiced today is geomancy. It has to do with determining the forces of the earth relative to the "lay of the land." Any construction project or land use should be made in harmony with these earth-forces. Some people dismiss this as speculation and nonsense, but there is a definite presence at the location of this lighthouse which is very strong. It seems to extend beyond the six senses.

I looked out the window at the lighthouse. What a strange feeling I had had up there.

11 May 1974. Heng Ju writes:

Heceta Head lighthouse has a single 1,000-watt bulb which reflects in 700 prisms. It can be seen all the way out to the horizon, some twenty-one miles. Behind the lighthouse is a very heavy asbestos curtain which is draped across the cliff. In case the light should ever stop revolving, its intense focus and power, much like a magnifying glass, could easily start a fire.

We bowed five miles, and then pitched the tent on a rocky cliff. Another storm coming in!

12 May 1974. Heng Ju writes:

The storm last night was terrible. The wind was blowing like a hurricane, and the walls of the tent were whipping around like sails. Below on the beach the waves were crashing against the rocks like thunder. It's a good thing that the tent is well sewn, or it would have come apart. In a sometimes very cold and merciless world, the tent is a five-pound bundle of warmth and security.

Today we stopped at the Cape Perpetua Visitor Center and looked at the displays which explain some of the myriad phenomena we have encountered here in Siuslaw National Forest.

The Evans family from Eugene gave us a bag of fruit and a note which reads: "You both deserve attention. We are sure, to the eyes and ears of Oregonians, the press, and God, that you will make it."

What I'm really concerned about, though, is mindfulness. This, besides personal conduct, is the crux of cultivation. It is a real challenge to be without selfish views, to not be rushed, to not worry about the future, to not reminisce about the past. Mindfulness is an attempt to perceive the world in its pure state without putting labels on everything or dividing experiences into good, bad, big and little, and various other opposites.

It's not easy to be mindful, because we have been conditioned to have points of view, and to perceive the world in a self-oriented way. Our minds are full of other people's ideas and other people's values. Our happiness is based on externals, and thus we constantly seek the "good" and shun the "bad." Our minds run out the doors of the five senses—the eyes, ears, nose, tongue, and body, seeking gratification in a world of phenomena which are impermanent; therefore no true happiness is found.

For tens of thousands of years, sages have taught that the most direct way to end suffering is to break attachments by getting rid of desire. The goal is to be mindful of what is and to want nothing. But desire is an extremely powerful force; it manifests in a million different forms, sometimes directly, sometimes very subtly. There is desire for food, fame, wealth, sex, and sleep. Desire is particularly sickening when it manifests in the world of religion. There we have desire for fame and power. People desire to be respected and to have great virtue, and they want to be patriarchs and matriarchs so badly that they can't see straight. Desire causes us people to grasp at everything that comes along, and our minds constantly whirl and scheme, creating new karma and strengthening the dark energies of old habits. The first step in mindfulness, then, is to be without desire.

We passed through Yachats today and made six and a half miles.

13 May 1974. Heng Yo writes:

Off to the left is our constant companion, the vast and beautiful Pacific Ocean. But beneath its awesome surface is a world of turmoil and suffering. Yesterday at Cape Perpetua, we discovered that all of the living beings in the ocean, except perhaps one in ten thousand, are eaten by other predators. According to the teachings of the Buddhadharma, to be born into such a situation is the just retribution for killing done in past lives.

Bernie and Eileen Bernstein took us into their home for lunch today. Bernie told us that he had become "fed up with the rat-race executive's life" back east, so he quit his job, sold everything, and came out here, where he has established a fix-it shop and boutique. His wife makes candles and jewelry, and Bernie carves wooden totem poles. He takes a log, passes over it with his light-weight torch, and goes over it with a wire brush. Looks just like the real thing.

Sometimes when we have stopped, people park near us and pretend to be looking at the sea. Then, when they think we are not looking, they stare at us in amazement. I can hardly blame them. If I saw two bald-headed, tattooed bowing-bhikshus clothed in Tang Dynasty robes having a vegetarian banquet on the asphalt of a scenic turnout parking lot, I might be alarmed, too.

14 May 1974. Heng Yo writes:

After another stormy night, we bowed into Waldport, population 1,100. Upon invitation, we went to Mike, Julia, and Christie Perola's house for lunch. Julia said that she dreamt about us several days before our arrival, and that she has been reciting Na Mo Guan Shi

Yin Pu Sa, the name of Guan Yin Bodhisattva. She said this method has served to calm and center her mind, and that it is particularly efficacious in difficult situations, for example when it gets very hectic in the restaurant where she works.

After lunch, we bowed through Waldport and across the Alsea Bridge. On the other side of the bay, we were greeted by a gathering of friendly folks who gave us fresh vegetables, tea, and homemade bread. One person named Mark, who is a disciple of a Tibetan teacher, kept saying, "What a fantastic *sadhana!* What a fantastic *sadhana!*" *Sadhana* is a Sanskrit word for a method of cultivation or purification.

There was another man who was concerned that Americans consume too much sugar in their daily diet. He felt that it was poisonous and addictive, and wished people would wake up and kick the habit. This reminded me of the time when some of us learned something about the nature of sugar, and about our own desire. It happened a few years ago at Gold Mountain Monastery, when times were rough. We sometimes looked through garbage bins for the perfectly good vegetables and other food which others discarded. When washed and prepared, there was no way to tell that it had been taken from the Safeway dumpster. Now Big Ju was a regular on the scavenging runs, because he seemed to have the ability to consistently pick out the bins which were the most productive. I don't know whether he was using his spiritual powers, or whether he was just hungry. Anyway, there used to be a candy bar factory near the monastery, and their garbage was a weekly stop for Ju, who'd bring back ten or twelve Big Hunks—a sticky cement of sugar and peanuts, guaranteed to pull out at least one tooth or filling per bar. This wasn't so bad, but one day as I walked by the kitchen, there was a seventy-five pound Big Hunk lying on the cutting table! Oh, no! People were buzzing around it like flies.

A verse the Master wrote a long time ago reads:

Everything's a test
To see what you will do;
Mistaking what's before your face,
You'll have to start anew.

This was indeed a test: the proper thing would have been to remain unmoved by desire. But really, the only testing which was going on was not that of concentration over desire, but how to EAT the thing!

Someone broke off a large piece and heated it in a pot. When it cooled and hardened, the candy and the metal fused, and the pot was ruined. Others attacked it with hammers, chisels, and hacksaws. After a few days of dishes such as asparagus in Big Hunk sauce, someone grabbed the remaining glob and threw it back into the garbage can where it belonged. Our aching teeth reminded us of the lesson we had learned, and the test some of us had failed. As the verse says, we started anew in our effort to recognize what is going on and to remain unmoved in the midst of desire.

At the day's end, Big Ju and I were sitting by the side of the road wondering where to set up camp, when Mr. and Mrs. Ed Thayer stopped to take us in for the night. Ed was originally from New York; he moved here some fifteen years ago, and built a fine home on Alsea Bay. He is "disenchanted with conventional religions."

15 May 1974. Heng Ju writes:

Last night Ed Thayer was telling us how he had become disillusioned with Western religions. He had found in reading a translation of the recently discovered Dead Sea Scrolls, that the doctrines of Jesus had been taught 100 years before Jesus' birth by a teacher named Appolonius, who was the leader of an Essene group of monastics. There is a part of Jesus' life that is left out of the Bible—about fifteen or twenty years—which was spent studying with this sect. After he left this group he started his own teaching career, incorporating a doctrine almost identical to the Pure Land School of Buddhism: the doctrine of rebirth in paradise. Jesus was indeed a most profound teacher, but it was the Church Councils and the emperor Constantine who made him into a deity. People at that time were in dire need of spiritual leadership, and since Constantine wanted to unite his empire, he brought them all together through the teachings of an all wise and powerful God. Ever since then millions of people have been looking up to this God, who revealed his will through Jesus. Ed Thayer said he is unhappy with the teachings as they exist today, because they have strayed so far from their source. He believes that although the Christian religions have done innumerable good for the world, people will have to turn to other methods for ultimate union with the divine.

Heavy, heavy rain today. A couple of elderly ladies invited us in for tea and asked us if our teachers threw spears at us as part of our training at the monastery. Apparently they have been watching a lot of gong fu on television. In the late evening a car drove up directly behind me as if to run me over. The two middle-aged men inside were cussing, honking, and gunning the engine. I continued bowing at normal speed and didn't look back. After a few minutes they went away.

16 May 1974. Heng Yo writes:

Today we bowed seven and a half miles through some strange weather: the bright sun and the rain were alternating every half-hour or so. As we passed through Seal Beach, quite a few people stopped to talk, among them Associated Press reporter Joe Frazier; a milk truck driver who gave us some raw milk; an older woman who told us about the old days when there was a stagecoach line which ran along the beach; a salesman who described his meditational experiences; and a girl who lectured Heng Ju as he bowed along the road. "Don't you believe Jesus was the son of God?" she asked impatiently.

When we arrived at the bridge over Yaquina Bay, before entering the town of Newport, Jim Newman and Roland Chase from a TV station out of Portland gave us a lively interview and shot a lot of film.

When I was in grade school and junior high, I was reluctant to get up in front of the class alone. When we had to give a report, I was scared and forgot everything I wanted to say, and ended up so flustered that it was all I could do to read my notes off the paper. Once, we were assigned to write a poem, and the teacher called on us to recite our poems in front of the class. I read mine quickly, and ran back to my seat. The poem was so short that the teacher said cuttingly, "Don't bump his arm, it must be really sore from writing such a long poem." He was certainly no help. I was the same way in high school, but I enjoyed playing trumpet in the band, because I wasn't alone up there.

My fear was basically a little quirk which I had blown up out of proportion; it was defensive armor to protect my "self." But today, when TV cameras started rolling and the mike was taking in my every word, it all seemed to fall into place like the pieces of a puzzle. Here were several thousand people watching, and I didn't even get nervous. Maybe this is because during the last few months, I have talked to so many strangers that I forgot about my "self" and perhaps have gotten an inkling of its unreality. This may not be important for others who seem to thrive in the spotlight, but for me, today marked a real personal triumph. To top it all off, Mr. and Mrs. Maxfield gave us a room in their West Wind Motel in Newport for the night. I must admit that today I am really happy.

17 May 1974. Heng Ju writes:

Bowed six and a half miles in the sunshine. This morning, just north of the Newport City Limits, I stopped to take a leak in the woods behind a modern-looking Lutheran Church. In passing, I noticed a sign on the Church which read: Mr. Olson, Pastor. I didn't think anything of it at the time. Later, I continued bowing northward, and after about two hours, a middle-aged couple stopped to ask me the usual questions. I noticed that they looked pretty bright, so I asked them if they were of any particular religious affiliation. "Yes," the man replied, "We are both Lutherans.

Now I have never been in Newport before, and I have no idea what prompted me to say it, but I said right back to him, "Oh, yes; Mr. and Mrs. Olson!" It was a direct hit; they both almost fell over. Of all the Lutherans in Newport it just happened to be them. I kept a straight face, and continued talking for a few minutes. They listened to every word!

Hung Yo and Jung Ju, two American Buddhist monks, are on the final part of their 1,100 mile journey for world peace. Every third step, Jung Ju kneels and bows to the ground in prayer and meditation following the example of a Buddhist monk in China who made a similar pilgrimage. Hung Yo and Hung Ju were seen on Goldman Dr. N.W. on Monday, July 8.

Buddhists Make Trek For World Peace

A pilgrimage for world peace has taken two Buddhist monks on a 1,100 mile journey from San Francisco to Marblemount, Washington. The monks, Hung Yo and Hung Ju, traveling six miles a day, have completed 900 miles of their pilgrimage. In two months they expect to reach their destination that will have taken 11 months to achieve. Their route has taken them to Belfair where they visited Hung Ju's parents.

For Hung Ju the 1,100 mile journey will have been accomplished by taking three steps, then kneeling and bowing to the ground. "The three steps represent the three aspects of Buddhism," stated Hung Ju. "To rid oneself of greed, hatred and delusion to attain morality, concentration and wisdom." The kneeling and bowing is a period spent in prayer and meditation. Hung Ju has worn out 12 pairs of gloves as he performs this ritual. He has settled on a pair of rubber gloves with cotton lining as being the most durable. "Leather gloves were the quickest to wear out," he said.

Hung Yo and Hung Ju are members of the Gold Mountain Monastery in San Francisco. Hung Yo was converted to Buddhism during his undergraduate work in Chinese studies. Hung Ju joined the monastary following a period in the armed forces and college studies.

The monks pilgrimage for world peace was to originally end in Seattle. Shortly after starting their journey, land was bequeathed to the Seattle Buddha organization for the construction of a monastary. Hung Yo and Hung Ju are traveling to Marblemount. They may return to San Francisco following the completion of their journey.

The petite Mrs. Cude came out to share some of her wealth with us. She gave us a bag of whole wheat bread, cheese, and fruits. Unfortunately, that wasn't all she wanted to share with us. She was intent on giving us a big hug, and we had to use all of the skillful means we could muster to fend her off. Two riders on chopped Harley-Davidsons talked with me for a few minutes. They seemed to appreciate the idea of being all alone out here on the road.

18 May 1974. Heng Ju writes:

Russ Jamieson from radio KMED in Medford taped an interview. A rookie sheriff's deputy stopped and put us in the back of his car. He radioed headquarters to have them check the computer and see if we were criminals. He thought we were either escaped convicts, AWOL sailors, or insane asylum patients. But there wasn't a thing he could bust us for, so he finally let us go.

As we passed through Depoe Bay, a Mrs. Walter met us at the northern city limits and warned us that there was a houseful of drunks waiting for us up ahead. She said that they had been drinking all day and were having a big party waiting for us to come along. Some of them had been throwing beer cans out on the road, others had been making mock prostrations on the shoulder. As we stood there discussing the issue, Mr. Baker, owner of the local motel, came running out and offered us a free room. I looked up ahead about one block and saw the group they were talking about. Every once in a while one of them would dart out on the road to see if we were coming. Yes, this was the age-old choice again; should we accept the milk of human kindness, or should we march off to war? I'd had enough milk for the day; I wanted action.

I told Yo, "Why don't you go back to the motel and start unloading the gear? I'll bow for another hour or so, and then walk back."

"Nothing doing!" replied Yo, "I'm going out there, and I'm going out there now!" He reached down, grabbed the pack and threw it over his shoulders, then he grabbed the buggy and started huffin' down the road directly toward the drunks.

"Stop! You boys are making a terrible mistake!" One of the ladies yelled. I put on my gloves, adjusted my trusty kneepads, and started performing my ritual down the highway. "Na Mo Guan Shi Yin Pu Sa." The words rattled through my mind like a freight train. Yo approached the group with unswerving determination. From my vantage point about a hundred feet behind, I could see there were about eleven of them. But they seemed to be pushed away as Yo approached. In fact it appeared that they were scared. Yo kept trucking straight at them, but by the time he got within fifty feet, they had completely scattered. Most of them headed back to the house. One of them tossed a few pebbles from a safe distance, but his heart wasn't in it. Yo stopped directly in front of the house and waited for me to pass. It was as if a bulldozer had cleared the way: I went by without any problem. Only a few remarks were mouthed, but they had no power to them. We were so energized from the encounter that we bowed another two and a half miles, making it an eight-and-a-half-mile day, our longest so far. Just as we prepared to set up camp off the highway, a carload of people who were at the party came out and apologized. Yo said, "Oh, don't worry about it."

19 May 1974. Heng Ju writes:

Gwo Hwei Weber's parents stopped to see us today. Mrs. Weber brought us groceries, and told us what a ridiculous time she had had trying to locate us. She said that everyone that she asked along the way had a different idea of what we are doing. One man said, "I don't know what they're doing, but there has got to be a better way to get to heaven." A young girl said, "Yes, I saw a man. He bows to every car that comes along." In the evening, a red-nosed old drunk came up to Yo and said, "I don't know what you guys are doing, but I hope that you keep doing it!" It's just these little words of cheer that keep us going.

20 May 1974. Heng Yo writes:

Lincoln City stretches for some seven miles along the coast. As we bowed through town, hippies, common folks, Hells Angels, old folks, and youngsters all came out to greet us. We stopped for lunch on a vacant lot in town, where a newspaper reporter interviewed us. Even the Sheriff of Lincoln County, Roy Sutton, shook our hands. He was impressed with Heng Ju's fitness, and was especially moved that we were able to go so far on one meal of vegetables per day. After lunch we continued bowing, and a television news team covered our progress through town. We were about through for the day when two cars almost collided because the drivers were not paying attention—to the road, that is.

After bowing seven and three-quarters miles, we are camped off the road in a peaceful little clearing.

22 May 1974. Heng Yo Writes:

The road turns inland for a few miles between Neotsu and Winema Beach. Today we bowed up a long hill before reaching Neskowin. The roadside defoliant was making us sick, and the hot sun continued to beat down. To make matters worse, we were out of water. I went up ahead to the top of the hill, and after a little exploring, discovered a cool, clear mountain spring. "Wait till Ju tastes this sweet dew," I thought. I filled our jug, went back to where I had parked the buggy, and started bowing. Ju finally came by after about a half-hour. He threw down his gloves, and sat down on the soft earth. I sensed something was wrong, so I didn't dare speak. A moment later I knew what it was: I'd gone too far up ahead. If something had happened to either one of us, the other person would be unaware. "Have some water," I managed to say. "It's really good." We drank in silence. Now that I look back on it, the mutually reinforcing bad feelings could have been ended right then and there, but I was too proud, too full of self to apologize. So there we were, sitting by the roadside, each righteously ready to bite off the other guy's head.

Perhaps petty anger seems unimportant; after a while it subsides, so why make a big deal out of nothing? But looked at on a larger scale, petty anger, if not checked, grows into hatred, and it is hatred which causes people to fight. Taken one step further, hatred and anger are the root of war. So if we eliminate venomous thoughts in our own minds, we'd have no reason for acts of violence on any scale.

It all sounds so nice on paper, but, as usual, applying the principle in daily life is a real challenge. After a while Ju looked at me, and I looked at Ju. He got up, looked around, spit, and continued bowing. God, I felt small.

Outside of Neskowin, a lady snarled at Ju, "What do you think you're doing?"

"Bowing for world peace," he replied civilly.

"Well," she snapped, "You can tell it to the State Police." She ran into her trailer house and grabbed the phone, but no police showed up. Later some Neskowin boys gave us a bag of fruit, and a Christian girl spent a while trying to convert me on the spot. I told her to contemplate everything as being made from the mind alone, but she couldn't hear me.

We bowed six and three-quarters miles today despite the roadside poison. We are camped south of Cloverdale, on a hill hidden from the road. We picked a bunch of just-ripening salmon berries for tomorrow.

23 May 1974. Heng Ju writes:

Bowed seven miles in the rain. The Cloverdale eighth graders talked with us on the school's front lawn, then later a kid from the high school interviewed Yo for their school paper.

In Hebo, we called Gold Mountain and told the Master about the poison along the road. He said that there was basically no problem, and suggested that I breathe while I'm up, and hold my breath while down. He encouraged us to be more sincere each day, and not to speak casually with reporters, as they sometimes tend to pick up on idiosyncrasies, and miss the important points. I told him that everything I do is an idiosyncrasy. He said not to worry about it.

Father Gerald, a Benedictine monk from Mt. Angel Seminary, introduced himself and found us a place to set up our tent. He asked his parishioners, the Hurlemans, if we could set up the tent in their cow pasture, and they thought it was a fine idea. Father Gerald, who has parishes in both Cloverdale and Tillamook, invited us to come see him when we pass through Tillamook.

Now it is late. A quiet rain is falling on the rain-fly which protects the tent. As they say on the boats, "All compartments report no leaks."

24 May 1974. Heng Yo writes:

It's been a miserable rainy day. We had lunch under a bridge, where it was somewhat dry. The road is narrow and winding, there are many large trucks, and we almost got hit a couple of times.

In the afternoon, Ju told me that a couple of cars stopped next to him while I was up ahead. A blond curly-headed man stuck his head out of the window and said, "Keep going! Keep going! Don't stop! Don't stop! Don't stop!" Then about a dozen of them got out of the cars and walked toward him. Ju thought it was a bunch of ruffians about to do him in, but then the curly-headed leader approached him, respectfully put his palms together, and said in a soft voice, *shanti* (an Indian word for peace). He handed Ju a lemon, and said, "We've been following your progress in the papers and think what you're doing is wonderful." Ju didn't say anything. The man returned to his van, and one of the people smiled and said to Ju, "You just met Ken Kesey."

Toward the end of the day, John Wheeler, a hard-working farmer, took us in out of the rain for the evening at his ten-acre spread east of Beaver. He has two brothers who were about to use their truck and a chain to straighten up a sagging old garage. I could see it all happening, but didn't say anything. They hooked the chain to a beam, pulled a little, and then a little more. They had it just about perfectly straightened out, and then decided to go just a mite further. Everyone watched in amazement as the whole garage came down with a loud crash. We slept in the hayloft in the barn with a herd of goats downstairs.

25 May 1974. Heng Ju writes:

An old truck with a wooden house on the back stopped and four shaggy-looking souls came out to greet us. The shaggiest of the group said, "Would you guys like some fresh goat's milk?"

"Yes," I said without delay. At that, he walked over to the back door of the truck, swung it open, and there inside was a real live nanny goat, with her stern section toward us. He reached in under her, procured an empty quart bottle, and proceeded to relieve nanny of just that much of her warm goods. Afterward, we stood in a circle and passed the bottle around. "It don't come no fresher," I remarked.

The tallest one, who looked like a transformation-body of Ben Hur, said: "Please tell us exactly what you have learned on this trip." My mind began to whirl as I flashed back on the hundreds of miles and thousands of people we had already encountered. What an incredible question to ask! There was no way I could answer it in a few words, so I just remained silent. There was a long pause as we all stood there. Finally, the tall one said, "We think what you two are doing is really worth it; we hope you make it!"

In the evening, Andy and Sheila Klein took us to their home and introduced us to their grandparents and friends. Gwo Hsi (Sheila) had recently taken refuge in Buddhism and shortly thereafter had recovered from a very serious back problem. Her doctor said it was a miracle.

26 May 1974. Heng Ju writes:

A young man from Tillamook stopped and asked me to explain briefly, in a practical manner, how one should practice Buddhism. We got into a conversation and I laid out the basics for him.

Rule #1: Try not to commit bad karma. Work to purify the mind and to purify all your activities, by freeing your actions from greed, anger, and ignorance.

Rule #2: Contemplate the mind as being like empty space, able to encompass all things the way the void holds all the planets. The true mind is magnanimous, great, unobstructed, and on the ultimate level there is "no knowing and no attaining."

Rule #3: Understand that there are no fixed methods and no fixed dogmas. We should hold to our precepts, practices, and vows, but at the same time see all things, including all religious teachings, as relative and illusory creations, not real in themselves.

Rule #4: Look at things in terms of the Middle Way. Life is full of extremes, full of dualities. Yet these are mere words and ideas that do not give an accurate picture. Good and bad, big and little, inside and outside, and all other pairs of opposites are merely labels, mere relative qualifications. They are nothing more than the standardized figments of someone's imagination, unreal labels pasted on a fundamentally undifferentiated reality. In Buddhism, people learn to see things from the middle ground, from the space of no-thought. As the Master says, "Above there is no Heaven, below there is no earth: Empty space is obliterated."

27 May 1974: Heng Ju writes:

Memorial Day. Heavy traffic and heavy winds. Drunks racing down the highway in both directions. We decided to knock off before we got bumped off.

We camped in a tall grassy field. Around midnight, a large rat (he must have weighed about 3 pounds) climbed up on the cart and started getting into things. We awoke to the sound of munching and crunching. Why, the dirty rat was into our food! I got out of the sack and grabbed a flashlight. I shone it out onto the buggy, which was only four feet from the front of the tent. There he was, the shameless scoundrel, standing on top of the buggy stuffing fistfuls of bread into his mouth! He had eaten through a nylon tote sack and several layers of plastic, and had already consumed a good deal of bread, too. I had the light shining right in his eyes, and Yo was out of the tent by now. Both of us were within three feet of him, and he continued to eat. He was really into that bread! In Buddhism this is called, "Knowing that something is wrong, but going ahead and doing it anyway." I held the light in his eyes with my right hand and with my left hand, after Yo had slipped a glove on it, slowly came around behind him. Just as I darted out to grab him, he made a bounding leap, and all I touched was his tail. Rats! He got away!

People can become rats, too. All they have to do is act like rats and they'll become rats. No need to wait for the next life. Become a rat without a tail in this very life!

28 May 1974. Heng Yo writes:

We pushed on through Hemlock and Pleasant Valley, on a long stretch of inland highway, toward the famous cheese town of Tillamook. Local elections are being held today, and early this morning we met a white-haired old codger who was walking into town to cast his ballot. He scolded us for not voting. Later in the day, the Kleins came over the hills from Portland to see us again.

Last week I mentioned desire. We read in the Sutras, and have been graphically taught by the Master, that desire, in its ten thousand disguises, not only conceals our inherent insight and wisdom, but also creates affliction in the process. For example, when that seventy-five pound candy bar appeared, desire soared, but the Master kept silent, and let us learn a lesson by ourselves.

Not obtaining the object of desire, we are disappointed. Obtaining what we do not desire, we are angry. We may invest much effort, time, and money to attain fine things, but ultimately are left unhappy and afflicted because the fire of desire rages higher with each object added to the flames. Going to excesses, we hurt ourselves as well as others.

It is not easy to accept that most of us who seriously follow the Buddha-dharma have not yet put an end to desire once and for all. Others see no use in doing so. "Why shouldn't I enjoy myself?" they ask. Lao Zi answers:

Only when we are sick of our sickness
Shall we cease to be sick
The sage is not sick, being sick of sickness;
This is the secret of health.

The sickness is desire. Unable to admit to ourselves that we suffer from it, we do nothing to get rid of it in order to become healthy. If someone doesn't believe he has cancer, why would he go to a doctor for treatment?

29 May 1974. Heng Ju writes:

Up before the sun. I bowed for a while, then stopped to rest underneath a bridge. After 10 minutes I continued on but suddenly my stomach began to cramp up. I walked back to the bridge and went underneath to rest some more, and discovered that I had left my mantra book there. My cramps soon left.

As we approached Tillamook, we encountered several dozen friendly people. Linda Glass brought a busload of students. By previous invitation, we stopped at Sacred Heart Parish to visit Father Gerald. He took us over to the high school, and we spoke in front of the sophomore class. When we had finished, Father Kenneth, the assistant pastor, led the class in prayer; "May these two men find that peace in Jesus Christ our Lord. Amen."

We made it all the way through town with no problem (a police car was in sight the whole time). We spent the evening with Ted and Ivy Mullan. It was a great night. Ted insisted on taking us up in his hand-built airplane, so one at a time we went up and flew north at three thousand feet looking down at our future path. Nothing but ocean beach and highway as far as the eye could see.

30 May 1974. Heng Yo writes:

Members of the local Citizen's Band radio club brought us some hot tea today as we inched our way northward along Tillamook Bay. There are about 200 CB members in the area, and they say the airwaves have been crackling as they keep tabs on our current location and condition.

Approaching Garibaldi, a little boy asked us if we were Shao Lin priests. He had learned a lot from watching Kung Fu on television, and he did not hesitate to tell us how proud he was that he had beat up his friend at school. He was obviously enthralled with this TV adventure of an outcast monk in the American west of the nineteenth century. Daoist and Confucian texts are quoted and misquoted, and the show is very popular, but if you look through the Chinese wrappings, it's just another weekly display of violence.

Children watch these programs hour after hour, day after day, even before they can talk or walk. They are programmed to think that violence is the way to get things done. And why? It stems from the desire of advertisers to sell their products. A popular show attracts more viewers, who are exposed to the advertising propaganda which goes along with it. I am not a media expert, but it is plain to see that subjecting children to this powerful and destructive influence as they grow up is a high price to pay in order to satisfy the greed of advertisers. I wonder if the Kung Fu writers are aware that Lao Zi, who they seemingly quote so often, said, "A man of violence meets a violent end."

Mr. and Mrs. Blackwell of Garibaldi offered us a room for the night in their house.

31 May 1974. Heng Ju writes:

Through Rockaway hundreds of folks came out to talk, including a very friendly Chief of Police. We have found that the best way to relate what we are doing is to talk to people in terms of their own religions. When Buddhism came to China from India, it incorporated the languages and ideas of Confucianism and Daoism, fusing them all into an inseparable whole. We have also found, after many encounters, that it is useless to get into arguments with people about religion. If they have already decided to come out and convert us, then they aren't going to be the least interested in hearing our views. I have found that the best thing to do, in most cases, is to just be friendly with them. I wish I could talk with them, though, and tell them that I'm not a believer in the right-wrong business. I feel that all religions are valuable, and that they can serve the needs of people as they grow spiritually. Buddhism itself is only a stepping stone. The Buddha likens his teachings to a raft; the teachings exist only to help people get to the other shore. It would be good if we weren't so quick to categorize each other. People are far too complex and beautiful for that nonsense.

1 June 1974. Heng Yo writes:

The road loops around Nehalem Bay and the land is low-lying and swampy, with eel grass and driftwood on the sandy earth. There are low hills in the hazy distance to the west.

In the afternoon, we made our way around a bend and down the hill into the small town of Wheeler, where it seemed like the folks had been waiting around to watch us bow through. The owner of the local grocery store offered us anything we wanted out of his store, so we got a razor. After a brief rest, the store owner's nephew, who was a former seminarian at the Catholic monastery Mt. Angel, interviewed us at length for the town paper. He asked some interesting questions.

As the interview went on, he commented once or twice, "Your philosophy is rather complicated." Unfortunately, my attempts to demonstrate the opposite failed as I tried to state simply the principles of karma, rebirth, and enlightenment. I began to feel helpless and frustrated, because the more I tried to explain how simple and uncomplicated Buddhism is, the more the opposite became fixed in the mind of the interviewer. Finally, we realized the whole thing had lasted too long already. "Let's go, Ju."

A little boy led us to a grassy field on a hill high above the town where we spent the night.

2 June 1974. Heng Ju writes:

Bowing six miles in an Oregon rainstorm is not necessarily a bad experience. I just don't pay any attention to the water, and after a while it's like it isn't even there. In fact, it's very quiet and contemplative. The rain washes off all the plants, making everything fresh and clean. Too bad most folks stay indoors every time they see the rain. They're really missing something.

3 June 1974. Heng Yo writes:

We bowed through the towns of Nehalem and Manzanita, and then up and over Neahkahnie Mountain, which is about 1,700 feet high. Now we are camped in a desolate area of Oscar West State Park, just short of the Tillamook-Clatsop county line. Ju's back is sore, and the rain has been getting us down a bit, but it is a comfort to know that we've come 776 miles so far. Despite all of the bitterness that is involved in this work, there is something about it that is overwhelmingly wonderful. Maybe it is the natural high which comes from living outside for so long, coupled with an illusory feeling of freedom which travel sometimes fosters.

We can go anywhere we want in our lives, do anything we wish, and yet we are still prisoners of our own ignorance, no matter where we go. It is said that by following a path trod by the ancient sages, we can see through our ignorance, and go places we never knew existed. We are told to take our eyes off the short-lived, illusory freedom of living without precept or rule, and look at the true freedom which is born of long-term effort and sacrifice.

I like to think that this bowing trip is a lot more than just a trek to Seattle. It has become clear that everyone we meet, whether they want to help us or hurt us, is involved in the trip just as we are. Our lives may appear individual and separate, but below the surface of our waking consciousness, we are karmically connected like the maze of roots of the cattail plant. Good deeds done in the present result in rewards for the future. The mendicants in Buddhist countries, for example, provided people with a chance to plant the seeds of good karma. By giving the mendicants food, people nourished their own virtue.

This may seem to be a mere walk to Seattle, but if we can do it in the proper manner, it is a path similar in substance to the path many ancient cultivators followed. They left ignorance behind and ultimately arrived at true freedom. They also influenced, aided, and led countless numbers of people along their own way to liberation. A pleasant thought as the cold rain seeps into the tent.

4 June 1974. Heng Ju writes:

Heavy storm, so we made no progress today. We are camped halfway between hell and nowhere in the dripping-wet Oregon salad. We didn't make a proper drainage ditch last night, so now we are in the process of submerging. There is an ever-growing pool of water in the back section of the tent. Not only that, but I burned a big hole in my foam pad while trying to light the SVEA stove with a little splash of fuel. For a few seconds it looked as if the whole tent was going to burn down. Lighting the SVEA inside the tent should be left only to those brave souls who have already cut off the cycle of birth and death! Once the little devil was running, I managed to scorch the oatmeal. Five minutes later I broke the salt shaker, liberating half a cup of salt all over the tent. What a day! We're sinking and bobbing in the sea of our own afflictions.

It is said that if people weren't afflicted, they would be enlightened. But the sea of afflictions can be endless. I remember that back at Gold Mountain there was a period of time when it seemed that every time I struck up a vain, idle, or afflicted thought, I would hear the Master's door slam shut. It was an amazing occurrence which took place hundreds of times. I would think to myself, "This is incredible! Who would ever believe that a teacher could teach his disciples by slamming his door?" But believe it or not, the teaching was there. There was no doubt in my mind. The symbolism of a Master shutting his door on a disciple was heavy enough in many instances to cause me to change my thinking and upgrade my behavior. In short, the method was effective.

5 June 1974. Heng Yo writes:

Cannon Beach: rain, hills, twisty road, a tunnel.
Pulling the cart uphill is like tugging oneself through an unpleasant task, while restraining the cart on the downgrade is like trying not to overindulge in pleasure. Walking with the cart on level pavement is like meshing with the universe; there is no thought of cart or of one who pulls it. It is not important to know whether

downgrades follow inclines, or inclines follow downgrades. The way I see it, the Middle Way consists in taking all grades as they come, just as if they were level. Pulling the carts of ourselves uphill, it is easy to become angry, because the work is hard and the progress is slow. Going downhill, it is easy to get going too fast and lose control. And so in cultivation: whether bearing the discomfort of sitting in full lotus in meditation, or dining on the finest heavenly delights, our minds should not move. Just as these hills are fluctuations of level ground, pleasure and suffering are fluctuations of the pure, still, bright mind. This is my study of samadhi.

6 June 1974. Heng Ju writes:

A newspaper reporter from Astoria stopped to interview us today. As we were all sitting by the side of the road talking, a car passed by and a passenger chucked a handful of stones at us. They missed Yo and me, but they got the reporter. Fortunately, he was wearing a heavy leather coat, so he wasn't hurt. As we continued into Seaside, we noticed that the car with the rock-throwing hooligans in it was shadowing us. It looked like they were getting ready for another strike. We had already made 8 miles, and another storm was brewing up, so we ditched them, and found a dry little cabin in the heart of town that no one was using.

It must be getting close to summer; the rain is getting warmer.

7 June 1974. Heng Yo writes:

Today I received a letter from my folks. It reads in part: "We enjoy hearing of your adventures. You know, when we first heard about your plans to make the trip, we were pretty uptight (we all are wary of things strange to us). Now, however, not only have we accepted it, but we have come to feel that it is a marvelous experience and opportunity for you and Heng Ju."

Tonight we are staying with Ju's relatives, the Fennertys, who live nearby. Their lifestyle seems to be an interesting and happy blend of rural aloofness and suburban convenience. A remodeled chicken coop is their house, and besides their large vegetable garden, they have goats, sheep, chickens, and a big mother pig with a lot of squealing babies. Gus Fennerty has constructed a sauna bath of his own design with a swimming hole in front.

We are planning to hit the road early tomorrow; the state of Washington is not far off.

8 June 1974. Heng Ju writes:

The Master from Gold Mountain arrived today. With him were three cars full of monks, nuns, and laypeople. It was a very spirited meeting. We secured bowing for the day and drove up to Saddle Mountain for a picnic lunch. After lunch we returned to the bowing area and asked for instruction on how to best perform this last part of our journey.

The Master said that we should make every effort to be extremely sincere and mindful. In our minds' cultivation, as well as in our travels, we should always go forward and never retreat. He said that if we really do the work of casting out all of our afflictions, his coming to America will not have been in vain. He said that the bowing journey is causing people all over the world to wake up. He cautioned us about receiving invitations into people's homes. If they can observe the five precepts during our stay, then we can stay there; otherwise, we should leave. I asked him how we should handle all this attention we are getting from the media. He explained that notoriety is neither good nor bad, it's what a person does with it that matters. One should neither want fame nor not want fame. If newspeople come seeking articles and pictures, then it is OK to oblige them. Just don't go seeking them. It's basically no problem.

Just before they all got into the cars to leave, we said goodbye to the Master, and he began rubbing our heads. He rubbed very softly for what seemed like five or ten minutes. Within the ancient tradition of Buddhism, to receive this rubbing of the forehead is a very rare and special honor. The rubbing had the effect of obliterating all my worries and fears, and once again I was filled with an overwhelming sense of peace and tranquility. Having loaded us with food, clothing, and Dharma, they departed, wishing us a hearty "Try your best!"

9 June 1974. Heng Ju writes:

Astoria, Oregon: It's a beautiful day. We bowed seven miles in the sun.

Last night we stayed with the Fennertys again. In the morning we talked to Gus about the principles of being a vegetarian. Swami Satchidananda explains it well. He says to simply look at the animals in the zoo. The meat-eating animals must be caged up. They are usually quite restless. In contrast, the grass- and herb-eating animals, such as goats, cows, and elephants, are innocent and mellow, yet they are quite strong with a gentle and useful strength. The tiger can kill the elephant, but what kind of quality is that?

Mrs. Ehrlich came by and offered us some fried chicken and a couple of soda pops. We declined the chicken. She asked if I had acquired "milkmaid knees." "Milk-person knees," I replied.

An evangelist gave Yo a long sermon this afternoon, and in summation said, "Now you should consider what I have said, and I will consider what you have said, ahh, ahh, even though you haven't said anything."

As we approached Astoria, hundreds of folks stopped to talk. Many of them asked how we are going to get across the four-mile long Astoria bridge. "We'll cross that bridge when we get to it," was the only answer we could come up with.

10 June 1974. Heng Ju writes:

Last night Eric Swedburg put us up in a freaky hotel that he manages in the heart of town. As we approached the Astoria bridge which spans the Columbia River into Washington, a red pickup rolled to a stop, and Eric's friends Ron, Marie, and Steve offered to give us a ride across. We would have preferred to bow, but there was no place to do it, so we accepted. On the other shore, we were welcomed by many news people, and a Mr. Harriet, owner of the local market, told us that we could have anything we wanted in his store.

I talked to a man who has been smoking for thirty years. His lungs are really ruined. It makes me really appreciate all the trouble that the Master has taken to teach his disciples to completely give up smoking, drinking, and drugs. The truth is that it only takes a short period of sustained effort to put down these habits, and then they are forgotten; but some people cling to the habits as if they were precious jewels. It's not fun and it's not easy to make people give up their hang-ups, but that's just another point where a true teacher is different from others. He cares about people and exhausts himself for their benefit.

11 June 1974. Heng Yo writes:

A hot day, good road, wide shoulder. A girl handed me a brown paper bag, jumped into her car, and zoomed off. In it were two oranges and a bible.

Up the road a ways, we came across a large sheet of butcher paper that was held down by some rocks. "Jesus was God in a human body!" it said. It went on to exhort us to let Christ answer for our sins, and to accept his salvation. This is good, but we are all responsible for working out our own karma.

In the afternoon, I went to a store for vegetables in Naselle. The store seemed to be a sort of social center. An older man asked me a few questions about Buddhism and then went on to tell me that he couldn't see how people in India could let cows run free when there were so many starving people. I could see that he was bent on arguing, so I didn't go into the matter.

We are camped in the trees next to the road. It certainly is quiet.

12 June 1974. Heng Ju writes:

A Sea Story

In the early morning, the submarine received permission to enter the enemy harbor and make an attack. It was still dark when several miles off shore, she vented her ballast tanks and slipped silently into the ocean's bosom.

This morning, Bobbie Yantze, a teacher at Naselle Youth Camp, invited us to come and speak to a group of boys. The camp is a state correctional facility for wayward young men, ages 14 to 18. Yo and I discussed the tactics and then stashed the gear in the bushes by the road.

Running slowly at periscope depth, the sub cruised silently into the enemy harbor. "Up scope", said the Captain. He beheld a fantastic sight: destroyers, cruisers and carriers; ships too numerous to count. "Man Battle Station Torpedo! Flood the bow tubes, open the outer doors! Stand by to fire!"

Miss Yantze picked us up and took us into the camp. We were introduced to the principal, chaplain, and some teachers. Originally, we had thought that we would be talking to a small class, but apparently the word had leaked out, and the whole institution was waiting to see us, several hundred in all. There was not enough room in their biggest hall, so we all gathered in a big assembly on the blacktop. Yo and I sat in full lotus and, facing the crowd, prepared to explain just what in the hell we were doing.

The Captain took the con, expertly maneuvering and exposing his periscope only long enough to estimate range and bearing. "Fire One! Fire Two!" The sub shuddered as the two-and-a-half-ton steel fish went screaming off at 45 knots to their targets. "Hot, straight, and normal", reports the sonar room. "Hit, sir, they're breaking up!"

Yo went first. He spoke loud and clear; his principles and analogies were solid. He said that life is a dream, an illusion. People think what is true is false, and what is false they think is true. Therefore it is necessary to wake up. Everyone listened intently. I could see that his points were hitting home.

Then the Captain turned the scope to the Engineer. Spinning the scope around, bobbing up and down, he called off his shots: "Fire Six, fire Seven, fire Eight!"

Ju spoke next. He explained that gong fu is not necessarily beating in someone's head. It is using one's own abilities to attain a state of dynamic concentration and unity with one's own inherent wisdom. The best kind of gong fu is "reversing the light and illuminating within."

Then the enemy struck back. The destroyers were throwing hot lead through the air, and the sub chasers were buzzing around like mosquitoes.

Then came a barrage of questions. One person asked Yo what we would do if some mean person came up to hassle us. "If people come out looking for a hassle, we just don't give them one." Yo replied sharply. The inmates and staff engaged with us in sporting enquiry. We cleared up a lot of questions, but there were still several people in the crowd who stared at us in total disbelief.

Having sunk and damaged many ships, the sub turned and ran full speed out of the harbor. Once into deep water she went down as far as her thin skin would allow and listened on her sonar to the chaos above. After things quieted down, she surfaced, lit off four engines, and commenced to head home at full speed. A radio message was received from the squadron commander. It read, "Outstanding job!"

After the assembly broke up, we were swamped by inmates and teachers. The bells were ringing but nobody was going back to class. Yo and I made a run for Miss Yantze's car. Just before we drove through the crowd, Mr. Biggs, one of the veteran instructors, came up to the car window and said, "That was the best thing for those kids I've seen in the whole time I've been here, and that's a long time. It really hit them. It really laid it on the line!"

Miss Yantze took us back to the bowing spot. We dug our gear out of the bushes, and continued bowing north.

12 June To 1 July 1974. Heng Ju writes:

In Shelton, we foolishly left our backpack by the side of the road, and while we were not looking, someone stole it. It contained, among other things, our Daily Log book. We are missing all the entries since the Naselle Youth Camp. However, Yo and I have reconstructed that portion of the trip as best we can remember.

After Naselle, and the talk with the delinquent boys, we continued north along Highway 101, a narrow, twisting nightmare of a road that is heavily laden with fast-moving logging trucks. During this period we bowed every day.

Jim Gatens, an independent logger from Naselle, stopped on several occasions to discuss the Dharma, and helped us repair our ever-ailing cart. Because Yo sometimes has to hit the ditch in a hurry, we have installed roll bars around the wheels to protect them. The buggy is getting quite strong, since we get a new stick of metal welded on in just about every town we pass through. But the big 26-inch spoke wheels are still a little fragile for this kind of application. They can't take much side pressure, and so we have been popping and bending a few spokes. In South Bend we had to get a new rim.

We bowed for several days without incident, then near the little town of Arctic, the frame cracked on the buggy. Within minutes after the break, however, a man from Weyerhauser stopped and took us and the cart down to the big plant for repairs. When we got to the machine shop, all work came to a halt as six of Weyerhauser's machinists hovered around the little buggy, hammering, filing and welding away. Within minutes the buggy was brought to perfection, and we were delivered back to the "spot."

Where the Smith River intersects with Hwy 101, there is a long narrow bridge. Every few seconds a car or a big truck goes roaring across, leaving no way for pedestrians to get across. We sat by the bridge for over an hour not knowing what to do. We had finally given up all hope and were getting ready to risk walking across when a white Chevrolet stopped, and a big jolly logger, who must have weighed at least 300 pounds, popped out and said, "Say, can I give you fellas a lift across the bridge? Ho Ho Ho Ho!"

At Montesano, we turned off Highway 101, and headed inland. Sarah Tripp, one of Yo's old friends from the Zen days, came out from Portland with her daughter. She brought us some Mexican food and then stayed for a while and did some bowing.

It was a late sultry Saturday afternoon when we came prostrating our way in to the little town of Montesano. We had already done over six miles that day, but we didn't feel like stopping. Yo was a ways back talking to a group of farmers, and I was just approaching the city limits when I felt a strange feeling in my stomach. I looked

up ahead, and there, about a quarter mile in front of me at the end of a bridge, was a small group of people. As I drew closer, I could see that it was a bunch of drunken men. They were staggering all over the highway, yelling profanities, and pissing everywhere. "My God!" I thought, "A reception committee!" I kept bowing and noticed that Yo was catching up. This would be another time when submarine training would carry through into the spiritual world. "Now, rig ship for deep submergence. Rig ship for depth charges. Shut the water tight doors. Double up the hatches!" I kept bowing, and as I reached the southern end of the bridge, Yo was alongside. We bowed across the bridge together, and then at the very end, we couldn't go any further. There were six huge, drunken loggers standing directly in our path. The biggest one roared, "If you boys don't start explaining what you're doing, real fast, we're gonna chop your little cart into a million pieces!"

Now, in my heart, I knew that we weren't doing anything wrong. We had just as much right to that piece of earth as they did. But I could also see that this was not a question of human rights or justice. This was a question of saving our scrawny little necks. These guys had the faces of enraged bulls. Ordinarily, there are two ways a person can go in a situation like this. He can respond with fear, cower and change, and do whatever the opposition demands; or he can respond with anger and try to fight his way through the situation. These are the two natural tendencies of the human mind. But at that moment, the conditions must have been right; there was some kind of magic in the air. I recalled in a flash what the Master had told me earlier during a phone conversation in Oregon. I had told him that we were getting into the thick of logging country, and that things were sometimes pretty hairy. I asked him if it would be permissible for me to defend myself, if absolutely necessary. He replied instantly: "No! If you fight, you cannot consider yourself my disciple. You must learn to use your great intelligence. Under no circumstances may you fight. If you get into a situation where there is heavy opposition, contemplate your own heart. If you are without the slightest flicker of fear or anger, then no one will be able to touch you. For your entire trip, I will personally guarantee it! Simply do your work and maintain your precepts. What is there to be afraid of?"

I looked over at Yo. He seemed to have things under control. More than anything else, I was surprised by my own reaction to the whole scene. These teachings really worked! My mind was not moving. It was not only what the Master had said, but it was the way he had said it, with total authority, that made it all so powerful. There was just no doubt about it!

Immediately some of the loggers began to realize that something was not going quite the way they had planned. Yo and I were responding to their attacks with open, straightforward, and friendly answers. It completely knocked them off guard. Pretty soon they were arguing amongst themselves; some of them were still trying to provoke us, while the others were trying to invite us down to the local tavern for a few beers. One of them hollered, "Hey Jesse! These guys have their shit together more than you think!" Finally Yo said, "Well now, you gentlemen will have to excuse us. We've got some more miles to go." And on that note, I got down on my hands and knees, and bowed right through them with Yo alongside.

The next morning a car full of them came out and apologized.

After a couple of days we reached the small town of Satsop. It was like a county fair when we went through: almost the whole town was out to see us. Hordes of kids on bicycles, and their dogs with them, flanked us on both sides. It was one of the sunniest, happiest days of the trip.

The city of Elma was also a scene. Hundreds of folks out on the sidewalks. Some smiling, some frowning, some talking it over. There was every response imaginable, from total frustration to states of bliss. In the heart of town, the Ladies Auxiliary prepared us a lunch of clamless clam chowder (it was the only vegetarian dish they could think of). It was mostly made of corn and milk. We stopped inside and ate while many curious faces peered in the window.

Toward the end of town, we noticed that there was a boy about twelve years old who had been following us all day. We asked him what was up. He said that his name was Chris and that he would like to tag along and help us through these parts. We told him that we didn't need any help, but he insisted, so we let him tag along. For the next three or four days he would appear at the bowing spot, bright and early in the morning, and help Yo with gear, etc. At nightfall he would go up ahead and help Yo find a spot to set up camp. He gathered firewood and built us fires. He was a real quiet kid. Heng Yo transliterated his name into Chinese. "Chris" changed to *Ke Li Shr*: Able to Benefit the World.

We bowed through McCleary and on into Shelton, where our backpack was stolen. In the pack, besides the daily log, was Yo's rag robe, some sutras, our pocket camera, and our clothes and sleeping bags.

We received quite a bit of flack in Shelton. It is getting close to the Fourth of July, and there are a lot of young kids with firecrackers. We make a good target. Mr. and Mrs. Graham gave us a place to pitch our tent in their backyard.

2 July 1974. Heng Ju writes:

Despite the loss of the pack, we are doing OK. The Grahams gave us some crackers and blankets to take with us.

Paul Everett stopped to offer any help that he could. He told us about his practices doing Christian meditation. He said that every day he sits and recites, "My soul doth magnify the Lord." He said that it has really helped to round him out.

A nuclear submarine sailor from Bremerton shipyards stopped in his blue Austin-Healey. He was surprised to find out that I was also a submariner. He said that his boat stays down for sixty days at a time, leaving plenty of opportunities for contemplation, and lately many of the men are seriously studying Eastern religions and demanding vegetarian meals. Instead of acting like the wild sailors of the past, many are turning to meditation and self-discipline.

3 July 1974. Heng Yo writes:

We were in a turnout for a rest when a state highway maintenance truck stopped nearby. We could hear the radio crackle: "Hey, George, you looking for Henry? ... Right, where is he? ... He's over by the gurus; don't run them over!" Laughter.

The word has gotten out about our backpack being stolen. One headline explains it rhythmically: "Belfair Buddhist wants his backpack back." Heng Ju's folks live in Belfair.

After leaving Shelton, we made our final bow on U.S. 101 and headed east on State Highways 3 and 302. At Purdy, we will head south for about ten miles, cross the Tacoma Narrows bridge into Tacoma, and then head north to Seattle on Highway 99. We chose this route because it was the best way around Fort Lewis, the big military installation, through which there is only freeway. We are passing hundreds of small peninsulas and islands and inlets and estuaries which are part of Puget Sound. The road is extremely narrow and crooked, dotted with wooden houses along its edge.

Berries are becoming ripe just about everywhere. It's a real test of concentration power to walk by a luscious blackberry without plucking it, but it is well worth it to resist, because if one is not in control of unimportant situations, how can he hope to be in control of important ones?

4 July 1974. Heng Ju writes:

My family came out to the bowing area and picked us up. We spent the Independence Day holiday with them at our home in Belfair. My mother took quite a liking to Yo, and helped him make a bhikshu shirt on her sewing machine. My dad fixed us up with a backpack and two sleeping bags. Even though it rained the whole time we were there, it was wonderful to be with the folks again.

7 July 1974. Heng Ju writes:

After three days at my parents' cabin, we are now underway. We bowed through Allyn and headed east through Purdy. Newspaper and television crews have been visiting us constantly as we approach the Greater Seattle area. This Seattle passage is going to be heavy.

Of the hundreds of questions that we receive every day, one of them is: "Do we believe in God?" Well, before I can answer that, it is necessary to define what God is, since God is different things to different people. If we conceive of God as the all-pervasive principle which fills the universe, which includes the big and little, the good and bad, the true and false, and which dwells in the hearts of all beings regardless of what creed or lack of it they follow, then yes, I believe in God. But although this "God" is everywhere, few people really know him. In Buddhism, we learn to study and practice the teachings so that we may directly experience "God." Actually, the terms we use are quite different. The experience is called enlightenment. It is the result of a long career in good conduct, diligent study, and contemplation. It means that one experiences the totality and deathlessness of one's own nature.

But Buddhism does not claim to have a monopoly on God. We acknowledge that all religions have their uses and that there are many roads which branch onto the path of wisdom. Some are long, some are short, some will take countless lifetimes before they reach perfection. We have to have a view of salvation as taking place after many eons of work. We've all been through so much, and yet we have a lot to go through; there is no getting out of it. Since we are human beings, why do we want to spend our lives dreaming about heaven or hell? We must accept ourselves as we are, and learn to make the best out of the materials available. Whether we call ourselves Buddhists or Christians is secondary.

To know God, then, is simply to know oneself. When the spiritual traveler actually and truthfully walks the road, and subdues, matures, and opens his mind beyond all worldly limits, he may know "God." Then God becomes more than just an image, a concept, or a dream. God becomes reality.

8 July 1974. Heng Ju writes:

An Alfa Romeo roadster packed with young acne-faced girls stopped. They approached us en masse, all giggles and wiggles.

Finally one of them said, "We think what you are doing is really neat." (pause) "What are you doing anyway?" Giggle, giggle.

Bhikshuni Heng Yin's parents passed by, and we talked to her dad, Mr. Baur, who helped us fix a wheel on the buggy.

Channel Five from Seattle did a news story on us. The reporter, Robin Groth, expressed genuine interest in our practice and did a very thorough job of reporting. One of the questions she asked Yo, with a big camera focused right on his face, was "How come you guys are so laid back? I really feel calm talking with you."

"Good Lord!" I thought, "There are a million people watching. How is he ever going to answer a question like that?" I was glad she hadn't asked me that one. Yo winced ever so slightly and then calmly replied, "Well, I didn't notice it myself, but if we are that way, perhaps it's because we hold the precepts against killing, stealing, sexual misconduct, lying, and intoxicants." What a fine reply!

Sam McCoy presented us with a statue of a white bird in flight and said, "You boys have touched my heart."

9 July 1974. Heng Yo writes:

Today we arrived at Purdy, where we leave the smaller, winding road for a larger, straight highway into Tacoma. Now that we know that Marblemount will be the future site of a monastery, we want to bow the extra 125 miles beyond Seattle to give our pilgrimage an auspicious ending.

Bob and Joanie Kurtis, old family friends of Heng Ju's from Gig Harbor, took us in for the night. Bob thought that leaving the home life to become a bhikshu meant that we were automatically afforded the opportunity to retire from the world and sequester ourselves somewhere with plenty of material to read and study. At Gold Mountain, this is not necessarily the case. The life of a bhikshu is devoted to teaching people how to attain enlightenment, based on self-cultivation according to the principles set forth by the Buddha. This means that a bhikshu does not desert other people. In addition to the duties of all those who live in a community situation, a monk is expected to be a model for others. He must be upright in conduct, speech and thought, so that others may be favorably influenced. He is also expected to explain the sutras to all those who request instruction. There is at least one formal lecture at Gold Mountain every day. Because of these and other responsibilities, a bhikshu is very much in the world, not retired or withdrawn. In this way, he can function in the mundane world without becoming attached, repelled, or otherwise moved by the matrix of forces and data which constantly bombard the senses.

I told Bob that when we were in the process of building Gold Mountain, Heng Ju asked the Master if he could put his desk in the storeroom where he would not be bothered. The world of ringing telephones, doorbells, visitors, and crying babies would not impinge upon the quietness of the storeroom. But permission was denied, and the desk was put in an already-cramped office. In this way, Ju could be in a situation to develop his concentration power by remaining unmoved in the swiftest currents and forces, instead of retreating from the world.

Later, Bob told us an old Indian proverb: If you can see Mt. Rainier, then it is going to rain; if you can't see it, it is already raining.

10 July 1974. Heng Ju writes:

As we approached the entrance to the Narrows Bridge, we were approached by four members of the Nichirin Shoshu movement. The oldest one, whose brothers both served with me on the submarine Rock, was named Harold Waller. He casually swaggered up to me, took a long pull on his cigarette, blew the smoke right in my face, and said, "Tim, let me tell you about real Buddhism!"

We tried talking with them, but it was to no avail. They were intent on making us give up our ascetic practices, se we finally started bowing again. Shortly thereafter, Balwant Nevaskar, a teacher of Sociology at the University of Puget Sound, picked us up and took us to his home in Tacoma. During the course of a most warm and enjoyable evening, Dr. Nevaskar invited some of his colleagues over and we all discussed the Dharma. Amongst them was John Magee, who invited us to speak to his philosophy class tomorrow.

Dr. Nevaskar, who is a native of India, was thrilled to see that Buddhism was taking root in this country, and he was one of the very few people we have met on the entire trip who knew the word "bhikshu." His small son Raja (King) was busy climbing all over the furniture with a backpack on, in imitation of Heng Yo.

11 July 1974. Heng Yo writes:

We had a very interesting morning at the University of Puget Sound with Dr. Magee's philosophy class. Ju explained a verse from the Sixth Patriarch Sutra, and I talked about Chan meditation. Using one of my favorite analogies, I explained that when the mind is focused in meditation, it becomes like the coherent light of the laser, which can be used to penetrate almost anything. The idea is to break through one's rings of ignorance, greed, hatred, stupidity and arrogance, until one finally becomes enlightened. This goal is reached by one's own efforts alone, and does not rely on anything external.

One of the students asked if special abilities accrue to one who is enlightened. I answered that there are six spiritual powers traditionally mentioned in regard to one who has met with success in his cultivation of the Way. They are: the Heavenly Eye, the Heavenly Ear, the ability to know past lives, the ability to know others' thoughts, the extinction of outflows, and penetration of the spiritual realm. The student then asked if I believed that these were real powers and abilities, or were just some kind of metaphysical building-block of Buddhist cosmology. I told him about a time a few years ago at the monastery, just after I became a novice monk. A large meeting of all the monks and lay people was being held, and the topic under discussion was a forthcoming trip to Canada to open a new temple and explain the Dharma. I was disappointed to hear that I was to remain at Gold Mountain instead of going along. I thought how wonderful it would be to travel with the Master. Not one minute later, out of context in regard to the topic under discussion, the Master looked right at me and seemingly through me, and said, "Kuo Tao, someday, when you learn what you are supposed to learn, and understand how to follow the rules, I will take you along with me." I was flabbergasted, my mouth dropped open, and my face was burning up. How did he know what I was thinking?

The class laughed at the story, and I said that they would have to make up their own minds about whether or not to believe that a sage can know the thoughts of others. But for me, it was another occasion on which this fact was proven.

Afterward, Professor Nevaskar bought Ju a new pair of Converse tennis shoes, and insisted that we stay the night at his home. It was pouring rain.

12 July 1974. Heng Ju writes:

Today we bowed through metropolitan Tacoma. Here and there large crowds would gather and ask questions: "What are you doing? Where are you going? What does the three steps signify? Do you take turns pulling the cart? Do you know gong fu? Can we take your picture?" Methodists, Baptists, ministers and laypeople, blacks and whites, all came out to offer their opinions or wish us luck. Mostly the latter. As we approached the thick of the downtown area, a woman, who must have been in her late sixties, came up to Yo and told him that she had come to lead us through town. She said that God had sent her "to guide us through Tacoma." And that's exactly what she did. Not only that, but early in the day, a chubby barefoot lad resembling Huckleberry Finn offered his services, and without another word, pulled the buggy all the way through town.

In the late afternoon, when we had made it through downtown and were bowing out through the flat, industrial harbor area, we experienced a really close call. About a half a block away, I happened to notice a man come out of a tavern with a case of beer under his arm. He got into a red 1960 Pontiac convertible, and spinning his tires, came roaring out of the parking lot. He turned around a corner and came squealing out onto the main road. Then, with his engine racing wildly, he accelerated in our direction. We were standing together on the curb. He was doing about fifty miles an hour as he approached us, when suddenly he cranked over on his steering wheel and jumped up onto the curb. He was going to mow us down! It all happened so fast that there wasn't time to think or move, or anything. We could only stand there and watch it happen. The red streak missed my leg by something like four to six inches. Then, just as suddenly as he appeared, he was gone.

Once again, I was amazed by my own reactions and Yo's, too. There was no fear. The event was empty. It was like watching a scene from a television show. There just didn't seem to be anything going on at all. Some people from the tavern came out and asked us if we were all right. We said yes. They had taken up a collection for us, and invited us into the tavern to say a few words.

Halfway through the mudflats area, we made camp under a bridge. Windy night, crackling fire, sitting in Chan.

13 July 1974. Heng Yo writes:

Screech! Crash! We were awakened by the sound of a car careening into the bridge rail above us. The driver had apparently been asleep or drunk at the wheel. He totaled out his new car, but escaped with minor injuries. Later on, two policemen gave us funny looks as we bowed by the wreck. They probably thought we had something to do with it.

Later in the day, as we bowed up the long hill out of Tacoma, Heng Ju's aunt Sister Mary Agnes, a Dominican nun, paid us a visit. She was glad to see Ju. We talked for a while and she described how her order is rapidly diminishing in numbers. The schools and convents are closing down, she said, and the nuns are forced by circumstance to go out in the world and work at secular jobs and wear ordinary clothes rather than teach in the parochial schools as they used to.

Mark Tatz, a professor at the University of Washington, and a couple of his friends, brought us some food and then we all sat down by the side of the road and talked about Buddhism.

14 July 1974. Heng Ju writes:

We are now passing through Federal Way, which is located halfway between Tacoma and Seattle. It's very hot outside. Yo found a weeping willow tree standing alone out here amongst this suburban jungle and crawled beneath its branches to find a very cool place to fix lunch. From within, we could see everything that was going on around us, but no one could see in. What a wonderful thing a weeping willow is!

I set up the stove and prepared lunch. First I cooked the pinto beans which had been soaking all night. To them I added chili and cheese and salt. Then I made some hot grilled cheese sandwiches. Not bad!

One of my old grade school buddies, Jimmy McCunn, stopped to rap for a while. He said that another friend of ours is now a Catholic priest, Father Mike Batterberry, and he's got his whole congregation praying for us!

In the evening, my brother Terry picked us up and took us to his home in Kent. Terry is three years younger than I. He works for a pump company. He installed a lifetime-guaranteed water pump on the buggy, which hand-pumps water out of our two-and-a-half gallon plastic water tank.

15-25 July 1974. Heng Yo writes:

We arrived in Seattle on July 15, and stopped bowing for a few days in order to help prepare for the Gathering for World Peace. Members of the Sino-American Buddhist Association had already been congregating in the Seattle area for the event. Dharma Masters Heng Kuan and Heng Kung were in the midst of an eighteen-day fast for world peace. On Saturday, July 20, the good old sun came out, bringing one of the most beautiful days Seattle had had in a long time.

In the morning, we all gathered in Seward Park, where several hundred spectators joined the monks, nuns, and laypeople in chanting mantras for world peace. After a vegetarian lunch for all participants, the Master, the monks and nuns, and members of the lay community of Gold Mountain gave speeches. The Consul from the Republic of China and Dr. Magee of the University of Puget Sound also addressed the gathering. It was a great success.

Afterward, we accepted an invitation by the Far East Department of the University of Washington and remained for three days to give instructional talks. Then, on the last day of their stay, members of the Sino-American Buddhist Association and the Bodhi Dharma Center of Seattle met and discussed plans for building a monastery at Marblemount.

On Monday, we began bowing again, working our way through the streets of Seattle. In the evening, Ju's cousins, the Works, stopped by to say hello, and his old friend Pete Preusser took us in for the night.

26 July 1974. Heng Yo writes:

Pete is happily married and lives in an elegant house overlooking Puget Sound. He is an engineer for General Electric. After Ju and Pete talked about old times, the discussion turned philosophical. Pete has a graphic explanation of infinity: he says that it is just space without any limits, and any attempt to define it is like trying to put a wall around this empty space. A wall has two sides, of course, and thus infinity is really not definable, because there always exists that which is not included by the wall, which is left out of the definition.

Our Buddha-nature is also like space: pure, clear, unobstructed; able to contain everything. Idle thoughts and discriminations are like a wall we construct which limits the realization of our Buddha-nature, because there is always that which is left on the other side of the wall. This is why the sages say that the Buddha-nature is to be realized, not merely discussed.

Ju and Pete grew up in the same neighborhood, went to the same schools and so forth, but now they are operating in different worlds.

27 July 1974. Heng Yo writes:

This is the longest built-up, urban area we will pass through. It looks like there are 60 to 70 miles of town for us to bow through.

Before now, I had more trouble bowing in the towns and cities than on the open road. But now I know that bowing in front of factories, houses, and stores all day is just the same as bowing next to trees and bridges. My apprehension was based on the idea that more people would confront us in the cities, but I've come to see that it just doesn't matter. If we are all from the same source, then who is bowing and who is confronting? As a matter of fact, it seems easier to become concentrated in populated areas like these.

Tonight we are camped in a big gravel parking lot full of large semi-trailers in the middle of Seattle. The ground was too hard to take a tent stake, so we just climbed into one of the empty rigs. In the middle of the lot was a large, out-of-place blackberry patch smothering an old fence. The berries were ripe to perfection, so we picked a couple of quarts for tomorrow's lunch.

28 July 1974. Heng Yo writes:

Progress has been relatively slow these last few days because so many of Ju's friends and relatives have heard that he is back in town, and they are all coming out to say hello. One was a road worker who popped out of a ditch he was digging to say hello as Ju bowed by, and another was so eager to convert us to Christianity on the spot that he got a ticket for making an illegal U-turn when he saw us. And through all of it, mile after dusty mile, Ju takes three giant steps with his palms together, makes a bow, gets up, and does it again. One, two, three, bow. One, two, three, bow. After all this time, it still amazes me.

29 July 1974. Heng Yo writes:

After bowing on Route 99 through Seattle, we headed through Bothell onto Highway 9, crossing the King-Snohomish County line. As we bowed along today, Upasika and Upasaka Pong drove up. Dedicated Buddhists for many years, they have established the Bodhi Dharma Center in West Seattle, and they are the ones who have donated the land in Marblemount. They invited us for lunch at their house, so we stashed the gear, and took a welcome break from the hot sun and dusty road.

Tonight we are camped off the road in a small clearing. It is very dark and silent. A myriad images rush through my head: the disciples of Maharaji who talked to us today; the portly Christian who "wanted to recruit" us; the little blond boy in the back of an old blue Falcon who couldn't stop staring. But there is something more important which I've just now remembered. It happened during the recitation of mantras at the Gathering for World Peace in Seattle. We were seated on the stage. After a few minutes of recitation, the Master motioned to me to look up. I was surprised to see that out of a clear blue sky, a strange-looking cloud had floated over the amphitheatre. It was long and narrow, and it just hung over everyone for about twenty minutes. When the recitation ended, the cloud dissipated without a trace. I wonder if the others saw it as well?

30 July 1974. Heng Ju writes:

Uncountable number of people have stopped to query us today. The weather has been good lately, and we have been making steady progress. One of the things that every cultivator of the Way must learn to deal with is anger. Of all the emotions, this is probably the worst, and we here on the bowing trip do not escape from it. On days when the going gets rough, anger can arise easily. Everyone has this tendency; it's how it is dealt with that's important.

The fire of anger is a primal urge which runs deep. It lies dormant below the intellect like the latent fire in a piece of wood. When it is sparked off, it colors all of our thoughts and views. It is like seeing through a red lens. When we are really angry at someone, it doesn't matter how much good he does; it all seems wrong. And once this powerful emotion becomes lodged in consciousness, it can be difficult to remove.

Just the other day, we saw an old woman who looked like she just plain hated everything. Her scowl had become a permanent feature of her face. Sometimes when I am bowing across intersections, I may hold up traffic for a minute or two, and it's unbelievable how

mad some of those drivers can get. They lay all over their horns, and look like they would like to kill me. Everyone has this ability to explode in rage. The root of the problem is that we have deep views of a self. When our views or desires get tampered with or obstructed we get angry. Today, modern psychology offers many sophisticated solutions to this problem, but the only real solution, and the one which doesn't cost $90 an hour to find out about, is patience. The character for patience in Chinese is a picture of a heart with a knife above it. Patience is a very rare and wonderful quality which can be perfected to an infinite degree. It is a quality found in sages, developed throughout lifetimes of work in the field of self-mastery.

About this problem the Master often says, "To endure suffering is to end suffering." This means we must bear it; when everything doesn't go the way we would like it to go, we must keep our cool. By patiently enduring difficulties, we forge a solid and indestructible character. By blowing our tops, we create hell.

Speaking of hell, I have come up with something to endure. I thought it would have happened long ago, but finally it has happened. I have developed a large swelling under my left kneecap. I don't know how long we can continue with it—it seems to be getting worse all of the time.

We are camped in a vacant lot off of the highway.

31 July 1974. Heng Ju writes:

We made a few miles this morning, but the knee is swelling bigger and looks as if it is getting infected. It's all purple and yellow. I called up my old high school friend Jon Myers. We went into the Navy together, and now he is a color television repairman for R.C.A. in the north end of Seattle. He came out here to Bothell Way and picked us up, and hearing about my leg, told us we should stay at his home until it is healed. It has been over five years since I've seen Jon.

1 – 4 August 1974. Heng Ju writes:

We spent the last three days at Jon's house. Although I have been soaking the knee every night, the swelling hasn't gone down. In my estimation it looks as if it will take two weeks or more to heal, considering, of course, that no bowing is done on it. In Buddhism, this is known as a karmic obstacle.

5 August 1974. Heng Ju writes:

Today we finally decided to seek the Master's advice. I called the temple and asked him what the best cure would be. I explained how my knee was swollen, how it would take a long time to heal, and how bowing would only make it worse.

The Master did not hesitate in his reply, "Basically, there is no problem. The best cure for your knee is to get out there and finish your bowing."

I was stunned by his answer. If it had been anybody else, I would have argued. But Yo and I packed up the gear, said goodbye to Jon, and got out there on Highway 9 where we had left off, just north of Bothell. I started bowing, and was surprised to find that there was no pain! I continued bowing and got in four miles before the day was over. The swelling had gone down. It was nothing short of a miracle.

6 August 1974. Heng Ju writes:

Our plan is to continue north on Highway 9 until we reach Sedro Woolley; then we will turn east and follow Highway 20 for 45 miles alongside the Skagit River to Marblemount. A passing motorist yelled, "Stand up and walk like a man!"

The Washington State Patrol stopped to rap and gave us some stewed raspberries.

A man by the name of Roland Strandell stopped on his big Moto-Guzzi motorcycle. He said that he had been studying Eastern religions for thirty years, and had been waiting to see something like this. He wrote a poem entitled "Harmony."

> *The vehicles pound the road*
> > *with a many minded drum beat,*
> *Echoing discordance through all*
> > *living creatures.*
> *Then the gentle flutter*
> > *of saffron robes*
> > *in the wind,*
> *And all the noise of creation*
> > *is muted by*
> > *the quiet thunder of Buddha.*

We stayed in the home of Goldie and Lynn Goldhammer, a very friendly, back-to-earth couple (he drives a dump truck) who lives near Arlington.

7 August 1974. Heng Ju writes:

We have reached Arlington, and the end of the trip is rapidly approaching. Looking at the maps, I remember the doubts and fears that haunted us earlier. They are gone now, and unless something very unusual takes place, it appears that we will make it.

During the first part of the trip I remember the butterflies I used to get at the thought of going out and facing all those people. I felt a need to try to explain myself to everyone. I could see by the disapproving looks on many of their faces that they did not like either me or what I was doing. Not only the bowing but the mere appearance of a monk with a shaven head was enough to set off a lot of scowls.

Things have changed quite a bit as we have worked our way north. The news media has played a great part in explaining to the people what's going on. People seem to know us already, having read about us for months preceding our arrival. They treat us like long-lost relatives, and the few that do scowl now we just don't pay any attention to.

8 August 1974. Heng Yo writes:

We were bowing along as usual today, when a man and a woman in a Toyota stopped to watch us pass slowly by. Then driving ahead about half a mile, they waited for us again, this time getting out and introducing themselves. They were friendly and respectful, and asked about our trip, and about Buddhism in general. Learning that Buddhist monks practice certain beneficial austerities—such as eating only one meal a day, and not lying down to sleep—the man, Bill, said that he thought these practices were too difficult for the average layman.

I told him that there are gradated rules and optional ascetic practices for both monks and laypeople which may seem impossible to follow at the outset. It's like climbing a mountain which is difficult at the beginning, but becomes easier the further you go. Nobody except Superman can leap from the bottom to the top of the mountain, so our progress must be step by step. It is easy to become discouraged, thinking, "I've been practicing so long and nothing has happened." But if something is easy, the result is not likely to be worth much, because anyone could do it. The difficulty can serve as a screen, filtering out those who are not truly determined to make it. Yes, it may be difficult, but we should not always try to get off easily, looking for an existential bargain.

I must have gotten a little carried away, and Bill said he'd have to think about it.

Later on, a big burly man stopped, got out of his pickup, and asked if we wanted some fresh pizzas. I tried to figure out how to be polite to him, thinking that they probably had meat and onions on them. "Yup", he said, "Brought them all the way from Yakima." The bag was opened, and lo and behold, a dozen fresh peaches! The man was a little soused and had slurred his words a bit.

9 August 1974. Heng Ju writes:

Near Bryant, a small boy named Byron walked with us today. He told us that when he saw our picture in the Everett Herald, he stared at it for about an hour; he didn't know why. Byron took care of us for the day. Being the local Huck Finn, he knew all the good spots. When we got to a certain bend in the road, he led us inland to one of the most beautiful swimming holes that I have ever seen. And I've seen a few. We took a long break and bathed our dusty bodies.

In the afternoon, a very long-haired man who called himself "Mr. Freedom Love" asked me what in God's name I was doing. After I explained, he told me that none of this was necessary. He said that God is love, and that it is all very simple: God is here, now, and that is all there is to it. He invited me to come and live on his farm.

10 August 1974. Heng Ju writes:

Kate Myers, whom I had once dated in high school, and who is Jon Myers' little sister, happened to stop by. She now has a husband, two kids, and a jeep. All I have now is a sore knee, and even that is going away. Things do change.

As we bowed past Big Lake, the owner of the local tavern came out to talk. He was real friendly; however, his customers, who were pretty well smashed, came out into the street and began mocking him. Imitating Yo, they put a sleeping bag in a little shopping cart and set to pulling it around the parking lot of the tavern. One of them yelled, "Hey Roy! You forgot your cart." Roy didn't pay any attention to them.

My knee has just about recovered now as we continue bowing into the Skagit Delta area. Mt. Baker looms ahead of us to the east, and the Olympics stand out to the west. As we pass by, the friendly folks say, "It won't be long now."

11 August 1974. Heng Yo writes:

Last night, we were just about gobbled up by 84,000 voracious, blood-sucking mosquitos. The tent has served to keep the water off us during the rains, and now its mosquito netting is the frail difference between a decent night's rest and the sheer insanity of having several of those creatures relentlessly buzzing our ears and tapping our veins.

Lately, we've been eating up the highway at the rate of seven or eight miles per day. We passed through Clear Lake, then over the Skagit River, and on into the town of Sedro Woolley, where we will pick up Highway 20 to Marblemount. As we approached Sedro Woolley on a long, flat stretch of road, scores of people stopped to congratulate us, donate food, or just look and take pictures. It was almost like homecoming week—we must have talked to hundreds of people today alone, and thousands since we've been in this county. The folks here are simple, hard-working people: farmers, loggers, and merchants, and most all of them seem to be solidly behind us.

We finally pulled into the town park at dusk and set up the tent. I looked at the cart which was laden with apples, bread, and garden-fresh carrots with their greens spilling over the side. These people may not know much about Buddhism, but it is clear that in their own ways, they are aware that our trip is a good thing, a positive thing. Perhaps it is this knowledge which really helped me out during the most discouraging parts of the trip. You could call it any number of things, but gratitude fits best: gratitude for the chance to make this journey; for the Master's expert guidance; for the chance to share the teachings of the Buddha with others; for the chance to learn how to deal with others by learning how to deal with myself; for the chance to practice with a good companion; and for everything, good and bad, which has happened.

12 August 1974. Heng Ju writes:

Today we turned off of Highway 9 and onto Highway 20. The Master has often said, "There are always two roads before you: one is enlightenment, the other is confusion." The idea of having a crossroad in front of us is not new. It is the age-old choice of doing right or wrong, good or evil. Sometimes, however, there doesn't appear to be a choice. Sometimes we reach a point in cultivation when there isn't any road at all in front of us. On the one hand, we've left behind all of what made up our lives: our families, friends, jobs, pleasures, and everything, in search of the ultimate. On the other hand, we have not reached the ultimate and are still basically common people. We get caught in no-man's land, halfway between the two. We've left the "world" but have not yet reached "the other shore." This is a difficult passage. There can be a tremendous pull to return to a "normal life." The world beckons with her vast array of sensual delights. The passions, now amplified with concentration power, surge up stronger than ever. The mind, that is to say, the self-mind, makes a strong bid to redeem itself. It wants to go back to the world and outline its identity. It doesn't want to let go. With a little bit of cultivation behind us, we awaken all kinds of latent talents and powers. We find that we are capable of doing all kinds of things. We find that we can apply ourselves in almost any direction, and truly succeed.

But this is not the ultimate goal. There is much more to Buddhist practice; there is much more to the practice of a monk. We must go on. This is only a stage in cultivation. This is the time to pick up our resolve and not forget our original goal. We want to transcend the cycle of birth and death. We want to become Buddhas. We want to separate from the dust. Therefore, we must have patience and continue onward.

13 August 1974. Heng Yo writes:

This North Cross Highway runs through the fertile Skagit Valley through the Cascade Mountains to Omak, and its lanes are filled with screaming logging rigs, campers, bicycles, and many cars. It is hot and dusty.

Off the road, Ju discovered a recently killed deer—someone had ripped off the top and back of his head just to get the horns. It was a sight I'll never forget. What makes people act so violently?

As we bowed through Lyman, and later Hamilton, there were a few snide comments by some of the local people. This was nothing unusual, but it started me thinking about the causes and conditions which bring about such actions, and about why that deer, which has been etched into my memory, met such a violent death. Perhaps the seeds of actions done in the past are coming to fruition. Bob Dylan said it very well in a song:

Oh, every foe who ever I faced,
The cause was there before we came.

14 August 1974. Heng Ju writes:

We bowed eight and a half miles, passing the town of Concrete. The summer heat is really bearing down on us and our skin is getting very dark. The intense heat also seems to relate to anger, as lately Yo and I seem to get irritated by the smallest things. Sometimes we get mad at each other without even knowing why. There is one thing that always makes me mad, and that is when I sense that he is trying to squeeze more mileage out of me. I may be imagining it, but I don't think so. Sometimes he will go farther up ahead than I would like him to, and then I have to bow that much farther before I can rest. Especially around lunch time, that last stretch before we eat is always a super-long one. I keep bowing and bowing and he keeps going way, way up ahead. I cannot help but think about the story of the man who dangled the carrot in front of the donkey. And it makes me furious.

Of course, when I get even the slightest bit mad, Yo picks up on it, even if I don't say anything. Then the whole trip turns sour, and he enters the Pisces blues. It is an interesting karmic obstruction to try to work through. The both of us, being so close together for so long, have many places where our minds overlap and interpenetrate. Often I cannot distinguish where his afflictions end and mine begin. The same is true of our joys. But in either case it makes for excellent contemplation.

As Bodhidharma said, "Enlightenment is just affliction, and affliction is just enlightenment." Of course, Bodhidharma saying it and our understanding it are often two different things. When Bodhidharma came into China from India and explained the Dharma in that manner, few people believed it. Even fewer understood it. Just where does affliction come from? Who is experiencing it? Where is the actual place of anger? There is ample time while bowing to consider these and other points, and to investigate the illusory boundaries of the human consciousness. But sometimes, when the afflictions just won't seem to go away, we stop the bowing and sit down and mix up some instant tea with sugar and fresh lemon. Although it is strictly an expedient worldly dharma, it works quite well.

15 August 1974. Heng Ju writes:

Another one of those hot, dusty days. Heavy traffic, logging trucks, and affliction everywhere. We bowed along Highway 20 into the little town of Van Horn. The Olsons, who own the general store and gas station, invited us in for a cool pop. There was a lot of activity around the place; these folks had been hearing about us for months. Kids and dogs were milling around everywhere. At one point, I noticed an old man, short, bearded, and bespectacled, wandering around outside the station. He was talking to the kids, and although I don't think he had ever been there before, he behaved like he was old friends with everyone. He had a white truck with a home-made trailer behind it, and two dogs that he was trying to give away. I was taken aback when he walked up to me and asked me if I called myself a Buddhist. I noticed that he was totally relaxed and centered.

"Why, ahh, ahh, yes." I replied, wondering what he was getting at.

"Do you want to hear what the Buddha taught in plain English?" he asked. I didn't want to say no, because that wouldn't be right. And I didn't want to say yes, because that would imply that I didn't already know. I looked around and there was a small crowd gathering. He had a mischievous gleam in his eye.

"What did the Buddha teach?" I finally said.

"The Buddha taught compassion. The Buddha said that we should stop knocking each other around, but most people don't buy it!"

I was sure this little man could see right through me, but I quickly replied, "Buy what?"

"What the Buddha taught!" laughed the little man. "I don't think that you are a complete convert," he said.

Boy, he was really putting me on the spot! "I didn't say I was perfect," I replied. I had shifted totally into my own defense. The little man paused, and then he moved closer and looked right into my eyes. I was beginning to steadily flash on how angry I had become toward Heng Yo during the last few weeks.

"The Buddha taught compassion. Be more compassionate!" he said.

Then he took off his glasses and stuck his face up about twelve inches in front of mine. "I'm not your enemy, I'm your friend. How many people do you know who would talk to you like this?"

By this time I was completely overwhelmed, not to mention embarrassed. I had never seen this guy before, yet he had zeroed right in on my number as if I was transparent. All the people were looking at me. Everything was quiet, and I was absolutely speechless. I didn't know what to do or say, so I went back out on the road and continued bowing. Only afterward did I begin to realize just how miraculous an encounter it was. Just as the Master had often done, this man was talking right through my false front, directly to my attachments. As I bowed along, I began to feel a sense of shame that I hadn't felt in a long time. I really had been mean to Yo in many, many ways. Most of the time it was very indirect and subtle: nevertheless, it was always very irritating. I felt terrible about it. I recalled a verse that the Master once wrote:

Truly recognize your own faults,
Don't discuss the faults of others.
Others' faults are just your own.
Being one substance with everyone
Is called the Great Compassion.

I scurried down the highway until I reached the spot where Yo was waiting with the cart. He had missed my little encounter with the old man, so I told him what had happened. We sat down and mixed up some lemonade powder with some fresh Skagit River water. I looked at him directly for the first time in a long time. For a short moment, we shared a smile of silent understanding. I felt old, old, old. Then we both got up and continued on.

16 August 1974. Heng Ju writes:

We made another eight and a half miles and are now camped past Rockport. We should make it into Marblemount tomorrow. We reported our progress to the Master on the phone.

"Good. Very good!" he said. "Would you like to go to Hong Kong, Taiwan, Singapore, Japan, India, Nepal, Ceylon, and Vietnam on a Dharma tour? We'll be giving talks and also going to visit some of the places where the Buddha lived." His voice crackled over the wires.

I was floored. "Yes, yes, we would love to go!"

"Traveling with me is a lot of suffering. Are you sure you want to go?" the Master said.

"Yes, I'm sure," I replied.

"Okay. If you're really not afraid of suffering, then when you get back here, we'll get ready and go."

Dennis Ammons, a resident of Hamilton, has been watching over us on this section of road. He parks his little green pickup truck ahead half a mile and waits for us to come along. When we get up close to him, he gets out, struts over puffing on his cigar, and, snapping his rainbow-colored suspenders, asks us what's up. "Don't want to miss none of the doin's," he says. Then he goes up ahead and waits some more.

Howard Miller, a county commissioner, came out to take our picture. Many other friendly folks gave us their welcome. They tell us that the Indians have a saying for these parts: "Once you drink water from this Skagit River, it's for certain you will someday return." We've been drinking it for days.

Letter from an observer
August 16, 1974

Dear Sirs:

On August 5 I had the privilege of meeting two monks from your monastery on Highway 9 between Lake Stevens and Arlington, Washington. I have forgotten their names; however, one was pulling a cart and the other had been kneeling and bowing every third step on their journey from San Francisco.

It was a very moving experience to see and talk with these two men who reflected serenity along the busy highway. I have enclosed a short poem I composed about the experience.

HARMONY
August 6, 1974
(On Seeing Two Buddhist Monks on the Road)

The vehicles pound the road with a many-minded drumbeat
Echoing discordance through all living creatures.
Then the gentle flutter of saffron robes in the wind.
And all the noise of creation is muted by
The quiet thunder of Buddha.

Respectfully,
Rowland Strandell

17 August 1974. Heng Yo writes:

Last night I heard a yell coming out of the sleeping Heng Ju. "Hey, there's monsters under this freeway!" he called out in a loud and clear voice. After he woke up, he told me that he had dreamed he was picking up the road, just as if it were a piece of rug, and beneath it were myriads of demonic-looking creatures.

We got up early and bowed through the little town of Marblemount before many people were up, and continued three miles to the monastery site without stopping to rest. The excitement was high, and we reached the property at 10:30 a.m. Ju made his final bow. We ended the trip by reciting the Great Compassion Mantra several times and transferring any merit we may have acquired to living beings everywhere. Then we had lunch on a big rock bank with the Skagit River flowing rapidly below us.

At the end of the day, we went up to the top of Sauk Mountain, where there is an unbelievably awesome view of the whole Skagit Valley and of the last 45 miles we had bowed. The sun was just beginning to set as we reached the summit at 5,500 feet. Oceans of pink and blue clouds were rolling in over the delta like giant puffs of cotton candy. We were surrounded by hundreds of giant mountains, all drenched in numberless shades of orange and purple. Mt. Baker loomed in front of us in deep samadhi. The stars were beginning to appear. Suddenly we noticed a strange light on the horizon. One minute it looked like a crescent, the next minute like a bouncing ball. It appeared and disappeared several times, then suddenly got very bright, and shot off like a ball of fire. To the left of it, we noticed a huge black and grey cloud formation perhaps 100 miles in length, which took the unmistakable form of a fire-breathing dragon. It looked like it was chasing the ball of light. Then darkness came, and with it, all of the rain which had been storing up for the last few weeks. It broke loose in the biggest torrent we had seen in a long time. I looked up in sheer wonder as the storm blew in.

The trip was over!

On May 7, 1977, Heng Sure[8] and Heng Chao,[9] two other bhikshus of Gold Mountain Monastery, began a second bowing pilgrimage from Gold Wheel Monastery in Los Angeles to the City of Ten Thousand Buddhas in Ukiah Valley, 110 miles north of San Francisco. They completed their two-and-a-half-year trip up the coast of California on October 17, 1979. Their journey is recorded in the eight-volume series *Journals & Letters on a Bowing Pilgrimage* (2007). Excerpts of their letters to Tripitaka Master Hua are recorded in the book *Highway Dharma Letters: Two Buddhist Pilgrims Write Letters to Their Teacher* (October, 2014).

Notes

1. The current Gold Mountain Monastery is located in the center of San Francisco Chinatown at 800 Sacramento Street.

2. Dr. Ronald Epstein, Ph.D., has taught at San Francisco State University. He is also Professor Emeritus and Chancellor Emeritus at Dharma Realm Buddhist University (DRBU) and author of the book, *Buddhism A to Z* published by the Buddhist Text Translation Society (www.buddhisttexts.org). He recently published a book called *Responsible Living: Explorations in Applied Buddhist Ethics — Animals, Environment, GMOs, Digital Media*, a collection of exploratory essays that uses applied Buddhist ethics to address modern issues.

3. Gwo Jou (David) Rounds was the editor (2001–2010) of *Religion East and West* published by Dharma Realm Buddhist University (www.drbu.edu), founded by Tripitaka Master Hua. He also edited *The Śūraṅgama Sūtra: A New Translation* (2009).

4. Gwo Hwei is now Bhikshu Heng Lai, President of *Vajra Bodhi Sea: A Monthly Journal of Orthodox Buddhism* published by the Dharma Realm Buddhist Association (www.drba.org). He currently manages Snow Mountain Monastery in Index, Washington.

5. The *Avatamsaka Sutra* is also known as the *Flower Adornment Sutra* or the "King of Kings" of Buddhist scriptures because of its profundity and great length with more than 700,000 Chinese characters. This sutra contains the most complete explanation of the Buddha's realization and the 52 steps in a cultivator's quest for awakening. With detailed explanations of every stage of the Bodhisattva Path, it is the ultimate handbook imparting valuable tools and methods of practical cultivation for monks, nuns and lay people seeking spiritual guidance.

6. Confucius saying translated by James Legge in The Four Books, Book VI, Chapter XXII.

7. Buddhist Text Translation Society has published three editions of the *Shurangama Sutra*
   a) *Shurangama Sutra* in eight volumes with commentary (1979), primary translation by Bhikshuni Heng Chih
   b) *Shurangama Sutra*, 9 volumes, revised edition with commentary (2003)
   c) *The Śūraṅgama Sūtra: A New Translation*, (2009), single volume edition, edited by Ronald Epstein, Ph.D. and David Rounds
   d) E-book (2012) available for free download at http://www.buddhisttexts.org/surangama.html

8. Rev. Heng Sure, Ph.D., is Director of the Berkeley Buddhist Monastery. He teaches at the Institute for World Religions. He has taught at Dharma Realm Buddhist University, at Graduate Theology Union (GTU) in Berkeley, and at Bond University in Australia. He lectures on the *Avatamsaka Sutra* and other sutras. He currently leads a team to translate the *Avatamsaka Sutra*. He is actively involved in interfaith dialogue and in the ongoing conversation between spirituality and technology.

9. The former Bhikshu Heng Chao is Dr. Martin Verhoeven. He is currently Dean of Academics and Professor of Buddhist Classics at Dharma Realm Buddhist University. He was as an adjunct professor of Comparative Religion at the Graduate Theological Union in Berkeley from 1997 to 2016. He lectures weekly on the Sixth Patriarch's Jeweled Platform Sutra and conducts a meditation class.

Glossary

Bhikshu.

One who has received the 250 precepts of a Buddhist monk.

Bhikshuni.

One who has received the 348 precepts of a Buddhist nun.

Bodhisattva.

An enlightened one among living beings who causes others to become enlightened. A Bodhisattva perfects the virtues of giving, morality, patience, vigor, meditation, and wisdom in order to become a Buddha.

Buddha.

One who is greatly enlightened. A Buddha understands all things, and with great compassion is resolved upon saving all living beings. All living beings have the Buddha-nature, all have the potential to become Buddhas.

Dharma.

A method for cultivating the Way to enlightenment, usually referring to those methods taught by the Buddha.

Dharma Master.

A title of respect for a Buddhist monk or nun. Literally, it means one who masters the Dharma and gives it to others and who also takes the Dharma as his or her master.

Gwo or Kuo (Guo 果).

"Fruit" or "result." The first word of the Dharma name given to all persons who take refuge with the Three Jewels in the Dharma Realm Buddhist Association, taking Venerable Master Hua as their teacher.

Heng (Heng 恆 or 恒).
"Always" or "constantly." The first name given to all persons who were ordained in the Dharma Realm Buddhist Association under Venerable Master Hua.

Sangha.
The community of Buddhist monks and nuns. Literally meaning "harmoniously united assembly."

Tripitaka.
The three categories of Buddhist texts: the *sutras*, which are the words spoken by the Buddha; the *vinaya*, or moral codes; and the *shastras*, which are commentaries on the *sutras*.

Three Jewels.
The Buddha, the Dharma, and the Sangha.

Upsaka and Upasika.
Respectively a layman and laywoman who have taken refuge with the Three Jewels and have received the five lay-precepts, which prohibit killing, stealing, sexual misconduct, lying, and taking intoxicants.

Introduction to the Dharma Realm Buddhist Association

Mission

The Dharma Realm Buddhist Association (formerly the Sino-American Buddhist Association) was founded by the Venerable Master Hsuan Hua in the United States of America in 1959. Taking the Dharma Realm as its scope, the Association aims to disseminate the genuine teachings of the Buddha throughout the world. The Association is dedicated to translating the Buddhist canon, propagating the Orthodox Dharma, promoting ethical education, and bringing benefit and happiness to all beings. Its hope is that individuals, families, the society, the nation, and the entire world will, under the transforming influence of the Buddhadharma, gradually reach the state of ultimate truth and goodness.

The Founder

The Venerable Master Hua developed the inclination to cultivate early on in his childhood. Influenced by the filial piety of Filial Son Wang (Great Master Chang Ren) of Shuang Cheng County, the Master vowed to follow his example. Every morning and evening after bowing to the Buddhas, he would make three bows to his parents. Later he took refuge with the Three Jewels and had deep faith in Buddhism. When he was nineteen his mother passed away, and he lived in a tiny hut by her graveside for three years in observance of filial piety. At that time he left the home-life with Venerable Master Chang Zhi and cultivated quietly and earnestly. He travelled widely to study under Elder Masters of great virtue. Later he received the transmission of Dharma from Venerable Master Xu Yun and became the Ninth Patriarch of the Wei Yang Sect, the 45th generation since the First Patriarch Mahakashyapa. In 1949 the Master went to Hong Kong to propagate the Dharma. He founded monasteries, delivered lectures on sutras, and engaged in other activities to benefit living beings, thus causing Buddhism to flourish in Hong Kong. In 1962 he came to America alone. Responding to the ripening conditions in the West, he worked to gradually actualize his vow to raise the banner of the Proper Dharma in the West.

Establishing Centers of Cultivation and Bringing People Together

The Venerable Master Hua's three great vows after leaving the home-life were to (1) promote and develop education in the Buddhist tradition, (2) translate the Buddhist Canon, and (3) establish a foundation for Buddhism in America. In order to make these vows a reality, the Venerable Master based himself in the Three Great Principles and the Six Great Guidelines. Courageously facing every hardship, he founded monasteries, schools, and centers in the West, drawing in living beings and teaching them on a vast scale. Over the years, he founded the following institutions:

The City of Ten Thousand Buddhas

Purchased in 1974, the City of Ten Thousand Buddhas is the hub of the Dharma Realm Buddhist Association. The City is located in Talmage, Mendocino County, 110 miles north of San Francisco. The grounds cover 488 acres, and there are approximately 80 acres in active use. In the Hall of Ten Thousand Buddhas at the City, there is a large image of Guan Yin Bodhisattva with a thousand hands and a thousand eyes. The four walls inside the Hall are covered with over ten thousand small Buddha statues. The four assemblies of disciples gather daily in this Hall for the morning and evening recitation ceremonies, and after evening recitation they listen to the Venerable Master's lectures on the Mahayana Sutras. Whenever there are intensive sessions for reciting the name of a Buddha or Bodhisattva, devotees from all directions come together to cultivate. During the annual Jeweled Repentance before the Ten Thousand Buddhas, the Hall is filled with the vigorous energy of cultivation. There are many other buildings and schools on the grounds of the City, including the elementary schools and secondary schools, the university, the

Sangha and Laity Training Programs, Tathagata Monastery, Great Compassion House, Joyous Giving House, Wonderful Words Hall, the Ordination Hall, the Library, Tower of Blessings (a seniors' center), and a vegetarian restaurant. There are more than seventy major buildings. The pure and peaceful atmosphere and the clean air at the City provide an ideal environment for study and spiritual cultivation.

Although the Venerable Master Hua belonged to the ninth generation in the lineage of the Wei Yang Sect of the Chan School, all the plans, Dharma events, and practices at the City give equal emphasis to the methods of cultivation of the Five Schools—the Chan School, the Pure Land School, the Esoteric School, the Vinaya School, and the School of Doctrine. Thus each person may choose the most appropriate method of practice to investigate and cultivate at a deeper level. That is also in accord with what the Buddha said, "The Dharma is level and equal, with no high or low." At the City of Ten Thousand Buddhas, the rules of purity are upheld strictly and carefully. All residents of the City undertake to regulate their own conduct and to cultivate with constant vigor. Taking refuge in the Proper Dharma, they lead pure and unselfish lives, and attain peace in body and mind. All residents are expected to dedicate themselves mentally and physically, follow the five precepts of Buddhism, and practice the principles of the City of Ten Thousand Buddhas. In this way they can nurture lofty moral character, activate their pure, inherent wisdom, and work for the prosperity of Buddhism.

Instilling Goodness Elementary School, Developing Virtue Secondary School, Dharma Realm Buddhist University

The Venerable Master Hua saw clearly that in order to save the world, the most urgent priority is to develop good education. If we want to save the world, we have to bring about a complete change in people's minds and guide them to cast out unwholesomeness and to pursue goodness. For this purpose the Master founded Instilling Goodness Elementary School in 1974, and he founded

Developing Virtue Secondary School and Dharma Realm Buddhist University in 1976.

The Master indicated that the elementary school should teach students to be filial to parents and respectful to teachers and elders, the secondary school should teach students to be good citizens, and the university should teach the principles of humaneness, righteousness, the Way, and virtue. Instilling Goodness Elementary School and Developing Virtue Secondary School merge the best of contemporary and traditional methods and of Western and Eastern cultures. Due to the emphasis on moral virtue and spiritual development, in addition to the required academic curriculum, courses are offered in ethics, meditation, Buddhist studies, and so on, giving students a foundation in virtue and guiding them gradually to know themselves and to explore the truths of the universe. At the City of Ten Thousand Buddhas, the elementary and secondary schools offer bilingual education (Chinese and English). Boys and girls are educated separately in order to avoid distractions and preserve their pure natures. Due to the many different cultures and nationalities that are represented among the teaching staff and student body, multiple grades are grouped together to allow students more flexibility in academic progress. Students learn to open their minds to respect and appreciate different cultural traditions. In offering an education based on virtue, Instilling Goodness Elementary School and Developing Virtue Secondary School hope to guide students to become good and capable citizens of the world, thus benefiting all of humankind. Aside from the City of Ten Thousand Buddhas, branches of the schools have also been formed at other affiliated monasteries with the aim of widely propagating filial piety and ethical education.

Dharma Realm Buddhist University does not merely transmit academic knowledge. It emphasizes a foundation in virtue, which expands into the study of how to help all people and all living beings return to their inherent nature. Thus Dharma Realm Buddhist University advocates a spirit of shared inquiry and free exchange of ideas, encouraging students to study various texts and use different experiences and learning styles to tap their inherent wisdom and fathom the meanings of those texts. Students are then encouraged to practice the principles they have understood and thus integrate the Buddhadharma into their lives. They will then be able to nurture their wisdom and become replete with virtue. The University aims to produce outstanding individuals of high moral character who will be able to bring benefit to all sentient beings.

The content of the courses taught by Dharma Realm Buddhist University consists primarily of the Proper Dharma. Faculty and students alike see this as the goal of their efforts in study and cultivation. Everyone investigates together in order to attain the ultimate state of wisdom and compassion. In such an environment, everyone's lifestyle is characterized by rigorous self-discipline. Whether students or teachers, monastics or laity, male or female, young or old, everyone is regarded with equal kindness. There are no distinctions of class and no personal differences. Every individual and the customs of every cultural tradition are respected. Beyond the physical manifestations of students, teachers, textbooks, and classrooms, the genuine and profound hallmark of the Dharma Realm Buddhist University is its spirit of taking the Dharma Realm as its substance and the Proper Dharma as its function. There is no place that is not a classroom, and nothing that is not a learning resource. There is no time when people are not mutually honing and refining each other's characters and talents. All people, events, and objects can be learned from and constantly give us good opportunities to accumulate blessings, grow in wholesome Dharma, and perpetuate wisdom.

Sangha and Laity Training Programs,
Proper Dharma Buddhist Academy

In the Dharma-ending Age, in both Eastern and Western societies there are very few monasteries that actually practice the Buddha's regulations and strictly uphold the precepts. Teachers of genuine wisdom and proper understanding capable of guiding those who aspire to pursue careers in Buddhism are also very rare. In order to raise the caliber of the monastic Sangha, cause the Proper Dharma to long endure, provide professional training for Buddhists from around the world that emphasizes practice as well as theory, and perpetuate the wisdom of the Buddha, the Venerable Master founded the Sangha and Laity Training Programs in 1982 and the Proper Dharma Buddhist Academy in 1988.

The Sangha Training Program provides left-home people with a solid foundation in Buddhist studies and practice, training them in the practical affairs of Buddhism and giving them a conception of Sangha management. After graduation, students will be able to assume various responsibilities related to Buddhism in monasteries, institutions, and other settings. Emphasis is placed on students' thorough knowledge of Buddhism, understanding of the scriptures, development of virtuous character, earnest cultivation, and strict observance of precepts, so that they will be able to propagate the orthodox Dharma and continue the Buddha's legacy. The Laity Training Program offers courses appropriate to laypeople, allowing them to develop proper knowledge and proper views, advance together in cultivation, and gain an understanding of the regulations of the monastery and the essentials of cultivation. After completing the Program, they will be able to serve humanity by contributing their abilities in Buddhist organizations. Proper Dharma Buddhist Academy, founded in Taiwan, focuses on the study and cultivation of the *Shurangama Sutra*. In the Dharma-ending Age, a time when deviant theories are rife, the Academy is devoted to training students to have clear and penetrating views and to be able to propagate the Proper Dharma.

International Translation Institute and
Dharma Realm Buddhist Books Distribution Association

The Venerable Master vowed to translate the Buddhist Canon (Tripitaka) into Western languages so that it could become widespread in the world. In 1973, he founded the International Translation Institute at Washington Street in San Francisco for the purpose of translating the Buddhist scriptures into English and other languages. In 1977, the Institute was merged into Dharma Realm Buddhist University as the Institute for the Translation of Buddhist

Texts. In 1991, the Venerable Master purchased a bank building in Burlingame (south of San Francisco) and officially established the International Translation Institute there for the purpose of translating and publishing Buddhist texts. To date the Association has published more than two hundred volumes of Buddhist texts translated from Chinese into English, French, Spanish, Italian, Polish, Vietnamese, Korean, and Japanese. Over twenty bilingual (Chinese and English) volumes of sutras, vinaya texts, and Dharma talks are also available.

One of the Venerable Master's three great vows was to translate the Buddhist scriptures. In China's past, this difficult and vast mission was directed and supported by the emperors and kings themselves. In the present, the Venerable Master encouraged his disciples to cooperatively shoulder this heavy responsibility, producing books and audio tapes and using the medium of language to turn the wheel of Proper Dharma and do the great work of the Buddha. All those who aspire to devote themselves to this work of sages should uphold the eight guidelines of the International Translation Institute—not being greedy for fame or profit, not being arrogant, not praising oneself nor slandering others, not establishing oneself as the standard of correctness and looking for flaws in others' work, taking the Buddha-mind as one's own mind, using the Dharma-selecting Vision to determine true principles, and requesting Virtuous Elders in the ten directions to certify one's translations, and endeavoring to propagate the teachings by printing sutras, shastras, and vinaya texts when the translations are certified as being correct. These are the Venerable Master's wishes, and they should be the goals that participants in the work of translation strive to achieve.

Certain wise individuals in Taiwan, seeing the degeneration of human morality in the Dharma-ending Age and wishing to avert the flood of disaster, organized and founded the Proper Dharma Buddhist Books Distribution Association in Taiwan in 1984. The Association's missions are to propagate the Six Great Principles promoted by the Venerable Master Hua and to improve and transform social trends. Based on a membership system, the Association accepts donations to print books and reproduce tapes produced by Dharma Realm Buddhist Association in order to make the Proper Dharma available throughout the world. Since 1990, in addition to printing Buddhist texts, the Association began to hold a variety of other Dharma activities.

The Institute of World Religions

Founded in 1994, the Institute is located near the University of California at Berkeley. The purpose of the Institute is to study the truths of religion in harmony with other religious groups, without rejecting or opposing any religion. The six principles of the City of Ten Thousand Buddhas serve as guidelines for the Institute. Propagating the spirit of the City of Ten Thousand Buddhas with expansive open-mindedness, the Institute invites the members of various religions to give presentations, deepening our understanding of their ideals and practices. The Institute of World Religions offers an hour of meditation twice daily and presents evening and weekend programs that foster conversation between religions, the sciences, and the humanities. All truth-seeking individuals who wish to discover their innate wisdom, benefit all beings, and bring harmony to the world are invited to come to study and cultivate together.

Affiliated Monasteries

In order to propagate the Proper Dharma, the Venerable Master not only trained and educated people, but also spent great effort in establishing various monasteries. He wanted to provide monasteries where people could cultivate in purity according to the Buddha's regulations as well as turn the Dharma wheel and carry out the Buddha's work. After coming to America, over the years he established the many monasteries of the Proper Dharma in the United States, Canada, and southeast Asia, including the following: Gold Mountain Monastery, Gold Wheel Monastery, Gold Summit Monastery, Gold Buddha Monastery, Avatamsaka Monastery, Long Beach Monastery, the City of the Dharma Realm, Dharma Realm Monastery and Amitabha Monastery in Taiwan, Prajna Guanyin

Sagely Monastery (formerly Purple Cloud Monastery) in Malaysia, and others. All of these monasteries firmly uphold the credo:

Freezing to death, we do not scheme.
Starving to death, we do not beg.
Dying of poverty, we ask for nothing.
We accord with conditions, but do not change.
We do not change, yet accord with conditions.
We adhere firmly to our three great principles.
We renounce our lives to do the Buddha's work.
We mold our destinies as our basic duty.
We rectify our lives to fulfill the Sanghan's role.
Encountering specific matters, we understand the principles.
Understanding the principles, we apply them to specific matters.
We carry on the single pulse of the patriarch's mind-transmission.

  The monasteries follow the Six Great Guidelines: no fighting, no greed, no seeking, no pursuit of personal advantage, and no lying. They also honor the Venerable Master's rules of eating only one meal a day and only before noon and always wearing the monastic robe or precept sash (*kashaya*). The monasteries have daily lectures on the sutras, turning the great Dharma wheel to universally rescue living beings.

  The Dharma is in decline and the world is under dangerous and evil influences. In accord with the mission of Dharma Realm Buddhist Association, the City of Ten Thousand Buddhas has been established as an international center for the study of Buddhism and for spiritual cultivation. It is open to those of all ages, faiths, ethnic origins, and nationalities. Individuals devoted to seeking the truth, helping humankind, and working for the prosperity of society and the nation are welcome to gather in the City to honestly study, cultivate, and put forth effort to rescue the world.

A Brief Account of the Life of the Venerable Master Hsuan Hua
(1918-1995)

One of the most eminent Chinese Buddhist masters of the twentieth century, the Tripitaka Master Hsuan Hua (1918-1995) was a monastic reformer and the first Chinese master to teach Buddhism to large numbers of Westerners. During his long career he emphasized the primacy of the monastic tradition, the essential role of moral education, the need for Buddhists to ground themselves in traditional spiritual practice and authentic scripture, and the importance of respect and understanding among religions. To attain these goals, he focused on clarifying the essential principles of the Buddha's original teachings, on establishing a properly ordained monastic community, on organizing and supporting the translation of the Buddhist Canon into English and other languages, and on the establishment of schools, religious training programs, and programs of academic research and teaching.

Born in 1918 into a peasant family in a small village south of Harbin, in northeast China, the Venerable Master was the youngest of eight children. His father's surname was Bai, and his mother's maiden name was Hu. His mother was a vegetarian, and throughout her life she held to the practice of reciting the name of the Buddha Amitabha. When the Venerable Master formally became a Buddhist, in his mid-teens, he was given the Dharma name An Ci ("Peace and Compassion"), and after becoming a monk, he was also known as To Lun (Du Lun—"Liberator from the Wheel of Rebirth"). Upon granting him the Dharma seal of the Wei Yang (also pronounced Gui Yang) Chan lineage, the Elder Chan Master Xu Yun (1840-1959) bestowed upon him the Dharma transmission name Hsuan Hua ("Proclaim and Transform").

When the Venerable Master was a child, he followed his mother's example, eating only vegetarian food and reciting the Buddha's name. When he was eleven years old, upon seeing a dead baby lying on the ground, he awakened to the fundamental significance of birth and death and the impermanence of all phenomena. He then resolved to become a monk and practice on the Buddhist path, but he acquiesced to his mother's request that he not do so until after her death. When he was twelve, he obtained his parents' permission to travel extensively in search of a true spiritual teacher.

At the age of fifteen, the Venerable Master went to school for the first time, and when he was sixteen, he started lecturing on the Buddhist sutras to help this fellow villagers who were illiterate but who wanted to learn about the Buddha's teachings. He was not only diligent and focused but possessed a photographic memory, and so he was able to memorize the Four Books and the Five Classics of the Confucian tradition. He had also studied traditional Chinese medicine, astrology, divination, physiognomy, and the scriptures of the great religions. When he was seventeen, he established a free school, in which, as the lone teacher, he taught some thirty impoverished children and adults.

At the age of eighteen, after only two and a half years of schooling, he left school to care for his terminally ill mother. He was nineteen when she died, and for three years he honored her memory by sitting in meditation beside her grave in a hut made of sorghum stalks. During this time, while reading the *Lotus Sutra*, he experienced a deep awakening. Subsequently, while seated in meditation, he had a vision of the Sixth Chan Buddhist Patriarch Hui Neng (638–713 CE). In his vision, Master Hui Neng came to visit him and to give him the mission of bringing Buddhism to the Western world.

At the end of his period of mourning, the Venerable Master took as his teacher Chan Buddhist Master Chang Zhi, and he entered Three Conditions Monastery as a novice monk. Chan Master Chang Zhi subsequently transmitted to him the Dharma of the Jin Ding Pi Lu Chan (Golden-crowned Vairochana Sect of the Chan School) lineage. During this time, the Master devoted himself not only to meditation but also to the study of the Buddhist scriptural tradition and to the mastery of all the major schools of Chinese Buddhism.

After a period of solitary meditation in the Chang Bai Mountains, in 1946 the Master began the long journey to the south of China. In 1947, he received full ordination as a monk at the Buddhist holy mountain Pu Tuo Shan. In 1948, after over two thousand miles of travel, the Master arrived at Nan Hua Monastery and bowed to Chan Master Xu Yun, China's most widely revered enlightened master. From him the Master received the mind-seal transmission as verification of his awakening, and later a more formal transmission of the Dharma of the Wei Yang lineage of the Chan School.

In 1949 the Master left China for Hong Kong. There he taught meditation, lectured on the Buddhist sutras, and sponsored their printing. He also commissioned the making of images of Buddhas and Bodhisattvas, and he aided monastic refugees from mainland China. He also built Western Bliss Garden Monastery, established the Buddhist Lecture Hall, and rebuilt and renovated Flourishing Compassion Monastery (Cixing Monastery).

In 1962, he traveled to the United States at the invitation of Hong Kong disciples who were then living in San Francisco Bay area, and he began lecturing at the San Francisco Buddhist Lecture Hall, which had been previously established as a branch of the Hong Kong Buddhist Lecture Hall. As the community at the Buddhist Lecture Hall in San Francisco grew, both in size and in diversity, the institution's name was changed, first to the Sino-American Buddhist Association and then, in 1984, to the Dharma Realm Buddhist Association. In 1970 the Venerable Master moved from Chinatown to the newly established Gold Mountain Monastery in the Mission District of San Francisco. In 1975 the Venerable Master established the organization's first branch monastery, Gold Wheel Temple in Los Angeles. In 1976 he established a new headquarter as well: the City of Ten Thousand Buddhas, in Ukiah, California.

In the summer of 1968, the Master began the intensive training of a group of Americans, most of them university students. In 1969, he astonished the monastic community of Taiwan by sending there, for complete ordination, two American women and three American men whom he had ordained as novices. They were the first Americans of that period to become fully ordained Buddhist monks and nuns. During subsequent years, the Venerable Master trained and oversaw the ordination of hundreds of people, both Asians and Westerners, from among those who came to California from every part of the world to study with him. These monastic disciples now teach in the twenty-seven temples, monasteries and convents that the Venerable Master and his disciples founded in the United States, Canada, Australia, and several Asian countries.

The Venerable Master was determined to transmit to the West the correct teachings of Buddhism, and he categorically rejected what he considered to be corrupt practices that had become widespread in China. He guided his disciples in distinguishing between genuine, scripture-based practices that were useful and in accord with common sense, as opposed to ritual superstitions that were unwholesome cultural accretions.

Among the many reforms in monastic practice that he instituted was his insistence that his monastic disciples accord with the ancient practice of wearing the precept-sash as a sign of membership in the monastic Sangha. He himself followed, and he required that his monastic disciples follow the prohibition against eating after noon. He considered a vegetarian diet to be of paramount importance. He encouraged his disciples among the Sangha to join him in following the Buddha's beneficial ascetic practices of eating only one meal a day and of never lying down. Of his monastic disciples he expected strict purity, and he encouraged his lay disciples to adhere to the five precepts of the Buddhist laity.

Although he understood English well and spoke it when necessary, the Master almost always lectured in Chinese. His aim was to encourage his Western disciples to learn Chinese and his Chinese disciples to learn English, so that together they could help to fulfill his wish that the Buddhist Canon be translated into other languages. So far, the Buddhist Text Translation Society, which he founded, has published well over two hundred volumes of translations, including several of the major Mahayana sutras with the Master's commentaries.

As an educator, the Venerable Master was tireless. At the City of Ten Thousand Buddhas, he established formal training programs for monastics and for laity, elementary and secondary schools for boys and for girls, and Dharma Realm Buddhist University. From 1968 to the early 1990's he himself gave lectures on sutras at least once a day, and he traveled extensively on speaking tours. Responding to requests from Buddhists around the world, the Venerable Master led delegations to Hong Kong, Taiwan, India, Southeast Asia, and Europe to propagate the Dharma. He also traveled to Myanmar, Thailand, Malaysia, Australia and South America. His presence drew a multitude of the faithful everywhere he went. He was also often invited to lecture at universities and academic conferences.

The Venerable Master was a pioneer in building bridges between different Buddhist communities. Wishing to heal the ancient divide between Mahayana Buddhism and Theravada Buddhism, he invited distinguished Theravada monks to the City of Ten Thousand Buddhas to share the duties of full ordination and transmission of the monastic precepts, which the two traditions hold in common.

He also insisted on inter-religious respect and actively promoted interfaith dialogue. He stressed commonalities in religious traditions, above all their emphasis on proper and compassionate conduct. In 1976, together with his friend Paul Cardinal Yu Bin, who had been archbishop of Nan Jing and who was the Chancellor of the Catholic Fu Ren University in Taiwan, he made plans for an Institute for World Religions that came to fruition in Berkeley in 1994.

In 1990, at the invitation of Buddhists in several European countries, the Venerable Master led a large delegation on a European Dharma tour, knowing full well that, because of his ill health at the time, the rigors of the trip would shorten his life. However, as always he considered the Dharma more important than his very life. After his return, his health gradually deteriorated, yet, while quite ill, he made another major tour, this time to Taiwan, in 1993.

In Los Angeles, on June 7, 1995, at the age of 77, the Venerable Master left this world. When he was alive, he craved nothing, seeking neither fame nor wealth nor power. His every thought and every action were for the sake of bringing true happiness to all sentient beings. In his final instructions he said: "After I depart, you can recite the *Avatamsaka Sutra* and the name of the Buddha Amitabha for however many days you would like, perhaps seven days or forty-nine days. After cremating my body, scatter all my remains in the air. I do not want you to do anything else at all. Do not build me any pagodas or memorials. I came into the world without anything; when I depart, I still do not want anything, and I do not want to leave any traces in the world. From emptiness I came; to emptiness I am returning."

Dharma Realm Buddhist Association Branches

[World Headquarter]

The City of Ten Thousand Buddhas
2001 Talmage Road
Ukiah, CA 95482 USA
Tel: (707) 462-0939
Fax: (707) 462-0949
www.drba.org
(Branch URLs and email addresses are available on the DRBA website.)

U.S.A.
California
Berkeley

Berkeley Buddhist Monastery
2304 McKinley Avenue
Berkeley, CA 94703 USA
Tel: (510) 848-3440
Fax: (510) 548-4551

Burlingame

The International Translation Institute
1777 Murchison Drive
Burlingame, CA 94010-4504 USA
Tel: (650) 692-5912
Fax: (650) 692-5056

Long Beach

Blessings, Prosperity, and Longevity Monastery
4140 Long Beach Boulevard
Long Beach, CA 90807 USA
Tel/Fax: (562) 595-4966

Long Beach Sagely Monastery
3361 East Ocean Boulevard
Long Beach, CA 90803 USA
Tel: (562) 438-8902

Los Angeles

Gold Wheel Monastery
235 North Avenue 58
Los Angeles, CA 90042 USA
Tel: (323) 258-6668
Fax: (323) 258-3619

Sacramento

The City of the Dharma Realm
1029 West Capitol Avenue
West Sacramento, CA 95691 USA
Tel: (916) 374-8268
Fax: (916) 374-8234

San Francisco

Gold Mountain Monastery
800 Sacramento Street
San Francisco, CA 94108 USA
Tel: (415) 421-6117
Fax: (415) 788-6001

San Jose

Gold Sage Monastery
11455 Clayton Road
San Jose, CA 95127-5099 USA
Tel: (408) 923-7243
Fax: (408) 923-1064

Maryland
Bethesda

Avatamsaka Vihara
9601 Seven Locks Road
Bethesda, MD 20817-9997 USA
Tel/Fax: (301) 469-8300

Washington
Index

Snow Mountain Monastery
PO Box 272
50924 Index-Galena Road
Index, WA 98256 USA
Tel: (360) 799-0699
Fax: (815) 346-9141

Seattle

Gold Summit Monastery
233 First Avenue West
Seattle, WA 98119 USA
Tel: (206) 284-6690

Canada
Alberta

Avatamsaka Monastery
1009 4th Avenue SW
Calgary, AB, T2P OK8, Canada
Tel: (403) 234-0644

British Columbia

Gold Buddha Monastery
248 East 11th Avenue
Vancouver, B.C., V5T 2C3, Canada
Tel: (604) 709-0248
Fax: (604) 684-3754

Australia

Gold Coast Dharma Realm
106 Bonogin Road
Mudgeeraba, Queensland 4213
Australia
Tel: 61-755-228-788
Fax: 61-755-227-822

Hong Kong

Buddhist Lecture Hall
31 Wong Nei Chong Road, Top Floor
Happy Valley, Hong Kong, China
Tel: (852) 2572-7644
Fax: (852) 2572-2850

Cixing Monastery
Lantou Island, Man Cheung Po
Hong Kong, China
Tel: (852) 2985-5159

Malaysia

Dharma Realm Guanyin Sagely Monastery
161, Jalan Ampang
50450 Kuala Lumpur, West Malaysia
Tel: (603) 2164-8055
Fax: (603) 2163-7118

Prajna Guanyin Sagely Monastery
Batu 5 ½, Jalan Sungai Besi
Salak Selatan
57100 Kuala Lumpur, West Malaysia
Tel: (603) 7982-6560
Fax: (603) 7980-1272

Fa Yuan Monastery
1 Jalan Utama
Taman Serdang Raya
43300 Seri Kembangan
Selangor Darul Ehsan, West Malaysia
Tel: (603) 8958-5668

Malaysia DRBA Penang Branch
32-32C, Jalan Tan Sri
Teh Ewe Lim, 11600 Jelutong
Penang, West Malaysia
Tel: (604) 281-7728
Fax: (604) 281-7798

Guan Yin Sagely Monastery
166A Jalan Temiang
70200 Seremban
Negeri Sembilan, West Malaysia
Tel/Fax: (606) 761-1988

Lotus Vihara
136, Jalan Sekolah
45600 Batang Berjuntai
Selangor Darul Ehsan, West Malaysia
Tel: (603) 3271- 9439

Taiwan

Dharma Realm Buddhist Books Distribution Society
11th Floor, 85 Zhongxiao E. Road, Sec. 6
Taipei, 11575, Taiwan, R.O.C.
Tel: (02) 2786-3022
Fax: (02) 2786-2674

Dharma Realm Sagely Monastery
No. 20, Dongxi Shanzhuang
Liugui Dist.
Gaoxiong, 84445, Taiwan, R.O.C.
Tel: (07) 689-3717
Fax: (07) 689-3870

Amitabha Monastery
No. 126, Fuji Street, Shoufeng
Hualien County 97445, Taiwan, R.O.C.
tel: (03) 865-1956
fax: (03) 865-3426

Subsidiary Organizations

Buddhist Text Translation Society
City of Ten Thousand Buddhas
4951 Bodhi Way, Ukiah. CA 95482 USA
web: www.buddhisttexts.org
email: info@buddhisttexts.org
catalog: www.bttsonline.org

Dharma Realm Buddhist University
City of Ten Thousand Buddhas
4951 Bodhi Way, Ukiah, CA 95482 USA
www.drbu.edu

Dharma Realm Outreach
City of Ten Thousand Buddhas
outreach@drba.org

Instilling Goodness and Developing Virtue School
City of Ten Thousand Buddhas
2001 Talmage Road, Ukiah, CA 95482 USA
www.igdvs.org

Institute for World Religions
2245 McKinley Avenue, Suite B
Berkeley, CA 94703 USA
web: www.drbu.edu/iwr
email: iwr@drbu.edu

Religion East & West (journal)
2245 McKinley Avenue, Suite B
Berkeley, CA 94703 USA
Tel: (510) 848-9788
web: www.drbu.edu/iwr/rew

Vajra Bodhi Sea (magazine)
Gold Mountain Monastery
800 Sacramento Street
San Francisco, CA 94108 USA
Tel: (415) 421-6117
Fax: (415) 788-6001